STRESS MANAGEMENT
FOR THE EXECUTIVE

STRESS

MANAGEMENT
FOR THE EXECUTIVE

edited by
EXECUTIVE HEALTH EXAMINERS

BERKLEY BOOKS, NEW YORK

This book incorporates material from
COPING WITH EXECUTIVE STRESS,
EXECUTIVE NUTRITION AND DIET,
and DIET EXECUTIVE FITNESS.

STRESS MANAGEMENT
FOR THE EXECUTIVE

A Berkley Book/published by arrangement with
McGraw-Hill Book Company

PRINTING HISTORY
Berkley trade paperback edition/October 1985

ISBN: 0-425-08396-9

Contents

Preface

Twenty-five years ago, in one of our preeminent medical research centers, resided a group of very special laboratory animals. Challenged constantly, forced to make decisions and act under pressure, they were the "executive monkeys." In one famous experiment, two monkeys were placed side-by-side in chairs equipped to give electric shocks. One of the monkeys—and only one—could prevent the shocks to both itself and its partner by pressing a lever. Under the psychological stress of being responsible for pressing the lever, this executive monkey developed duodenal ulcers.

The close correlation of behavior patterns in animals and humans has been thoroughly documented by scientific research. It has been shown that information obtained from animal research can be successfully applied to human research and experience. The study of animal behavior, for example, can result in a better understanding of the behavior of the individuals who go out each day to lead our governments, industries, and unions.

Few of us have ever watched chimpanzees in their natural habitat, the jungles of Africa. If we could observe these animals, we would see that they wander around, nibbling a few nuts here, a few berries there, eating continuously in small amounts. What they do *not* do is neglect eating for long periods and then pour raw alcohol onto the tender mucosal linings of their stomachs. They do *not* smoke several cigarettes, and thereby increase the outpouring of hydrochloric acid. They do *not* then consume large quantities of food, try to exist on insufficient sleep, and undergo rapid changes in environment. If they did, they would very likely suffer the same fate as a number of American executives under observation at a major research center who, possessing one or more of these habits, died before the study could be completed.

Medical science has accumulated an enormous amount of significant data from studies on animals and humans. As always, though, the important task is putting that knowledge to use in practical ways that can most benefit humankind. Executive Health Examiners was founded more than twenty years ago for the primary purpose of making medical knowledge available to a particular group—executives. Over the years our medical staff has examined executives from every kind of business and profession and at every level. From this vast experience it has become apparent to us that these executives—men and women alike—are often *simultaneously* exposed to all the life-threatening habits that chimpanzees naturally avoid. And it is this circumstance that, in our opinion, makes executives unique. Other groups are, of course, subjected to some of the same threats to their health, but, in our experience, only in the executive lifestyle do these threats converge at the same time.

The conviction that executives are unique, that their lifestyles are different and therefore have special health needs, led us to prepare this book specifically for executives. In this volume we combine solid medical fact with our years of professional experience to provide practical, proven approaches to solving health problems. Each section deals with an area of health where executives are especially vulnerable. Executive Nutrition and Diet is a commonsense program for nutrition and diet that has been highly successful for thousands of executives. All the special problems of executive lifestyle are dealt with in this basic, balanced discussion of sound nutritional habits and healthy diet. *Executive Fitness* is a flexible, workable exercise program designed for busy executives. Within a basic format, it offers a wide variety of exercise options, all of which are certain to result in increased stamina and productivity. Coping with Executive Stress provides the most current medical information on stress and its effect on both the mind and body to show executives how to recognize and cope with stress in executive life.

There is no question that the demands of executive life make good health maintenance difficult. Having guided hundreds of thousands of executives to positive and lasting changes in their lifestyle, however, we know that the habits of eating properly, exercising regularly and coping with stress can be successfully acquired. The volumes in this series offer sound information gained from long and specific experience with executives. We view these books as a kind of survival kit for executives. It is our hope that they will enable every executive to enjoy a longer, healthier, more productive and satisfying life.

Richard E. Winter, M.D.
Chairman

STRESS MANAGEMENT

FOR THE EXECUTIVE

PART I

Executive Nutrition and Diet

Introduction

Every executive knows it: What we put into the gut each day does more than stoke the body's furnace.

Today executives, as well as the general public, are becoming increasingly aware of the impact that nutrition has, both directly and indirectly, on health and disease—on heart disease, stroke, high blood pressure, diabetes, cancer, etc., as well as on vigor and longevity.

But confusion abounds. Almost weekly, new self-proclaimed diet prophets clamor for our attention. Food fads come and go. We hear endlessly about the pros and cons of vitamins and substances passed off as vitamins, of minerals, of fibers, and of food additives. The media is full of advice, much of it conflicting, about what to eat and what not to eat.

At Executive Health Examiners, many of our clients have expressed the need for reliable guidance not just to cut through the general confusion, but to help them deal with the special nutritional problems arising from the executive lifestyle and executive activities.

It was to address those problems that several years ago we set up a special department for nutritional counseling to supplement the work of our examining physicians. The material that follows in this section stems from that counseling and the positive results experienced by many of our executive clients. We have tried to make it concise, direct, and practical.

1.

Nutrition and the Executive Lifestyle

How America Eats

Not long ago, in a series of articles on current eating patterns, a *New York Times* reporter wrote that although millions of Americans were supposed to have become concerned in recent years with good nutrition, there was no clear evidence "that even those people who say they are interested in improved nutrition have altered their eating habits." According to D. Mark Hegsted, M.D., of the Human Nutrition Center of the U.S. Department of Agriculture, who was quoted in the *Times* article, "Americans now seem to be as fat as ever."

Writing in the *National Food Review*, two Agriculture Department scientists, Betty B. Peterkin and Ruth M. Marston, reported that Americans are managing to ignore all warnings that they are eating too much. "The caloric and most nutrient levels of the U.S. diet are the same or higher than last year and ten years ago."

The Record

Here are a few figures worthy of inclusion in the *Guinness Book of World Records*:

- American sugar consumption, now at its highest rate ever, averages 850 calories per person per day. Added at the table? Some, yes. But 82 percent of it goes into processed foods. Nor is it a matter of concern only in candies, ice cream, and baked desserts; sugar is an important ingredient in soups, sauces, cold breakfast cereals, vegetable juices, crackers, breads, and even salad dressings.

- Salt intake is excessively high; some estimates put it at an average of 15 grams (half an ounce) a day, far beyond any actual body requirement. Plenty is added at the table; plenty more is found in processed foods.

- Fat consumption, also at record levels, averages 52.6 pounds per person per year.

- Whereas the American per capita consumption of fresh fruits once averaged 134.7 pounds, this figure has recently hit a low of 83.2 pounds.

- Vegetable consumption has increased, but the bulk of vegetables being consumed are processed vegetables, the consumption of which has shot up from 14.5 pounds per person in 1910 to 62.5 pounds recently.

- Look what has happened to potato consumption: Even as late as 1950, almost all potatoes (94 percent) grown in the United States were eaten fresh; now most (60 percent) are processed, largely as frozen french fries, which from the tonnage standpoint have become the country's most-consumed vegetable.

In 1977, concerned about a national diet rich in meat, dairy products, and processed foods laden with fats, cholesterol, sugar, salt, and calories, the U.S. Senate Select Committee on Nutrition and Human Health issued its "Dietary Goals" report.

The report advised Americans to cut down on fatty meats and dairy products, eggs, salty foods and snacks, and nutritionally deficient sweets and alcohol.

On the positive side, it advised eating more lean meats, fish and poultry, fruits, vegetables, whole grains, and other foods rich in complex carbohydrates, fiber, vitamins, and minerals, and low in fat and refined sugars.

A controversial report! It had many in the food and dairy industries and even some independent scientists up in arms, arguing that such broad recommendations for dietary change on a vast national scale had to be considered premature and that enough clear evidence to provide justification was still lacking.

Yet, almost 3 years later, in what has been termed a "historic joint enterprise," two federal departments—the Department of Agriculture and the Department of Health, Education and Welfare (since renamed the Department of Health and Human Services)—joined forces to issue a "Dietary Guidelines for Americans" report.

Largely reinforcing the earlier report, the "Guidelines" urged: "Eat a variety of foods; maintain ideal weight; avoid too much fat, saturated fat, and cholesterol; eat foods with adequate starch and fiber; avoid too much sugar; avoid too much sodium (salt); if you drink alcohol, do so in moderation."

In his first major speech, Secretary of Health and Human Services Richard S. Schweiker said: "By taking five simple steps, by not smoking, by using alcohol in moderation, and by eating a proper diet and getting the proper amount of exercise and sleep, a 45-year-old man can expect to live 10 or 11 years longer than a person who does not make these choices."

Executive Eating (and Drinking) Patterns

While Americans in general have nutritional problems, those problems are aggravated for executives.

Consider the problem of R.S., a 54-year-old controller with an occupational hazard.

The company where R.S. works owns three gourmet restaurants in the New York metropolitan area that are notorious for their huge portions of prime-cut beef and other rich foods. One of the "better" fringe benefits is free food whenever an employee wants it.

As a result, R.S. had watched his weight increase by 2 pounds each year for the last 25 years. He knew he was at least 50 pounds over his ideal weight, but when his physician at Executive Health Examiners discovered an elevated fasting blood sugar, or glucose, level of 160 milligrams per deciliter of blood serum, he became frightened because diabetes runs in his family. The physician referred him to the nutritionist to discuss a weight-loss program, the primary treatment for adult-onset diabetes.

At Executive Health Examiners the nutritionist worked with R.S. on modifying his diet to include smaller portions of food at mealtimes. Gradually he was able to eliminate snacks and most of the desserts constantly available. He cooperated fully at home by cooking the foods suggested by the nutritionist. Within 9 months, R.S. lost 38 pounds and his blood glucose fell into the normal range (60 to 120 milligrams per deciliter of blood serum). He continues to work on losing that final 12 pounds but is gratified that he has maintained a 38-pound weight loss and normal fasting blood glucose.

You can do as well even if you eat as many restaurant meals as R.S.

The Business Lunch and Other Restaurant Meals

When a study of a large group of executives in one corporation was made by a senior nutritionist at the Massachusetts Institute of Technology, the biggest nutritional problem proved to be overabundance— of calories, fat, and protein.

The prime mistake of the executives was the consumption of excessively large portions of food—as much, for example, as 12 to 16 ounces of meat per meal, which is far beyond a normal serving of only about 4 ounces of boneless, cooked meat.

Over-generous portions are to be found in many restaurants. Nor is it an easy matter for anyone brought up from childhood to "clean his or her plate" to do the opposite and reject excess.

Moreover, to many, it seems that when entertaining or being entertained it is inappropriate to appear "picky." Business meals often provide a rationale for eating what one should not because to do otherwise would be to "insult" one's host or guest.

There is also the element of time. Sitting over a meal for an extended period while business is discussed can invite more food consumption, even the ordering of an extra course.

Restaurant meals, furthermore, are often rich. Not only are desserts calorie- and fat-laden but gravies, sauces, and salad dressings as well. Even potatoes and other fresh vegetables may be prepared with fat.

Theoretically, broiled dishes should have a minimum of fat, but for restaurants, labor costs are greater than food costs and, whenever possible, methods of cooking are chosen on the basis of how expeditious they are. So it is often easier to broil something using a whole stick of butter than just a dab. With little butter, great care is needed if foods are not to dry out, stick, and become messy to clean up. It may help, when ordering, to specify that broiling be done without butter, in wine or lemon juice.

And Maybe—Now and Then—a Fast-Food Lunch

Millions of such lunches, of course, are eaten every day across the country. On occasion, when a business lunch is not scheduled and there is no time pressure, even an executive may duck into a fast-food emporium for a "hamburger and..." or may send out for a lunch to be eaten in the office.

Again, this is no bargain if you are watching your weight or your blood level of cholesterol and triglycerides.

Take the "quarter-pounder" hamburger. According to a recent U.S. Department of Agriculture sampling, you can count on getting 420 calories, 45 percent of which will come from fat, the vast proportion of it saturated fat. You will get a nice serving of cholesterol as well— 77 milligrams worth.

Or take a quarter-pounder with cheese: the calories, 559; the proportion from fat, 49 percent; the milligrams of cholesterol, 110.

French fries to go with your burger? Figure on about 250 calories or even a bit more, with as much as 49 percent of them coming from fat—plus 12 milligrams of cholesterol. Potatoes have no cholesterol themselves and extremely small amounts of fats; the content of fats and cholesterol in french fries reflects the use of fat in the deep fryers.

Oh, yes, you may have condiments added to your burger. The calories vary, but they can range as high as 105 for one chain's special sauce and 159 for the mayonnaise usually added by another chain.

Alcohol

When he was asked whether alcohol makes much of a difference in the executive diet, Fredrick J. Stare, M.D., of the Harvard University Department of Nutrition, observed that next to meat, alcohol is the second major source of calories for the typical businessman.

"And," he went on, "you don't have to be a drunkard to get most of your calories from alcohol. Yesterday I had lunch with some board members in New York, and we went to a luncheon club. Practically every person I saw there had two drinks at lunch, big drinks, and there's a good 300 calories.

"You get home and you have another good drink, a nice strong martini, say, and that's another 150. Now we're up to 450.

"Then, if you have wine with dinner, you're going to get another 100 calories, and you're up to 550. In the evening, people often have another drink while they're looking over the papers, another 150 calories, and maybe another one as a nightcap. So there's 800 or 900 calories—which is a third of my daily caloric requirement—from alcohol."

Dr. Stare made those comments some years ago. From our observations at Executive Health Examiners, we think there has been some moderation since then in drinking by executives. Still, in many cases, alcohol contributes a significant number of calories—and no nutrients. The consumption of alcohol can be a particular problem for executives who do extensive traveling.

Travel

Among executives, travel is commonly very much part of the job. It is not unusual for them to spend as much as 25 percent or more of their time away from home.

Certainly, it is not impossible to eat well and moderately and to control one's weight while traveling, but it can be more difficult.

When people travel, they often have a pronounced tendency to eat differently than they do at home.

Many of those who rarely have more for breakfast than juice, cereal, and coffee find themselves indulging in multi-course breakfasts. Dinners taken in restaurants are often more lavish than those eaten at home.

Some individuals may feel expansive about eating because it goes on the expense account; for others, indulging themselves by eating large meals of rich food may seem to offer some compensation, however little, for being away from home.

A SPECIAL NOTE ABOUT TRAVEL

Particularly during long flights, air travel can present a special problem: *dehydration*.

As much as 2 pounds of water can be lost by evaporation through the skin during even a 3½-hour flight in a commercial jet. This results from the rapid circulation of very dry air in the ventilating system.

Dehydration (fluid loss with insufficient replenishment) can, if allowed to progress, become severe enough to produce one or more symptoms such as flushing, dry skin and mucous membranes, cracked lips, decreased urination, lethargy, fatigue, low blood pressure, and muscle cramps.

But, far short of that, it can make for under-par feelings and can contribute to jet lag. One cannot depend on thirst to signal the need for adequate water consumption in this situation.

The emphasis should be on *water* consumption. It is not wise to depend on alcoholic beverages, since these, in fact, can contribute to further fluid loss. So can coffee, tea, and many soda beverages which contain enough caffeine to act as diuretics, increasing fluid excretion.

Insipid as airplane water may taste, drink it, or ask for bottled water or club soda.

From article by A. H. Hayes, *New York Times*, June 19, 1981.

The Woman Executive

Not only do women executives have problems similar to those of men (business lunches, frequent traveling), they may have some additional ones as well.

Women executives have even more reason for concern about their weight than do men. Generally, women have less lean body mass and lower metabolic rates, and it is easier for them to develop weight-control problems.

Women have more concerns, too, about meeting nutritional needs. They have greater susceptibility to anemia during the child-bearing years, because of inadequate iron intake to compensate for the loss in menstruation. Later, they are more susceptible to osteoporosis, or bone thinning and bone fractures.

For some, premenstrual tension may be a problem. The symptoms, such as irritability and fluid accumulation during the week or ten days prior to menstruation, often can be relieved, and in some cases even completely eliminated, by reducing salt intake, but this can be difficult for women who must frequently eat in restaurants and corporate dining rooms or take all their meals out while traveling.

WHAT ABOUT WATER?

About 60 percent of total body weight is water, and all the chemical reactions in your body that convert food to energy and body tissue require its presence. The body retains the amount of water you need at any given time, and when you are running low, you feel thirsty. When you have taken in more than you need, the kidney receives a hormonal message to rid your body of the excess as urine.

Though some elderly or ill people can develop thirst-control abnormalities, most people go a lifetime without any water metabolism problems.

Executive Health Examiners recommends that, unless advised against it by a doctor, adults drink between 6 and 8 cups of liquids daily. Coffee, tea, cola beverages, and alcohol do not count as satisfying this requirement.

2.

The Three Basics: Proteins, Fat, and Carbohydrates

Of the many myths and misconceptions surrounding nutrition, these three are among the most common:

• Because protein is the quintessential nutrient, there is no such thing as too much.

• As for fats, when it comes to good health, it's all just a matter of eating fewer saturated and more unsaturated fats.

• Carbohydrates (starchy foods) are our major miscreants: high in calories, not really needed, to be avoided as much as possible.

All three are total nonsense! Proteins, fats, and carbohydrates are the vital dietary components, the calorie carriers, the three central substances of nutrition. Not only do all three have fundamental roles to play in the body's economy, so do their interactions.

Proteins

The myth: Second only to water, protein is the most important nutrient.

The facts: Protein is important all right, but the body's need for it is quite limited. Many Americans, thinking there can't be too much of a good thing, consume far more than they need. The excess, however, is converted into sugar and fat, which are stored by the body if they are not immediately needed for energy.

Also, most high-protein foods include more fat besides the fat from the conversion of excess protein. It is stored, too, if it is not immediately needed.

Thus, besides adding extra calories to the diet, eating excess protein results in the addition of extra fat in more than one way.

What Proteins Do

The heart, liver, kidneys, muscles, brain tissue, hair, and nails all consist mainly of protein. No cell in the body can survive without an adequate protein supply. The very wall of a cell is protein, and protein makes up 20 percent of total cell mass.

Proteins build and maintain all body tissues by contributing the essential amino acids of which they are made. The amino acids are used to make enzymes (which further the body's chemical reactions), hormones, and body fluids. They help form antibodies to combat disease and blood hemoglobin to carry oxygen to tissues. They also contribute to the regulation of digestion and other body functions.

What Proteins Are

The most complex of natural compounds, proteins are built of small constituent units called amino acids (often referred to as the "building blocks" of protein) which contain nitrogen, carbon, and other elements.

What determines the nature of any particular kind of protein is the number and arrangement of those building blocks. For example, the protein albumin (a major constituent of albumen, or egg whites, and other animal-product foods) consists of 418 amino acids strung together in a particular way to form each albumin molecule.

It is not the complexity of proteins, however, which counts in the diet, but rather their amino acid constituents. As you digest proteins they are quickly broken down into their amino acid constituents, from which the body then builds the particular types of proteins that it requires—structural proteins and connective tissue proteins—as well as hormones, antibodies, enzymes, and other body substances. In fact, according to current estimates, in this building process the body produces as many as 50,000 different types of proteins.

More than twenty different amino acids are to be found in proteins. The body can synthesize many of them from sources of nitrogen and from the intermediate compounds that form as carbohydrates are broken down.

But there are some amino acids which the body is unable to synthesize and which are therefore dietary essentials. These "essential" amino acids include lysine, valine, isoleucine, leucine, threonine, tryptophan, methionine, phenylalanine, and histidine. Two other amino acids can be derived only from amino acids which are dietary essentials: tyrosine from phenylalanine and cystine from methionine.

Protein Sources

All flesh—from fish, fowl, cattle, and other mammals—is rich in proteins. Cow's milk has a high protein content—in fact, three times as much as human milk. Some cheeses have still more. Cereals contain about 5 to 10 percent protein by weight. Fruits contain little protein— about 1 percent by weight. Vegetables, particularly peas and beans, have a greater proportion than fruit.

Foods that contain large amounts of the essential amino acids are known as *complete protein sources*. These include such animal-product foods as meat, eggs, and milk.

Vegetable proteins are incomplete; that is, no single vegetable contains all of the essential amino acids, but all of the amino acids can be obtained from a mix of vegetables. For example, Mexicans have a complete protein intake when they eat tortillas (corn bread), which are low in lysine, along with beans, which are rich in lysine and low in methionine.

Other complete protein sources include the following combinations of foods: peanut butter and whole wheat bread, rice and beans, nuts and beans, macaroni and cheese, and cereal and milk.

Too Much Protein?

Most Americans get plenty of protein. In the United States, approximately 15 to 17 percent of total caloric intake is in the form of protein—some 90 to 100 grams a day.

According to a recent report by John D. Palombo and George L. Blackburn, M.D., of Harvard Medical School, "Ninety-seven percent of healthy Americans consume much more protein than is required; the amount of extra dietary protein consumed may approach 40 to 50 grams per day."

It is also a fact that the kind of protein consumed has changed since the turn of the century. More than two-thirds of dietary protein now comes from animal sources, as contrasted with one-half in 1900, when grain consumption was greater.

Extra protein contributes to obesity. A gram of protein has an energy value of about 4 calories, which is exactly the same as the energy value for a gram of carbohydrate. Moreover, foods don't contain protein alone:

- In terms of calories, T-bone steak is about 20 percent protein and 75 percent fat.

- Cheddar cheese is 25 percent protein and 75 percent fat.

- Filet of sole, on the other hand, is only 10 percent fat.

- Chicken has more protein ounce for ounce than steak, while steak has 2½ time more calories and twice as much fat.

- In other foods high in protein, carbohydrates provide most of the calories. For example, skim milk is 40 percent protein and 60 percent carbohydrate; kidney beans, 25 percent protein and 70 percent carbohydrate; whole wheat bread, 16 percent protein and 80 percent carbohydrate.

Nutritionists generally recommend that proteins constitute between 10 and 15 percent of the daily caloric intake; the Senate Select Committee put the desired figure at 12 percent; and, as already noted, the Food and Nutrition Board's RDAs for protein are under 10 percent.

Reducing protein intake will, at the same time, almost certainly reduce the intake of fat, which so often goes along with protein. That should bring a significant reduction in total calories, since fat contains more than twice as many calories as does protein or carbohydrates: 9 calories per gram.

Fats

The myth: Maintaining a good ratio between saturated and unsaturated fats is an "open sesame" to good health.

The facts: The ratio between saturated and unsaturated fats is significant, true, but equally important is the *total intake* of fats.

The American diet has a higher fat content than almost any other in the world. Although agreement is not universal, many scientists blame our high-fat diet for a number of our major health problems, including obesity, heart disease, and possibly cancer of the colon and the breast.

What Fats Do

Fats serve many important and diverse purposes. Among other things, they do the following:

- Carry essential fatty acids the body needs but cannot produce for itself.

- Become the primary form of energy reserve once they are absorbed. They are highly efficient energy storers. Any given weight of stored, or depot, fat will yield about 2¼ times as much energy as an equivalent weight of protein or carbohydrate.

- Form essential constituents of cell membranes that regulate cellular intake and excretion of all nutrients.

- Act as an insulator to maintain body temperature by being stored as reserves, mostly in fat layers under the skin.

- Hold organs, such as the heart and the kidneys, in place and protect them.

- Transport and aid in the absorption of essential fat-soluble vitamins; A, D, E, and K.

- Spare protein from use by the body for purposes other than tissue biosynthesis.

- Improve the palatability of food and stimulate the flow of digestive juices.

- Contribute to the health of the skin.

What Fats Are

Fat molecules are similar to carbohydrates in that they contain carbon, hydrogen, and oxygen, but there is less oxygen in fat molecules. Also, the structural arrangement of fat molecules is such that carbon atoms are mostly tied to hydrogen atoms in a long string, whereas in carbohydrate molecules, oxygen atoms are mostly tied to hydrogen atoms. Thus, without hydrogen-oxygen links, there is no water held in fat molecules.

In effect, they are "dry," or at least relatively water-free; hence, they burn better and provide greater caloric energy—more than twice as much as carbohydrates (or proteins). For example, an ounce of fat can supply 240 calories, compared to 110 calories supplied by an ounce of carbohydrate or protein.

The carbon, hydrogen, and oxygen atoms in fats combine to form glycerol (a form of alcohol) plus fatty acids, which can be classified as *saturated* or *unsaturated*.

The saturated fatty acids have molecules constructed with single bonds between the carbon and hydrogen atoms and they contain all the hydrogen they can hold; in other words, they are saturated with hydrogen.

Unsaturated fatty acids, on the other hand, have some double bonds. They can take on more hydrogen under certain conditions. Some contain one double bond and are known as *monounsaturated*; others contain two or more double bonds and are called *polyunsaturated*.

All the common unsaturated fatty acids are liquid at room temperature. If hydrogen is added to unsaturated fatty acids, they become saturated and are converted into solid fats. This process is called *hydrogenation*.

Research has indicated that unsaturated fats are less likely than saturated fats to be harmful to the body. It appears that the normal blood concentration of cholesterol is increased by saturated fats, which are found mainly in meat, butter, and lard. On the other hand, unsaturated fats, found in large amounts in such vegetable oils as corn and safflower oil, help reduce the amount of cholesterol in the blood.

Some investigators believe that eating foods rich in cholesterol itself, such as egg yolks and liver, kidney, and other organ meats, also increases blood cholesterol levels. Excessive blood cholesterol is believed to be a major factor in atherosclerosis, in which fatty deposits form in arteries such as those feeding the heart muscle, impeding blood flow and leading to coronary heart disease and heart attack.

Sources of Fat

Dietary fats come from cooking fats and oils, butter, margarine, salad dressings and oils, meats, whole milk, cream, cheese, ice cream, nuts, chocolate, and avocados.

Fat Requirements

Although Americans have become increasingly fat-conscious, most of us consume far more fats than we realize—or need.

In 1901, fat made up 32 percent of the American diet; currently, it constitutes 42 percent. The increase has resulted chiefly from greater use of vegetable oils. Thanks to them, we consume much more poly-unsaturated fat than before but without cutting back significantly on saturated fat and hydrogenated oils.

Animal-fat intake has remained around 100 grams per person per day. The proportion of animal fat to vegetable fat in the total fat supply decreased from 5 to 1 in 1909 to 1.5 to 1 in 1974. Vegetable fat used in margarine, shortening, oil, and salad dressing has supplanted much of the fat previously supplied by dairy products, butter, and lard.

But total fat intake is still too high.

Guidelines developed for the general public by the American Heart Association and the Inter-Society Commission for Heart Disease Resources recommended that only 30 to 35 percent of calories be supplied as fat.

Dietary goals recommended by the U.S. Senate Select Committee on Nutrition and Human Needs include a 25 percent reduction in fat intake.

Carbohydrates

The myth: Foods containing lots of carbohydrates—both from starches and from sugars—are high in calories and low in nutritional values.

The facts: They are neither. On the contrary, carbohydrate-containing foods are effective carriers of many vital nutrients and are our major source of plant fiber, vitamin C, and the B vitamins—niacin, thiamin, and riboflavin—as well as of many important trace elements.

Ounce for ounce, carbohydrates are no more fattening than protein and have less than half the calories of fat.

Eat a 5-ounce potato without butter or sour cream, and you consume 110 calories. A 5-ounce steak, on the other hand, contains 500 calories because steak has more fat than protein. Yet weight watchers too often mistakenly leave potatoes on the plate and eat every last bit of steak.

What Carbohydrates Do

The major role of carbohydrates is to supply energy. In so doing, they spare protein so it can be used for its primary purpose of building and repairing body tissues. Carbohydrates also help the body utilize other nutrients, such as fiber, vitamins, and minerals.

The body's method of dealing with carbohydrates is to convert them to blood sugar, or *glucose*. Starches are converted into glucose by enzymes in the intestine; the body could not absorb them otherwise. Cane or beet sugar (sucrose) is converted into glucose plus fructose by the enzyme sucrase; the liver then changes the fructose into glucose. The enzyme lactase converts milk sugar into glucose plus galactose, and the liver then changes the galactose into glucose.

Energy from carbohydrates is quickly available and quickly used. Generally, within about a dozen hours the last of the carbohydrates from a meal have been burned up. Unless more energy from carbohydrates has become available in the meantime, fat stores are then ransacked for energy.

Supplying energy by burning fat is not highly efficient. In the process, ketone bodies (toxic breakdown products of the burning) are produced and have to be excreted by the kidneys. In those who follow faddist low-carbohydrate diets, ketone bodies can accumulate in the blood, causing nausea, fatigue, and apathy.

If for lack of adequate carbohydrates, the body also has to turn to proteins for energy, there can be more than one penalty. The amount of protein available for building and replacing tissues is reduced, and with the burning of protein, nitrogen is left over that must be excreted by the kidneys, which further adds to their burden.

What Carbohydrates Are

Carbohydrates, which include all sugars and starches, are made up of carbon, hydrogen, and oxygen. Just as in water, there are two hydrogen atoms for each atom of oxygen. Carbohydrates get their name because, in effect, they are hydrated (watered) carbons. They are best pictured as long chains of small building blocks. For example, starch, a large carbohydrate molecule, is a string of smaller, simpler sugar molecules.

There are many sugars: *Fructose*, the sweetest sugar (also known as *levulose* and *fruit sugar*), occurs in honey, ripe fruits, and many vegetables; *lactose* is a sugar in milk; *maltose* is a sugar from malt or digested starch; and *sucrose* is the table sugar in sugar cane and beets (from which comes table sugar), the sap from maple trees, and sorghum.

The starches, which are made up of complex sugars (polysaccharides rather than disaccharides such as sucrose), are not sweet like the simpler sugars. There are starches in tubers such as potatoes; in seeds such as peas, beans, peanuts, and almonds; and in roots such as carrots and beets. Our principal sources of starch, however, are cereal grains— wheat, rye, rice, barley, corn, millet, and oats—with which more than two-thirds of the world's croplands are planted.

Carbohydrate Requirements

Traditionally, carbohydrates have been the principal source of calories. Even now, for many in the world, 60 to 75 percent of food calories come from carbohydrates.

In the United States, however, carbohydrate consumption has fallen off markedly. At the turn of the century carbohydrates provided close to 50 percent of the calories in the diet; more recently the figure has fallen to 46 percent. The most marked decline has been in the consumption of nourishing complex carbohydrates, which has been partly offset by an increase in the consumption of "empty" calories in presweetened foods.

As a recent "white paper" of the American Dietetic Association points out, 1 pound of sugar was consumed in 1909 for every 10 pounds of fruit, vegetables, and cereal products, but "we now eat 1 pound of sugar for every 5 pounds of fruit, vegetables, and cereals. We are not eating the starchy vegetables and cereals that provide a balance between complex and simple carbohydrate, and also provide vitamins, minerals, and fiber."

The dietary goals recommended by the Senate Select Committee on Nutrition and Human Needs call for carbohydrates—especially the complex starches and naturally occurring sugars in fruits and vegetables—to make up 60 percent of our daily caloric intake.

FACTS ABOUT COMPLEX CARBOHYDRATES

- Unrefined or whole fruits, vegetables, and grains are important for supplying fiber, carbohydrate, vitamins, minerals, and calories.

- Enrichment of refined carbohydrates restores only a few of the vitamins and minerals lost in the refining process.

- The American diet has become very high in refined carbohydrate and, therefore, very low in dietary fiber.

- Low-fiber diets have been associated with constipation, diverticulitis, cancer of the colon, appendicitis, hemorrhoids, and hiatus hernia.

- Dietary fiber tends to hold water and produces stools that are bulkier, softer, and pass more quickly and easily through the intestines.

- A sudden, large increase in dietary fiber may cause uncomfortable flatulence, cramping, and distention. Add fiber *gradually* to your diet.

- Drink plenty of liquids, especially with more fiber in your diet. Liquids help to avoid gas, constipation, and intestinal blockage.

- The best way to increase dietary fiber is to increase unrefined, high-fiber foods such as whole grains, whole fruits, and vegetables.

- Whole grains spoil and turn rancid more quickly than refined grains. Store tightly sealed in a cool place.

Sugar—Sweet and Dangerous

Sugar was once affordable only for the rich—and even they couldn't get much of it. Apothecaries were the only sellers, and they measured it out by the ounce. In Elizabethan times, England consumed a grand total of only 88 tons of sugar a year.

Then, less than a century ago, Latin America began to cultivate sugar cane and a process was worked out in Europe for refining sugar beets. By 1850 annual world production had reached only 3.5 million tons, but by 1950 it was up to 35 million tons. Currently it is more than 70 million tons.

Per capita consumption of sugar per year in the United States, and in many other Western industrialized nations, now averages almost 140 pounds, more than 2 pounds per week.

Sugar and Obesity

Sugar is certainly not the only contributor to obesity—no one particular food is—but a larger proportion of daily calories is provided by sugar than by anything else.

One of the best-known opponents of sugar is Britain's John Yudkin, M.D., biochemist and physician. Many people, Dr. Yudkin believes, could lose excess weight simply by giving up or severely restricting their intake of sugar. If, he points out, you take just 1 spoonful of sugar in each cup of coffee or tea and drink only 5 cups a day, you could lose more than 10 pounds a year by eliminating the sugar.

Diabetes and Heart Disease

Aside from possibly contributing to diabetes and heart disease via obesity, does sugar do so directly? There have been some suggestive, but not definitive, studies.

Investigations in Israel found that the incidence of diabetes among Yemenites immigrating there was low. Sucrose is not a part of the traditional diet in Yemen, but the consumption of sucrose by Yemenites immigrating to Israel increased within a short time after their arrival there to the level common in Israel. Within a few years, the Yemenites had a diabetes incidence matching that of other Israelis.

The Israeli investigators, led by A. M. Cohen, M.D., of the Hadassah Medical School in Jerusalem, also undertook laboratory studies and determined that animals on a typically Yemenite, no-sugar diet for 2 months remained normal, while some of those on a western, high-sugar diet developed diabetes symptoms.

The symptomatic animals were probably genetically susceptible. "And this," says Dr. Cohen, "is undoubtedly true of humans. Eating sucrose can bring on diabetes in the genetically prone person. On the other hand, proper dieting—cutting the consumption of refined sugars down to 5 percent of total carbohydrates, not 50—can prevent the onset of diabetes in the genetically prone.

"Currently," Cohen says, "there is no way to tell who is genetically prone to diabetes and who isn't. Therefore, we must all be careful about the consumption of sugar."

Some years ago Dr. Yudkin studied death rates from coronary disease in fifteen countries in relation to sugar intake. The annual coronary death rate per 100,000 persons, he reported, increased steadily from 60 for an intake of 20 pounds of sugar per year to 300 for 120 pounds and then more sharply to about 750 for 150 pounds of sugar per year.

Despite their findings, these and other studies undertaken to date have left many scientists still skeptical about a direct link between sugar consumption and diabetes or coronary heart disease. That doesn't mean, however, that excessive sugar consumption plays no role at all.

Perhaps the views of many scientists are summed up well by Sir Richard Doll, Regius Professor of Medicine at Oxford. "I am not," says Sir Richard, "a believer in the hypothesis that sugar is a specific cause of either. But I think sugar does come into the picture because it makes it easier to eat too much, and if we lower total intake of food, we are more likely to avoid coronary heart disease and diabetes."

3.

Nutrition and Weight Control

"If you're overweight, you're ill. And I mean seriously ill. Oh, that's not to say you won't get away with it for a long time. Or that you won't feel perfectly well. . . . But in the end, the fat will get you."

So wrote physician Robert E. Fuiz some years ago.

His reasons: "Carrying extra weight batters your arteries, plunders your heart, predisposes you to diabetes, and pounds away at the weight-bearing joints so that in the end a fat man wobbles where a thin man runs. It's sad, really. . . . Being fat is being sick. Honest."

The Obesity Epidemic

In the United States today, it is a rare person who does not diet or does not know someone else who diets. At any given moment, some 20 million Americans are on one kind of diet or another. Although women have been the mainstay of the diet industry, men are becoming increasingly concerned about their weight, too.

About 40 percent of all Americans, it is estimated, are at least 20 percent above their ideal weight. For some age groups, including men from 38 to 48 and women from 50 to 60, the figure is 65 percent.

The Bad News

Although there must be a thousand or more programs to help people lose weight in what has become a leading minor growth industry at $10 billion a year, the record of success in losing and keeping off weight is abysmal.

Writing in the specialty journal, *Obesity & Bariatric Medicine* Margaret Mackenzie, M.D., observes: "Losing weight is easy; keeping it off is impossible for more than about 2 percent of those who try. Two years later, almost all who have successfully lost weight have not only regained it, but have added more as well."

Ironically, Americans, generally considered the most diet-conscious people on earth, are not getting thinner, as the Metropolitan Life Insurance Company discovered when it conducted a study of its policyholders going back 30 years. Over that time period, the average weight for men increased by 11 pounds, from 160 to 171 pounds, and the average weight for women rose by 5 pounds, from 129 to 134 pounds.

The Good News

In spite of depressing statistics, obesity is not incurable—far from it. There is nothing inherently insurmountable about it.

What does seem to be insurmountable is the misguided faith placed by so many people in fad diets, in the latest "quickie" panaceas, which rarely, if ever, do more than make their inventors rich.

Precisely because they result in quick losses of weight and do not permanently substitute good eating and drinking habits for poor ones, fad diets seldom achieve stable weight loss.

However, for the executive who is determined to achieve it, stable weight loss is possible. We know this is true from our experience at Executive Health Examiners.

The Penalties of Obesity

The stereotype of the jolly fat person may be the most inaccurate myth in American culture. Perhaps Cyril Connolly came closer to the truth when he said, "Inside every fat person, there is a thin person, screaming to be let out."

Beyond whatever psychological discomforts it may cause, obesity is associated with health hazards, among them the following:

Breathing Difficulties   The greater the weight in the chest wall, the greater the work involved in breathing. Because of their increased breathing difficulty, obese people have less tolerance for exercise.

Coronary Heart Disease   Excess weight is a risk factor for coronary heart disease and the heart attacks which that disease may produce. In the government's long-term Framingham Heart Study, which has been following more than 5000 originally healthy people in that Massachusetts community for more than 30 years, men who were 30 percent overweight turned out to have a 2.8 times greater risk of developing coronary heart disease within 10 years of their becoming that overweight than those who were 10 percent or more underweight during the same period of time. Obesity may promote coronary heart disease because it adds to the burden of the heart, which must provide circulation for the extra fatty tissue. Blood-fat abnormalities also are more common among the obese.

High Blood Pressure   The blood pressure of the obese is often elevated. High blood pressure contributes to coronary heart disease and is also a major factor in stroke and kidney disease.

Gallbladder disease   Obesity is associated with increased production of cholesterol and, hence, with increased concentration of cholesterol in bile, which is produced in the liver and stored in the gallbladder. If the concentration of cholesterol becomes great enough, the cholesterol may precipitate out of the bile as gallstones.

Diabetes   Obesity is clearly related to the most common form of diabetes mellitus—adult-onset diabetes. Obesity, research indicates, seems to lead to resistance to the action of insulin, which normally transfers glucose (blood sugar) to the body tissues.

Are You Obese?

By definition, an obese person is one who weighs 20 percent or more than what he or she should weigh.

Even if you are not obese, it may still be worthwhile for you to lose 10 pounds or so of whatever excess weight you are carrying. Chances are that if you are overweight at all, you will gain more weight in the future, and it is easier to lose 10 pounds now than 20, 30, 50, or more pounds in the future. Here are some easy ways of checking on your weight:

The Mirror Test   Usually, your mirror can provide you with a fairly good clue to whether you are too heavy. Remove all your clothes and take a look—back, side, and front—in a full-length mirror. Stop holding your breath and sucking in your gut. Examine the real you.

Desirable-Weight Chart   Consult the table on page 29 to determine if your eyes have deceived you. Note that this table, unlike some others, gives "desirable" rather than "average" weights. What is "average" tends to include more and more fat as you progress from age group to age group, and that is *not* desirable. Also, average-weight tables reflect the weight of overweight individuals, who skew the average upward.

The Pinch Test   Grasp a fold of skin with your thumb and forefinger— at your waist, stomach, upper arm, buttocks, and calf. At least half of body fat is directly under the skin. Generally, the under-skin layer (which is what you measure with the pinch, since only fat, not muscle, pinches) should be between ¼ and ½ inch thick. Since you get a double thickness with your pinch, it normally should be ½ to 1 inch. A fold much greater than an inch indicates excess body fat.

The Ruler Test   This test is based on the fact that if there is no excess fat, the abdominal surface—between the flare of the ribs and the front of the pelvis—normally is flat. If you lie on your back and place a ruler on your abdomen, along the midline of the body, it should not point upward at the midsection. If your stomach holds up the ruler so it doesn't lie flat, you need to slim down.

DESIRABLE WEIGHTS BY HEIGHT
FOR ADULT MALES AND FEMALES*

Height without shoes		Weight without clothes			
		Men		Women	
in	cm	lb	kg	lb	kg
58	147			102 (92–119)	46 (42–54)
60	152			107 (96–125)	49 (44–57)
62	158	123 (112–141)	56 (51–64)	113 (102–131)	51 (46–59)
64	163	130 (118–148)	59 (54–67)	120 (108–138)	55 (49–63)
66	168	136 (124–156)	62 (56–71)	128 (114–146)	58 (52–66)
68	173	145 (132–166)	66 (60–75)	136 (122–154)	62 (55–70)
70	178	154 (140–174)	70 (64–79)	144 (130–163)	65 (59–74)
72	183	162 (148–184)	74 (67–84)	152 (138–173)	69 (63–79)
74	188	171 (156–194)	78 (71–88)		
76	193	181 (164–204)	82 (74–93)		

*Average weight ranges in parentheses.
SOURCE: George A. Bray, 1975.

Factors that Contribute to Obesity

Obesity can have many contributing causes, one or more of which may predominate in a given individual. Some of those causes are well established; research is turning up others.

Genetic Predisposition

That a hereditary influence—a genetic predisposition—can be at work in some cases of obesity has been shown by studies of obese identical twins. Some were raised together; others, apart. Despite environmental differences, both groups tended to become obese.

Still environment is influential too. Studies have shown that genetically predisposed youngsters raised by nonobese adoptive parents do not become as obese as predisposed youngsters placed in families with obese adoptive parents. Also, children who are not genetically predisposed to obesity tend to be heavier when raised by obese adoptive parents than nonpredisposed children raised by nonobese adoptive parents.

Fat Children and Fat Cells

Many of us become obese only in adulthood, but others get an early start, even in the first months of life. The latter can be the particularly unlucky ones—fat in the sandbox, fat through school, fat now, and facing a very tough fight if they are not to die fat.

One reason for their difficulty is an excess of fat cells, tiny structures that are located throughout the body, with large concentrations in the abdomen and around such organs as the kidneys and the heart.

We all have such cells, which collect and hold fat from food intake, keeping it in storage for use when needed. Whether we all have the same number at birth is unknown. However, two facts about the cells have become known recently. One is that once a fat cell appears in the body, it remains for a lifetime, although the amount of fat stored in any given cell can vary from day to day and from year to year.

The second fact is that the number of these permanent fat cells can multiply—doubling or even tripling—in the first months of life. Such multiplication, it appears, can cause problems. The baby who is fed moderately so that no such multiplication occurs is far less likely to have trouble with obesity throughout life than the infant fed too much and thereafter burdened with an excess of fat cells.

Studying obese children, Jerome Knittle, M.D., of Mt. Sinai School of Medicine, New York City, removed small amounts of tissue from under the skin with a special syringe. He found 2-year-old obese children with double the number of fat cells of normal-weight children of the same age and 5-year-olds with more fat cells than normal adults.

There is some evidence that excess fat cells may communicate with the appetite center in the brain, signaling a need to be filled. An overabundance of such cells, then, may lead to excessive appetite.

Physical Inactivity

Many studies of both children and adults have shown that the obese commonly are less active than the lean. Interestingly, too, studies of people who have deliberately eaten to excess in order to become obese have shown that physical activity tends to decrease as obesity increases.

Glandular Disorders

In some cases, endocrine gland disorders can play a significant role in obesity. Underfunctioning of the thyroid gland (hypothyroidism) can make weight loss difficult unless it is corrected. Rarely, disorders of other glands—the adrenals, pancreas, or pituitary—may contribute to obesity. However, glandular dysfunction is considered by most authorities to be highly overrated as a cause of obesity; it is responsible at most for no more than 1 percent of excess weight.

The "Habit Belly"

Virtually all of us do some eating without hunger, but many of the obese far surpass us. They often eat in large measure because of the environmental cues—time of day, odors, palatability of food, sight of food. They may nibble without thinking while reading or watching television. They may eat simply because it is mealtime, and they may finish everything in front of them even though they are not hungry. They commonly eat when feeling depressed, bored, or lonesome.

This is learned behavior. It may be learned even in early childhood. Newborns naturally react to hunger pangs by sucking on breast or bottle until they feel comfortably full; then they stop. Even during infancy, however, external clues may intrude and trigger eating. If parents praise their children for finishing their bottles, the children may come to do some of their eating thereafter not out of hunger but in seeking praise. If children are given sweets to comfort them when they fall and hurt themselves, they may be learning to assuage pain—both physical and emotional—with food. And parents who give their children crackers or cookies to ease teething pain may be leading them into the habit of eating without being hungry.

A New Possibility—An Enzyme Defect

A biochemical defect that changes the way the body burns food for energy may result in a predisposition toward obesity, according to Havard Medical School researchers Mario DeLuise, Jeffrey Flier, and George Blackburn. Their discovery suggests that some people with weight problems may burn up fewer calories for energy than do normal people and may store more calories as fat.

Obese people, the investigators found, have a significantly lower level of an enzyme which helps to chemically balance the internal and external environments of cells. Called the *sodium-potassium-pump*, adenosine triphosphatase (ATPase) is an enzyme which transports sodium and potassium across the membrane of every living cell, keeping sodium levels low and potassium levels high.

In its work, ATPase uses from 20 to 50 percent of each day's food intake and generates heat as a by-product, thereby sustaining normal body temperature. Overweight people, suggest the investigators, may expend far less energy to maintain the sodium-potassium balance than do people of average weight.

They studied twenty overweight (47 to 177 percent higher than ideal weight) adult volunteers and twenty others with normal weights. The obese subjects were found to have a markedly lower level of ATPase in their red blood cells, and the heavier the individual, the lower the level.

The researchers now plan to go beyond red blood cells and study ATPase in other body tissues of obese and normal people. They hope to learn which hormones regulate the enzyme levels and whether age has anything to do with varying levels.

The ATPase discovery may have significance beyond understanding weight gain. The enzyme plays a role in other biological processes, and if the blood-cell abnormality is also found in other body cells, it may be linked to disorders common in overweight people, such as hypertension and diabetes.

Fad Diets and Diet Pills

Dieting has been called the number one national pastime, and fad diets have been referred to as "true pollutants of national health."

New diets appear almost weekly and are followed—often one right after the other—always with hope, however bizarre, self-defeating, and even health-impairing they may be.

"Magic Pair" Diets and Crash Diets

"Magic Pair" diets, such as the Beverly Hills diet, claim to produce quick weight loss if you eat only certain pairs of foods, such as grapefruit and lamb chops, eggs and spinach, or bananas and skim milk. On a crash diet, you may eat nothing but grapefruit and drink nothing but water, or you may only eat celery and drink water, or you may eat only cottage cheese, or something similar. While the idea of both kinds of diet is to melt away a lot of fat in little time, the actual effect is to make the dieter miserable and place him or her at risk of malnutrition. Also, fat that is quickly lost is usually quickly regained.

High-Protein Diets

These are diets which restrict food intake to steak, eggs, and other high-protein foods. Any diet restricted to a single category of foods is dangerous because it omits other necessary food groups. High-protein diets are also high in animal fat, salt, and cholesterol. They leave out essential nutrients that come from fresh fruits and vegetables.

"Eat Fat" Diets

Supposedly, this kind of diet puts the fats you eat to work, somehow miraculously melting away fat deposits in the body. Americans have spent millions of dollars on books advocating such diets. There is no evidence whatever that any one type of food has special value in stimulating the burning off of fat stores.

Low-Carbohydrate Diets

A diet sometimes called the Air Force Diet is one of many such diets, but it is vigorously disclaimed by the Air Force. It calls for restricting the intake of "carbohydrate units" but allows you to eat anything else you want. However, carbohydrate restriction may upset digestion and impair body fluid balance. Carbohydrates, moreover, are needed to help metabolize fats; in their absence a dangerous condition called *ketosis* may develop as fat metabolism becomes incomplete and products of the incomplete metabolism accumulate in the blood. Furthermore, low-carbohydrate diets tend to concentrate on foods high in fats, especially saturated fats, which may be harmful to the coronary arteries.

There are endless variations on these diets, purveyed under eye-catching new names in countless magazine articles and books. But however attractive their claims may sound, they are self-defeating, even when they are not outright dangerous. They may appear to be successful initially in removing weight, but the initial weight loss is due to water loss (rather than loss of body fat) and/or a decrease in appetite and thus in calorie intake. Because of the radical change in eating habits dictated by these diets, no one can, or should, continue on them for a long time. Also, as old eating practices are resumed, weight lost on these diets is quickly regained.

Diet Pills—Are They of Any Value?

To many people, the true wonder drug would be one that could melt away fat, making weight control entirely effortless, but it simply is not available nor is it ever likely to be. However, there are many drugs that have been used for this purpose.

Amphetamines For a while some years ago, amphetamines were claimed to be valuable as appetite suppressants, and in fact, those who took them felt less hunger. Then serious side effects were recognized, including increased blood pressure and heart rate, drug dependency, and bouts of depression when the pills were withdrawn.

Amphetamine-like Agents There are a number of other appetite-suppressant drugs, such as diethylpropion and phentermine, that are available for physicians to prescribe. Almost all are derivatives of amphetamine.

Tolerance develops in a few weeks, so they lose their effectiveness unless potentially dangerous large doses are taken. These drugs can be habit-forming. Among the adverse reactions to them are palpitations, elevation of blood pressure, restlessness, insomnia, tremor, headache, hives, and impotence.

Some 200 studies of amphetamine-like agents recently reviewed by the Food and Drug Administration indicate that taking such drugs results in only an extra half pound of weight loss per week. As some authorities point out, since tolerance develops and drug makers therefore suggest only a short course of 2 to 4 weeks, the average added benefit of appetite suppressants is only 1 to 2 pounds of weight loss—hardly worth the risks they entail.

Diuretics   These prescription agents have no real value in weight control. They only promote excretion of water, with no effect on fat, and the water is replaced promptly when use of the drug is stopped. Indiscriminate use of diuretics can upset the body's mineral balance, leading to serious losses of sodium and potassium. They may also cause nausea, weakness, and dizziness.

Thyroid Compounds   These speed up metabolism and may lead to some weight loss. But, except in persons who actually need them because of low thyroid function, thyroid compounds can produce hyperthyroid symptoms such as irritability, diarrhea, and abnormal heart rhythms.

Nonprescription Products   These contain one or the other of two agents: benzocaine or phenylpropanolamine.

Benzocaine, a local anesthetic sometimes used to soothe skin irritations, can be found in special chewing gums or candy. It is supposed to dull the taste buds and discourage eating.

Phenylpropanolamine (PPA), an amphetamine-related drug which has been used as a nasal decongestant in cold remedies, can be found in popular diet pills such as Dexatrim, Prolaine, Spantrol, and Appedrine. The drug is supposed to depress the appetite center in the brain. It has been found to elevate blood pressure in normal subjects.

Drug companies warn against use of these drugs by people with high blood pressure, diabetes, diseases of the heart, kidney, or thyroid, or other diseases. Such conditions often afflict the overweight, in many instances without their knowledge. The drugs also should not be used during pregnancy.

Even if they did no harm, do these drugs do much good?

No. At best they may serve as a temporary crutch. The phenylpropanolamine and benzocaine preparations that you can buy without a prescription are to be used for strictly limited periods—no longer than 3 months.

For long-term weight control, they are completely useless.

MASSAGES AND HOT BATHS

Massage does not help take off fat. Once the fat is off, however, massage may tone up the skin and muscles and help the body adjust to its new, slimmer contours.

The effect of hot baths lasts very briefly. They serve only to eliminate some water, which almost immediately is regained. In addition to being useless for permanent weight reduction, these methods can put a strain on the heart and circulation. Sauna baths, for example, expose the body to high temperatures and produce violent sweating—a shock to the body—sometimes doubling the pulse rate. Saunas have long been popular in Finland; however, the Finns use them over a lifetime rather than starting suddenly in flabby middle age. Saunas do little for obesity.

The Exercise Factor

For years, the role of exercise in weight control has been commonly misunderstood, but today regular physical activity is known to be important for maintaining health and preventing many diseases.

As for weight control, it can be said that while diet is part of the battle and helps you on your way, exercise contributes vitality and drive and helps take you where you want to go. See the complete discussion of exercise and executive fitness beginning on page 125.

Calorie Control

Your Diet—What Is Sensible for You?

It may be that by continuing to eat everything you now eat but with a little moderation—a cutback here and there—you can lose weight.

There is no need to rush. It took a long time for you to become over-weight. You should expect it to take a reasonable time for your weight to drop down to the desired level.

It makes no sense to try to give up, all at once, all the foods you love. You are likely to feel tortured and unlikely to stick for long with such deprivation. As long as you are already eating a balanced and varied diet, it makes sense just to eat a bit less of most of the things you are eating now.

Or you may do best with a daily meal plan. If so, you will find that the guidelines we have used successfully at Executive Health Examiners may work for you.

An Essential Variety

When "Nutrition and Your Health: Dietary Guidelines for Americans" was issued recently by two government departments—the Department of Agriculture and the Department of Health and Human Services—it listed as the very first guideline: Eat a variety of foods.

It is a concise, vital statement—very worthwhile excerpting here:

> You need about 40 different nutrients to stay healthy. These include vitamins and minerals, as well as amino acids (from proteins), essential fatty acids (from vegetable oils and animal fats), and sources of energy (calories from carbohydrates, proteins, and fats). These nutrients are in the foods you normally eat.
>
> Most foods contain more than one nutrient. Milk, for example, provides proteins, fats, sugars, riboflavin and other B-vitamins, vitamin A, calcium, and phosphorus—among other nutrients.
>
> No single food item supplies all the essential nutrients in the amounts that you need. Milk, for instance, contains very little iron or vitamin C. You should, therefore, eat a variety of foods to assure an adequate diet.
>
> The greater the variety, the less likely you are to develop either a deficiency or an excess of any single nutrient. Variety also re-duces your likelihood of being exposed to excessive amounts of contaminants in any single food item.
>
> One way to assure variety and, with it, a well-balanced diet is to select foods each day from each of several major groups: for example, fruits and vegetables; cereals, breads, and grains; meat, poultry, eggs, and fish; dry peas and beans, such as soybeans,

kidney beans, lima beans, and black-eyed peas, which are good vegetable sources of protein; and milk, cheese, and yogurt.

Fruits and vegetables are excellent sources of vitamins, especially vitamins C and A. Whole grain and enriched breads, cereals, and grain products provide B-vitamins, iron, and energy. Meats supply protein, fat, iron and other minerals, as well as several vitamins, including thiamine and vitamin B$_{12}$. Dairy products are major sources of calcium and other nutrients.

TO ASSURE YOURSELF AN ADEQUATE DIET, eat a variety of foods daily, including selections of fruits; vegetables; whole grains and enriched breads, cereals, and grain products; milk, cheese, and yogurt; meats, poultry, fish, and eggs; and legumes (dry peas and beans).

Cutback Maneuvers

Now, assuming you are getting variety, consider what moderation can do.

Look at the cutbacks in eating habits for examples of what individual small omissions can accomplish in terms of weight loss over a period of 1 year. Would several of these be enough to accomplish your weight-loss goal?

Remember that slow loss is not really a luxury. It gives you a chance to lose fat, not just muscle tissue or body fluids—and to form new, better eating habits.

If cutback maneuvers are not likely to be enough, you might want to try substitution maneuvers.

Substitution Maneuvers

In many cases, the caloric content of similar foods varies greatly despite the fact that the looks, tastes, and satisfactions may be quite similar. So substitutions often can be made readily and can prove quite satisfying, while saving many calories and contributing markedly to weight control.

At Executive Health Examiners, we have found "The Executive Calorie Countdown Guide" to be helpful for many executives.

CUTBACKS: CHANGE YOUR EATING HABITS JUST A LITTLE BIT

Food	If you omit	How often	Loss per year
Butter or margarine	1 pat	Daily	3½ lb
Bread or toast	1 slice	Daily	6 lb
Scrambled egg	1	Once a week	1½ lb
Medium-fried bacon	2 slices	Once a week	1½ lb
Pork and beans	½ serving	Once a week	2½ lb
Rice	½ serving	Once a week	1 lb
Bread stuffing	½ serving	Once a week	1 lb
Baking powder biscuit	1	Once a week	2 lb
Creamed cottage cheese	1 cup	Once a week	3 lb
Yogurt (plain)	1 cup	Once a week	2 lb
Avocado	½	Once a week	2½ lb
Oil and vinegar salad dressing	1 tbsp instead of 2	Twice a week	1½ lb
Whole roasted peanuts	¼ cup	Once a week	3 lb
Potato chips	10 medium	Once a week	1½ lb
Crackers	2 instead of 4	Twice a week	1 lb
Most cheese	1 oz	Once a week	1½ lb
Wine	3 oz	Once a week	1 lb
Beer	12-oz can	Once a week	2½ lb
Carbonated drinks	8-oz glass	Once a week	1 lb
Ice cream soda	1	Once a week	5 lb
Chocolate cake with chocolate frosting	1 slice	Once a week	4 lb
Sugar	1 tsp	Daily	1½ lb
Doughnut	1	Once a week	2 lb
Pie	½ slice	Twice a week	3½ lb
Jam or jelly	1 tbsp	Twice a week	1½ lb

THE EXECUTIVE CALORIE COUNTDOWN GUIDE

High-calorie choice*	Lower-calorie substitution*	Calories saved
APPETIZERS AND SNACKS		
1 cup New England clam chowder (275)	1 cup Manhattan clam chowder (100)	175
1 cup split pea soup (200)	1 cup consommé (25)	175
1 oz Swiss or American cheese (105)	1 oz farmer's cheese, plain (70)	35
1 tbsp cream cheese (53)	1 tbsp cottage cheese (18)	35
10 mixed nuts (94)	10 pretzels, very thin sticks (10)	84
2 tbsp roasted peanuts (172)	2 tbsp raisins (58)	114
1 cup buttered popcorn (172)	1 cup plain popcorn (82)	90
BEVERAGES		
1 cup whole milk, 3.5% fat (160)	1 cup skim milk or buttermilk (85)	75
1 gin and tonic, 8 oz (185)	1 wine spritzer, 2 oz wine (49)	136
1 Manhattan or martini (160)	3½ oz dry wine (85)	75
12 oz beer (150)	12 oz light beer (95)	55
8 oz cola, tonic water, or bitter lemon (100)	8 oz club soda (2)	98
½ cup grape juice (75)	½ cup tomato juice (25)	50
MEAT, FISH, POULTRY, EGGS		
3 oz grilled hamburger on bun (400)	3 oz roast beef on roll (300)	100
6 oz Swiss steak (630)	6 oz veal cutlet in wine (235)	395
½ fried chicken (464)	6 oz broiled chicken (257)	207
5 oz breaded fried perch (320)	5 oz broiled fish (240)	80
6 oz fried shrimp (380)	6 oz broiled shrimp (200)	180
1 fried egg (120)	1 poached or boiled egg (85)	35
2 strips bacon, crisp (96)	1 slice Canadian bacon (65)	31
BREADS AND STARCHES		
1 slice bread or toast (60)	2 pieces melba toast or Rykrisp (40)	20
1 Danish pastry (250)	1 plain roll (110)	140
1 cup granola-type cereal (500)	1 cup corn flakes (95)	405
½ cup fried rice (175)	½ cup rice, plain (70)	105

High-calorie choice*	Lower-calorie substitution*	Calories saved
VEGETABLES		
20 french fries (270)	1 medium baked potato, plain (90)	180
½ cup potato salad (125)	½ cup vegetable salad, raw, no dressing (20)	105
½ cup cole slaw (65)	½ cup shredded raw cabbage (15)	50
½ cup corn kernels (70)	½ cup green beans, cooked (14)	56
½ cup candied sweet potatoes (150)	½ cup winter squash, mashed (50)	100
DESSERTS AND SWEETS		
Apple pie, ⅙ of 9-in. pie (410)	1 baked apple, sweetened (160)	250
1 piece chocolate cake with icing (400)	1 piece angel cake (121)	279
2 chocolate chip cookies (104)	3 vanilla wafers (51)	53
½ cup vanilla ice cream (145)	½ cup orange ice (72)	73
½ cup chocolate ice cream (150)	½ cup chocolate ice milk (102)	48
1 chocolate ice cream bar (144)	1 twin popsicle bar (95)	49
1 caramel candy (42)	1 hard candy, butterscotch (21)	21
SAUCES AND COOKING INGREDIENTS		
2 tbsp meat gravy (82)	2 tbsp soy sauce (16)	66
½ cup sour cream (227)	½ cup yogurt, low-fat (65)	162
¼ cup heavy cream (211)	¼ cup evaporated milk (70)	141
1 tbsp butter (100)	Spray-type oil (PAM) (2 seconds) (8)	92
1 tbsp mayonnaise (101)	1 tbsp mayonnaise-type dressing (Miracle Whip) (61)	40
1 tbsp olive oil (124)	1 tbsp vinegar (2)	122

*Numbers in parentheses are "calories," or "large calories," as meant in common discussions of nutrition; each "calorie" is actually equivalent to 1 kilocalorie (kcal), or 1000 calories.
SOURCE: Riska Platt, M.S., R.D.

GOOD DIET/BAD DIET

A good diet is one that:

- Is nutritionally sound—which means that it provides all the necessary nutrients and therefore contains a wide variety of foods. The aim of a reducing diet is to help decrease body fat without damaging body structure.

- With some, additions can become a basic pattern of eating for the rest of your life.

- Consists of foods that are appetizing and pleasant to eat.

- Helps train the appetite and encourages you to develop a pattern of eating at regular intervals.

- Provides food with staying power—the power to satisfy your appetite and prevent excessive hunger.

- Is built around a nucleus of familiar foods. It should be adaptable to your living situation.

- Can be matched to the individual. Different people lose weight at different calorie levels, and diets should be planned accordingly.

A bad diet is one that:

- Has a limited choice of food—which leads to feelings of deprivation and monotony and does not provide all necessary nutrients.

- Requires special foods that make it difficult to follow in most living situations.

- Leads to rapid weight loss, which may be detrimental to your health.

- Does not establish a pattern to follow for life.

Riska Platt, M.S., R.D., EHE nutrition consultant

When You Dine Out

It is often said that executive business lunches and other restaurant meals make weight control impossible.

That is not true.

Many weight-conscious executives are very successful dieters. It is not uncommon to find executives who eat 10 or more meals weekly at restaurants and still manage to control their weight.

Most of them are assertive. They make special requests, and if the requests are not strictly honored, they find other restaurants that are happy to comply with them. Finding such restaurants is becoming easier and easier as patrons are becoming more and more demanding about good nutrition.

There is no reason to have any hesitation about specifying how you want your food prepared—baked, broiled or steamed, for example, instead of fried and with sauces and salad dressings served on the side.

In addition to avoiding such high-calorie extras, as sauces, crackers, rolls, sour cream, butter, and dressings, weight-conscious executives often leave unfinished a significant part of oversized portions. They make menu selections carefully. When being host or hosted at even the finest steak and chop house, for example, they may order broiled fish, spinach salad without bacon bits, and white wine and have a fine meal, free of excessive calories.

Weight-conscious individuals should choose beverages carefully, too. Many have conceded that martinis and other alcoholic beverages contribute nothing but calories to the meal and therefore have switched to club soda or to one of the mineral waters that are currently popular. Others have cut calories by drinking wine spritzers, which contain only an ounce or two of wine with calorie-free soda water.

When You Travel

Travel can make weight control more difficult, but many executives have learned to cope effectively by using some of the following techniques:

- Plan ahead. Most executives have an agenda which includes many scheduled meals. It is usually easy to predict the type of meal (sometimes even the actual foods) that will be served. Plan for light meals or snacks when nothing is scheduled.

- Retain the same eating habits you have established at home, if they are good ones. For example, do not eat a huge breakfast if you normally have only a small bowl of cereal.

- Limit alcohol intake. Alcoholic beverages are high in calories and do not enhance mental acuity for conducting business.

- Exercise. Jog, use a jump rope, or climb the hotel stairs if your physician approves. Otherwise, walk as much as possible.

- Do not use food to compensate for being away from home; it is not an adequate substitute anyway. Even if large and frequent meals are included with the hotel room or on the expense account, an executive who eats them all will end up paying for them in more ways than one.

- Be assertive. Request in advance the special meals that are readily available on airplanes and ask for substitutions at restaurants.

Behavior-Modification Techniques

We have found at Executive Health Examiners that changing eating habits through behavior-modification techniques is very important in successful weight reduction and weight control. We put major emphasis on it.

Commonly, eating too much is a learned behavior, a habitual response to stimuli in the social environment. Behavior modification applies the principles of psychology to changing the habits that make for overeating.

All of us sometimes eat without being hungry. It appears that the overweight, however, eat in large measure because of environmental cues—time of day, odors, palatability of food, or sight of food. They often nibble without thinking about it, while watching television or reading.

Write It Down

Take an inventory of your eating habits. Keep a written diary of everything you eat each day, noting:

- the type and amount of food

- where and when the food is eaten

- the time spent eating

- any activity while eating

- people you eat with

- your mood when you eat—how you feel at the time

- any events precipitating the eating

- how hungry (or not hungry) you are when you eat

A bore and a bother? It may well be at the very start, but you are likely to find that it is not only valuable but interesting as well.

For one thing, just monitoring intake of food helps many people to cut down. You may find that you are less likely to order a rich dessert at lunch or down a handful of peanuts in the evening when you realize you are obligated to yourself to write it down.

You will also be getting, as you may never have had before, an accurate picture of those eating habits that are causing trouble.

You may be surprised at what the record tells you about yourself. You may find that you eat more often or much more quickly than you thought you did or that you get a desire for food under certain circumstances—on passing the refrigerator, when you're fatigued or bored, or at some particular time of day—even though you're not hungry at all.

This behavior profile can help you to detect any eating behavior which is associated with circumstances or emotional stress rather than with hunger.

Once aware of what is going on, you will recognize, of course, that food is not a suitable response to fatigue or boredom. You can exert control when it is needed and, in the process, find more appropriate responses.

If, for example, you find from your record that you do considerable snacking when you settle down to watch television, you can find a solution for that. One obvious possibility, of course, is to watch television less.

Slow Down!

Eat slowly and enjoy your food. Many studies indicate that when you make a deliberate decision to eat and then take the time to enjoy the eating thoroughly, you will experience a greater sense of satisfaction, even though you may be consuming fewer calories.

Eating slowly gives your appetite a chance to be satisfied. If you eat a meal in less than 20 minutes, you are eating too fast to enjoy it. Moreover, it takes about 20 minutes for the brain to register "Enough." Therefore if you finish a meal in less time, you are more likely to reach for seconds because you still feel hungry.

Some Behavior-Modification Suggestions

- Take small bites.

- Chew your food longer, savoring each bite.

- Use your napkin more often.

- Put your fork or spoon down after each bite and wait until you have swallowed before taking another forkful or spoonful of food.

- Take sips of water—or plain tea or coffee—between bites.

- Pause for a few minutes in the middle of a meal.

Modified Attitudes

Changes in behavior are more important in the long run than immediate weight changes.

- Develop a tolerance for mild hunger. Think of it as a positive feeling.

- Make deliberate decisions to eat; don't eat absentmindedly.

- Do not immediately stop eating all of your favorite foods. All of us have "sin" foods—bread or pizza or sweets. Many people on diets forbid themselves such favorites, until their craving for them finally gets out of control and they binge. Afterward they feel guilty, and many then stop dieting.

- Plan in advance to indulge yourself occasionally—and to make up for it by eating less of something else.

- Concentrate on your eating. Avoid watching television or reading.

- Request your family and friends not to offer you seconds at meals or food between meals. Let them know that while offering food may commonly be equated with affection, you will regard it as far more affectionate if they don't offer you food.

- At home, choose one place to eat all meals and snacks.

- Sit in a chair when you eat—never stand, even for snacks.

- Use a plate and utensils—again, even for snacks.

- Even at home, avoid "family-style" eating and, instead, have food portioned on plates before it is brought to the table. Keep serving platters and bowls in the kitchen.

- At home and in restaurants, always leave at least a small amount of food on your plate.

Underweight

If you are markedly underweight or are losing weight, medical advice is important.

A chronic underweight condition or sudden loss of weight can be an indication of a health problem. It may signal the presence or onset of disease, for example, diabetes, thyroid gland overactivity (hyperthyroidism), or chronic infection.

Finding the cause and correcting it are the job of a physician.

Determining if You Are Underweight

Quite possibly, you will need the help of a physician to determine whether you are really underweight.

It is likely, of course, that you are if you are 10 to 15 pounds or more below the figures in the table on desirable weights and if, in addition, bones stick out all over your body, or your muscles do not provide adequate resilient protection to your back, thighs, and buttocks, or your face is thin and drawn.

The weight figures in the table alone may not be enough to indicate underweight. You could be the long, lean type whose weight normally falls below those figures.

Your physician, after a physical examination, including observations of the size and bony framework of your body, can determine fairly accurately whether you are underweight. Some people worry needlessly over an underweight condition that does not actually exist, because of a "diagnosis" by well-meaning friends or relatives.

What to Do about It

If extreme thinness is not the result of an underlying medical problem, it is very likely due to not eating enough of the right kinds of food. Your physician undoubtedly will have suggestions, including some for a change in diet.

How you eat can also be important. It takes time to eat proper meals and enjoy them. A 5- or 10-minute mealtime is hardly conducive to eating more without feeling stuffed. Longer and more relaxed mealtimes may help solve your problem.

Relaxing *before* meals can be helpful, too. It is difficult to eat adequately when you are either all steamed up or tired.

You may find that large portions discourage you from eating—or, on the other hand, you may have difficulty taking seconds and do better with large servings. It could be helpful, if you don't know, to determine which type you are and to determine, too, whether you eat more at family-style meals, or when food is served in predetermined portions.

Eating More

If you now eat relatively little, that can be a matter of habit—and habits can be changed. By taking an extra slice of bread or a second helping—even quite a small one—you may begin to change your eating patterns.

High-Calorie Foods

Certain vegetables—among them peas, lima beans, and potatoes—are higher in calories than others, particularly leafy vegetables. Try to increase your intake of higher-calorie foods, but continue to eat salads as well.

If your physician finds you have no blood-fat problems, you may find it helpful to increase your intake of such high-calorie foods as chowders, cream soups, mayonnaise, sauces, and rich desserts.

Snacking

Snacks can add weight, and you should look for some that you will enjoy.

You may find that some—such as candy, cake, and ice cream— tend to satiate you, dulling your mealtime hunger, but there are others you can try. Peanut butter and fruit, for example, are valuable for supplying essential nutrients as well as extra calories.

Smoking

Particularly when excessive, smoking can dull the appetite and the taste buds as well. You might try cutting down. At the least, try to avoid smoking just before and during meals.

Alcohol

For some people, sipping an aperitif, such as a glass of sherry, before dinner helps stimulate their appetite. For others, a leisurely cocktail or highball is helpful. Obviously, however, alcohol should not be substituted for food.

4.

Nutrition and Cardiovascular Disease

High Blood Pressure

Hypertension is a major threat to health, contributing significantly as it does to heart attacks and to strokes and kidney failure as well. It ranks as our greatest single cause of death.

The Normal and the High Pressures

Blood pressure is the force exerted against artery walls as blood flows through the blood vessels. The pressure is produced primarily by the pumping action of the heart and is needed to push the body's 5 quarts of blood through more than 60,000 miles of blood vessels.

Each time the heart beats, pressure increases. This higher pressure is known as the *systolic* pressure (systolic, from the Greek word for contraction). The pressure is at its lowest when the heart relaxes between beats. This is known as the *diastolic* pressure (from the Greek word for expansion).

Normal systolic pressure at rest is the range of 100 to 140, and normal diastolic pressure is 60 to 90. A blood pressure reading is expressed by both figures, with systolic over diastolic: 140/90, for example. Because blood pressure varies normally under different circumstances, a single reading above 140/90 does not indicate abnormal pressure. But when the pressure is continuously elevated, hypertension is present.

The Silent Killer

Hypertension is stealthy, readily detected by a physician taking measurements, but otherwise not likely to be apparent to the victim. Mild elevations, and often severe ones also, commonly produce no symptoms at all for long periods. The symptoms, including headaches, dizziness, fatigue, and weakness, are common to many disorders. So, even when they do appear, they may not be recognized as related to elevated pressure.

But, even though producing no symptoms, elevated pressure over long periods can have serious effects. It requires the heart to work harder to pump blood. So the heart muscle thickens and increases in size as a consequence. For a time, despite its increased work, the heart accommodates well. But at some point it can become fatigued, no longer fully able to meet the strain. The result may be congestive heart failure — reduced blood circulation to body tissues — which can lead to such symptoms as loss of energy, shortness of breath on exertion, wheezing, and fluid accumulation in body tissues.

Hypertension may have another effect on the heart. As the heart muscle increases in size the coronary arteries supplying it do not. They have space capacity, and that may be enough. But, in some cases, it may not be. Coronary insufficiency may then develop, with resulting chest pain (angina pectoris).

Persistent hypertension can reduce blood supply to the kidneys, impairing their function, sometimes leading to complete kidney failure and uremic poisoning and death. High pressure may also lead to rupture, or blowout, of a brain artery — in other words, a stroke.

Moreover, recent research has been assigning a critical role for hypertension in atherosclerosis. Other factors, of course, play a part: obesity, high blood-fat levels, cigarette smoking, sedentary living. But many studies have shown that a very large proportion of people who experience heart attacks, the end result of atherosclerosis of the coronary arteries of the heart, have elevated pressure. On the other hand, in the federal government's long-term study in Framingham, which for many years has been following more than 5000 people in that Massachusetts community, men and women with normal blood pressure have experienced only one-fourth the rate of coronary heart disease generally found among people of their age and sex.

How does hypertension foster atherosclerosis? One possible way is by the abnormal pounding that excessive pressure exerts on the inner linings of arteries. This pounding is severe enough, some investigators believe, to damage the lining surfaces and open the way for the fatty, clogging deposits to be laid down.

The Kinds of Hypertension

In only about 10 percent of people with elevated blood pressure can the trouble be traced to a definite physical cause. There may be pinching, or coarctation, of a portion of the aorta, the body's main trunk-line artery emerging from the heart. Narrowing of the kidney artery can elevate pressure. So, too, can a tumor of the adrenal gland. Such abnormalities often can be corrected by surgery, and blood pressure then returns to normal.

In the remaining 90 percent of patients, the hypertension is of unknown cause and is called *essential* or *idiopathic hypertension*. Essential hypertension can be treated effectively with antihypertensive drugs, but medication may not always be required. Evidence has been growing that overweight and excessive sodium (salt) intake can be significant factors in many cases of hypertension, and the elimination of one or the other, or of both, may be all that is needed to bring blood pressure down to normal.

Overweight and Blood Pressure

Physicians have long had the impression that hypertension and obesity may be related. Today there is no longer any doubt that excess weight is an important contributing factor to the development of high blood pressure.

The Framingham study confirmed this impression. Framingham participants with hypertension were found more often to be obese than people with normal blood pressure. Also, the prevalence of hypertension at all ages increased with relative weight.

Other studies as well have shown that most people with essential hypertension, even adolescents, are overweight. Conversely, the overweight are more likely than normal-weight individuals to have hypertension or to develop it over a period of a few years. And people who are overweight and hypertensive are more likely to have severe hypertension than hypertensive patients of normal weight.

Significantly, too, many physicians over the years have observed the effectiveness of weight reduction as a treatment for hypertension. The Framingham experience also confirmed this observation. About 60 percent of Framingham hypertensives who were able to achieve a substantial weight loss were able to lower their blood pressure below hypertensive levels.

Further confirmation has come from a recent study in Israel, where 81 hypertensive patients who were 10 percent or more above their ideal weight were put on a weight-reduction program. Over a 2-month period, all lost at least 6.6 pounds, and the mean weight loss was 23 pounds. All but 2 of the 81 patients had a significant fall in blood pressure.

In the Israel study, not only did 75 percent of the obese hypertensive patients who were not on medication return to normal blood pressure when they lost weight, but, in addition, 61 percent of those who were hypertensive despite medication returned to normal blood pressure when they lost weight, with no change in medication.

The Role of Salt

Many investigators today believe, on the basis of a sizable body of evidence, that excessive salt intake plays a major role in hypertension, particularly when coupled with genetic predisposition to elevated blood pressure.

The late Lewis K. Dahl, M.D., of Brookhaven National Laboratory, who did a lot of the pioneering work linking salt with hypertension, first became interested in salt in 1948. At that time a rice-fruit diet was being used with some good results to treat hypertension.

What was the ingredient in the diet, Dahl wondered, that accounted for the blood pressure-lowering effect. In 4 years of investigations, Dahl and other researchers discovered that the diet had *no* special ingredient. Instead, it was its very low salt content that made it work. When the same diet was used but with salt added, there was no beneficial effect on hypertension.

Dahl began to wonder. If low salt intake could lower blood pressure, might high salt intake be a cause of hypertension?

Over the next several decades, he worked with more than 32,000 rats. Thousands became hypertensive with chronic salt feeding. As the work continued Dahl noticed that in unselected rats the response to salt ranged from no effect at all to gradually increasing blood pressures to rapid, severe elevations. About one-quarter of the animals showed no elevation, even after consuming a very high salt diet for most of their lives. The remaining three-quarters developed varying degrees of elevation, with 2 to 3 percent dying of hypertension after just a few months on salt.

This suggested genetic variances—hereditary influences.

Dahl then mated members at both extremes of the response range, producing two distinct strains of rats: a resistant strain which could be fed a high-salt diet with no significant increase in average blood pressure—and a sensitive strain which showed significant rises in blood pressure with moderate salt intake and early death with high salt intake.

Dr. Dahl suggested, and many authorities now believe, that human beings react the same way.

At one extreme, there may be people with so strong a genetic predisposition to hypertension that they need very little in the way of an inciting factor, such as salt intake, to develop it. At the other extreme, there may be people with no predisposition to hypertension, who do not develop elevated blood pressure even after eating high levels of salt all their lives. And there may be people with a slight predisposition, who may or may not develop hypertension depending upon how great their salt intake is.

Incidence of Hypertension

Many studies worldwide have found that among populations with minimal salt intake hypertension is rare; among those with high intake it is common.

Geographically diverse populations which exhibit virtually no hypertension and have low salt intake range from South Sea Islanders to Brazilian Indians to Alaskan Eskimos. In contrast, some populations with a lot of salt in their diets, such as the northern Japanese, have a very high incidence of hypertension.

Researchers recently studied residents of different villages of the Solomon Islands in the South Pacific. Most natives of the Solomons have not adopted the western custom of adding salt to their food. In villages on the hill, the researchers found no high blood pressure and no rise of average pressure with advancing age, as occurs in the United States and all westernized countries.

In a village located on a lagoon, however, a significant incidence of high blood pressure was found, along with a rise in average pressure with advancing age. The lagoon villagers boiled their vegetables in seawater.

A Cutback for You?

Is there enough evidence to recommend that Americans should reduce their intake of salt?

As you have seen, many studies indicate that excessive salt intake is an important factor of hypertension, but none has absolutely proved the relationship. There may never be definitive proof, since that would require studying thousands of infants, half on lifelong salt restriction and half on the usual high-salt American diet, for as long a period as 30 to 40 years. Such a study would be virtually impossible to perform.

The evidence is strong enough, however, to convince many authorities that universal reduction of salt intake is justified.

To be sure, many people will never develop elevated blood pressure, even if they eat large amounts of salt all their lives. But others not yet hypertensive will become so.

Presently, there is no way to predict who is and who is not susceptible; there are only some clues. Blacks, as a group, have a higher incidence; so do overweight people. A family history of hypertension increases the risk.

Since most Americans eat more salt than needed, it will do no harm and may do much good for all of us to reduce our intake of salt.

How Much Salt Are You Eating Now?

Americans love salt. Each of us on an average eats an astonishing quantity—8½ pounds a year, or 2 to 2½ teaspoons a day.

In a review for the Food and Drug Administration, a committee of experts estimated American consumption as "not less than" 10 to 12 grams (equivalent to 2 to 2½ teaspoons) of sodium chloride per person per day. Since salt is about 40 percent sodium, a salt intake of 10 to 12 grams means consuming at least 4 to 5 grams of sodium each day.

Many people are confused by the difference between sodium and salt. Health concern is with the *sodium* content of foods. Sodium occurs naturally in many foods and is also added via salt and other sodium-containing ingredients. Common among the latter are sodium nitrate (a curing agent and preservative), sodium benzoate (a preservative), monosodium glutamate (MSG, a flavor enhancer), sodium bicarbonate (baking soda, a leavening agent), and sodium phosphate (a wetting agent for quick-cooking cereals).

Sodium is not all bad. In fact, it's an essential nutrient without which we could not survive. It helps regulate blood and other body fluids and plays a major role in nerve-impulse transmission, heart action, and body metabolism of protein and carbohydrates.

A daily human sodium requirement is difficult to establish, because need can vary depending on such conditions as excessive sweating and diarrhea (which may require additional sodium). As a result, the National Research Council, rather than recommend a specific daily amount, has issued an estimate of an "adequate and safe" sodium intake for adults of 1000 to 3300 milligrams a day (1.1 to 3.3 grams), as compared with the 4 to 5 grams of sodium per day that Americans consume on an average.

In its report to the Food and Drug Administration, a committee of experts remarked: "It is the prevalent judgment of the scientific community that the consumption of sodium chloride in the aggregate should be lowered in the United States."

The committee's report added: "The average daily intake of sodium expressed as sodium chloride from all sources . . . exceeds estimates of the amount that may elicit hypertension in susceptible individuals."

The commissioner of the Food and Drug Administration, Arthur H. Hayes, Jr., M.D., recently met with representatives of 200 food industry associations to discuss lowering the salt content of processed foods.

"We are looking into the need of new regulations," he said, "to require that the sodium content of food be declared on the label," adding that this was an important step to "help people help themselves to become healthier."

The Hidden and the Obvious

The salt that pours out of your salt shaker at dinner or during cooking counts for only about one-third of all the salt in your diet. Some salt occurs naturally in food and in some drinking water, but up to one-half comes from processed foods.

According to information furnished to the Food and Drug Administration by one manufacturer, one serving of chicken or turkey noodle, tomato, chunky beef, vegetable beef, or cream of mushroom soup contains over 1000 milligrams of sodium.

Besides canned and dried soups, some other processed foods that contain large amounts of sodium are canned vegetables, cheese, tomato juice, dill pickles, olives, canned tuna and crab, sauerkraut, frozen dinners, and condiments such as soy sauce, catsup, and salad dressing. Items such as instant pudding, breakfast cereals, ice cream, cookies, cakes, and bread also contain significant amounts of sodium.

Laboratory analyses done for one consumer publication recently turned up some surprising information. You would expect salt in cocktail peanuts, but how about finding nearly twice as much sodium in a 1-ounce serving of corn flakes (260 milligrams) as in 1 ounce of peanuts (132 milligrams)? Or 234 milligrams in 2 slices of white bread versus 194 milligrams in a 1-ounce bag of potato chips? Or 404 milligrams in ½ cup of chocolate-flavor instant pudding, 102 milligrams more than in a three-slice serving of bologna? Or 315 milligrams in just 1 tablespoon of a bottled Italian dressing, 1152 milligrams in a frozen fried chicken dinner, or 1510 milligrams in a Big Mac hamburger?

Cholesterol

Cholesterol has come to be portrayed as a kind of coronary time bomb.

Virtually everywhere in the world that populations have been studied, those with high occurrence rates of atherosclerosis and coronary heart disease have been found to have high levels of serum (blood) cholesterol.

HOW TO CUT DOWN ON SODIUM

• Learn to enjoy the unsalted flavor of foods. They may taste different, but they are not tasteless. An acquired taste for salt can be changed.

• To condition your taste to less sodium, gradually reduce the amount of salt you use at the table. Set your goal to avoid adding any. The conditioning takes approximately 2 weeks.

• When preparing foods, start cutting down by using just half the amount of salt called for in recipes.

• Use other seasonings in place of salt. Natural spices, herbs, and condiments such as pepper, parsley, chili, horseradish, and cloves contain only negligible amounts of salt and can be used liberally to make food tasty and satisfying.

• Replace salty snacks with unsalty ones, such as raw vegetables. Substitute peanuts in the shell for salted peanuts.

• Avoid canned soups or soup powders; they contain large amounts of salt (except for special brands of low-salt soup powders). In restaurants, avoid eating soup.

• Avoid eating canned, smoked, pickled, or cured meat and fish products as much as possible; they are usually high in salt. Preserved or pickled vegetables also almost always contain salt; frozen vegetables contain little or none.

• Ask the person in your home who shops for food to read labels carefully for additives containing sodium and to avoid products that list salt, sodium, or a sodium-containing additive near the top of the list of ingredients.

The reverse has proved equally true: Among peoples with low serum cholesterol levels, the occurrence rates of atherosclerosis and coronary heart disease are low. In Japan, for example, where blood serum cholesterol levels average almost 100 milligrams per deciliter lower than in this country, the death rate from coronary heart disease is one-tenth our rate.

Many studies in the United States have shown that the risk of coronary heart disease rises sharply with increasing cholesterol levels. The Framingham study, for example, determined a frequency of disease seven times greater in persons with cholesterol values above 259 milligrams per deciliter than among those with values below 200 milligrams per deciliter.

If you could look into an atherosclerotic artery, the involvement of cholesterol would be obvious. You would find it as the chief fatty constituent of the fibrous fatty plaques that bedevil the vessel.

How Atherosclerosis Develops

Atherosclerosis used to be called *arteriosclerosis,* which translates literally as "artery hardening." *Atherosclerosis* is a more accurate descriptive term for the disease process, which starts with soft swelling (*athero-*) and then progresses to hardening (*-sclerosis*).

In a normal artery, a smooth lining of flattened cells (the *endothelium*) keeps the blood and its contents flowing through the artery. Surrounding this lining, a thin sheath of muscle cells contracts or relaxes to control the artery diameter and help regulate the rate of blood flow.

When atherosclerosis begins, the earliest change visible to the eye is the development of fatty streaks—thin, slightly raised, yellowish lines—in the lining of the artery. These streaks are made up largely of cholesterol and cholesterol compounds (cholesterol esters).

As the disease progresses, the lining becomes thickened by soft deposits of fatty and cellular material called *atheroma* or *atheromatous plaques*. The cellular material consists of overgrown new muscle cells engorged with cholesterol. Damage to the artery lining causes the muscle cells to overgrow; one possible cause of damage is high blood pressure.

Studies in animals indicate that damage to the lining often is repaired spontaneously, but the damage persists or becomes worse when high blood cholesterol levels are present.

As disease progresses, the artery bore, or channel, is narrowed by the growing plaques and the scar tissue that may form around them. Blood flow is impaired. At some point, it may be cut off, and the area of heart muscle or other tissue normally nourished by the artery suffers injury or death.

Any artery can be affected by atherosclerosis, but those most often— and most seriously—affected are the larger vessels serving the heart, brain, legs, and kidneys.

The rate at which plaque develops varies considerably from one artery to another in the same person and from one individual to another.

The Long Buildup

Obvious manifestations of atherosclerosis rarely appear before age 40, because blood flow usually becomes seriously impeded only when there is more than a 75 percent narrowing of a vessel. The process begins in childhood, goes on slowly for years, and reaches an advanced stage in middle life or later, when manifestations appear, mainly as coronary attacks and strokes.

In the United States and other affluent western countries, one or more of the clinical manifestations affect one of every three men before age 60. In those countries, half of the annual death toll is traceable to disease of the heart and blood vessels, chiefly the result of atherosclerosis.

Women generally tend to lag 10 years behind men in developing manifestations of the disease, for reasons still not clearly defined. On undergoing menopause, they tend to lose their comparative immunity.

Friend and Foe

Despite the bad reputation it has gained because of associations with atherosclerosis, cholesterol is a vital material.

It is contained in almost every cell in the body and may play a part in regulating the passage of nutrient materials into and out of the cell through the cell membrane.

It is found in high concentration in the brain and probably acts there in some important though not yet well-understood capacity.

Cholesterol is also a material from which many other important body materials are manufactured; for example, the corticosteroids, or hormones of the adrenal gland, such as cortisone, are derived from cholesterol. The sex hormones are derived from the sterol nucleus of cholesterol.

Cholesterol is also changed by the body to bile acids, which are excreted in the bile that flows into the intestine to help in the digestion of fats.

So, a certain amount of cholesterol is essential, and the body produces its own as well as deriving some from food.

BLOOD CHOLESTEROL TESTS

Blood cholesterol tests are now an integral part of heart disease prevention programs, yet many physicians do not include them in your annual checkup. Your cholesterol level may be normal, but if you don't know, ask for a test. It's simple and requires only a blood sample that is sent to a laboratory for study.

The range between 125 and 220 milligrams per deciliter of blood serum is considered a safe cholesterol level by most cardiologists, but most middle-aged Americans (85 percent) have a cholesterol level well above 200 milligrams per deciliter. If this is true of you, you can begin to lower your cholesterol level today by eating more polyunsaturated and less saturated fats. Only a few months of careful eating will bring about an improvement.

HDL and LDL: "Good" versus "Bad" Cholesterol

For many years, physicians were puzzled: Why did some people remain unaffected by atherosclerosis despite a seemingly dangerous level of serum cholesterol? Only recently has there been an explanation for this apparent paradox.

What is critical is not so much the total amount of cholesterol in the blood but rather how it is carried in the blood—the amounts of the various chemical "toters" of cholesterol, the substances which transport it in the blood.

Cholesterol is a fatty substance. Fatty substances do not mix with water, so the blood cannot carry them. In order to transport cholesterol and other fats from the liver to other organs and tissues, the body attaches them to proteins which are able to dissolve in blood.

Fats are known chemically as *lipids*, and the fat-protein combinations found in the blood are called *lipoproteins*. What has been known for some time is that there is more than one kind of lipoprotein—that, in fact, cholesterol is transported in two major types: high-density lipo-proteins (HDLs) and low-density lipoproteins (LDLs).

As far back as 1951, one perceptive investigator, Donald P. Barr, M.D., of Cornell University Medical College in New York, considered that the two might not play the same role in atherosclerosis and that one, HDL, might be noninjurious, possibly even beneficial.

It was years before there was evidence to support that claim. It came from the Framingham study.

As we noted earlier, for many years, starting in 1948, investigators have been closely following a group of more than 5000 men and women residents of this Massachusetts community, all healthy at the start. At the beginning of the study, the researchers noted facts about the residents' habits, lifestyles, blood pressures, and cholesterol levels, and they have been correlating such data with subsequent illnesses and deaths ever since then.

It was the Framingham study which established the significance of obesity, smoking, hypertension, and elevated cholesterol as risk factors for atherosclerosis.

In 1977, Framingham investigators discovered a striking new correlation: In virtually all of the 142 new cases of coronary heart disease which had developed in residents during the previous 8 years, HDL levels were low.

The average HDL level for American men is 45 milligrams per deciliter (about one-tenth of a quart) of blood plasma. For women, it is 55 milligrams.

Of the 79 men who developed coronary heart disease, 70 had levels below 45 milligrams, and of the 63 women, more than two-thirds had levels below 55 milligrams.

As William P. Castelli, M.D., laboratory director for the Framingham study, noted: "The most surprising finding of our study was the observation that the cholesterol contained in HDLs was inversely related to the incidence of coronary heart disease. As the HDL went up, the rate of coronary events went down."

More on HDL

The Framingham study and other investigations as well have found that newborn babies have about half of their total cholesterol in the form of HDL. But as they grow into adulthood and live a typically American life, the level of HDLs falls and that of LDLs increases.

Women tend to maintain higher HDL levels longer than men, which may influence their lower rates of coronary heart disease. Eventually, however, increasing numbers of women, as well as many men, reach the point of having only about one-fourth of their cholesterol in HDL form.

In addition to the Framingham study, other recent studies—in Evans County, Georgia; Albany, New York; San Francisco; and Hawaii—have confirmed the importance of maintaining as high an HDL/LDL ratio as possible.

Moreover, C. J. Glueck, M.D., of the University of Cincinnati, has established that in families noted for longevity and freedom from heart and blood vessel diseases, levels of HDL are very high—usually 75 milligrams or more per deciliter of blood plasma.

How does HDL protect?

Although more remains to be learned, LDL seems to be involved in transporting cholesterol to—and depositing it in—tissues, including blood vessel walls. On the other hand, HDL is apparently responsible for the reverse traffic, removing cholesterol from sites where it is in excess and carrying it back to the liver for disposal.

Thus it appears that HDL may act to thwart the atherosclerotic process by removing cholesterol from artery walls and helping to keep the arteries clear of deposits.

Raising Your HDL Level

Since HDL is good for you, how can you raise your HDL level?

- Change your diet to one that emphasizes vegetables, cereals, and fish, with relatively little meat and no foods such as hot dogs and potato chips that are packed with saturated fats.

- Quit smoking and lose excess weight.

- Get more exercise.

Studies of exercise often have found no great impact on total cholesterol and blood fat levels. However, at Stanford University, Peter D. Wood, M.D., and his colleagues checked on forty-one very active men, aged 31 to 59. Many had not been particularly active earlier in life, but in the past year each had run at least 15 miles a week. They were compared with men of similar ages randomly selected from northern California communities.

The runners had an average total cholesterol level of 200 milligrams, compared to 210 milligrams for the other men—not much difference. But they had a much higher mean level of HDL—64 milligrams versus 43 milligrams for the others. The very active men had a lipoprotein profile much like that of young women largely free of coronary heart disease, rather than of sedentary middle-aged men.

A recent major study of 10,000 people at ten U.S. and Canadian medical centers, sponsored by the National Heart, Lung, and Blood Institute, examined the link between HDL and factors affecting coronary heart disease. The following observations were made:

- Both smoking and obesity were associated with significantly lower HDL levels.

- HDL levels for smokers averaged 4 to 8 milligrams per deciliter lower than those for nonsmokers.

- Thin people had HDL levels 3 milligrams higher than those for people of average weight and height, and the average people, in turn, had HDL levels 3 to 4 milligrams higher than those who were obese.

- Moderate drinkers (about two mixed drinks a day) had higher HDL levels than nondrinkers. Among the drinkers, mean HDL levels were 55 milligrams per deciliter, as compared with 42 milligrams for nondrinkers.

The Diet Influence

How strong is the evidence that a fat- and cholesterol-rich diet contributes to heart disease? Population studies have shown that in countries where the diet is rich in animal fats and cholesterol, the coronary death rate is much higher than where far fewer animal products rich in cholesterol and saturated fats are consumed.

Studies of Japanese migrating to the United States have shown major jumps in serum cholesterol levels and heart disease after their arrival in America—evidently, researchers believe, because of the switch from an oriental to an American diet.

In animal experiments, monkeys fed a typically American diet have been found to develop coronary artery disease similar to that of human beings. Taking the monkeys off the American diet reversed the disease process. Dietary studies in humans have shown that serum cholesterol can be predictably altered upward by an increase of saturated fats and cholesterol in the diet.

Despite such studies, it has been difficult to demonstrate conclusively the relation of diet to blood fat levels and coronary heart disease in free-living Americans. Some investigations of Americans not placed on any special diets have failed to show any clear-cut direct relationship between diet and heart disease. Several reasons for this have been suspected. Most investigations have looked at only what the participants ate in a single day, yet there can be considerable variation from day to day in fat and cholesterol consumption. Procedures for measuring diet in people eating freely have not always been accurate.

New Evidence

A recently reported study which analyzed deaths among 1900 American men whose diets and cholesterol levels were first examined 20 years earlier provides new evidence of the importance of dietary factors.

Called the Western Electric study, the investigation was one of the largest and longest of its kind. Supported by the American Heart Association, the National Heart, Lung and Blood Institute, and other organizations and private donors, it was carried out by scientists of the Rush-Presbyterian-St. Luke's Medical Center, Chicago; the University of Michigan; Harvard Medical School; and Northwestern University Medical School.

The 1900 men who took part in the study were employees of the Western Electric Company's Hawthorne works near Chicago. They ranged from 40 to 55 years of age at the start of the study.

For each man, a detailed dietary history was carefully taken—not just for a single day but for 28 days. More than 195 specific foods were reviewed to determine the number of times in the past 28 days each had been eaten and the usual size of the portions. Wax models of common foods and dishes of varying sizes were used as aids. Supplementary information about ways of preparing food was obtained by a questionnaire sent to each participant's wife. Restaurant meals were carefully checked.

Each man's diet was analyzed to determine usual caloric intake and consumption of animal and vegetable protein and fat, cholesterol, saturated and unsaturated fat, and vitamins. In each case, the blood cholesterol level was measured. A year later, the same procedures were repeated.

The status of the men was then checked on the twentieth anniversary of the first examination. It appeared that those who had had the lowest intake of cholesterol and saturated fats had a 33 percent lower death rate from coronary heart disease than the men with the highest intake.

As the investigators noted in their report of the study: "The results support the conclusion that lipid (fat and cholesterol) composition of the diet affects serum cholesterol concentration and risk of coronary death in middle-aged American men."

Richard B. Shekelle, M.D., senior author of the report, observed: "The message of these findings is that it is prudent to decrease the amount of saturated fats and cholesterol in your diet."

Proof and Prudence

Unquestionably, it would be nice to have incontrovertible proof of a cause-and-effect relationship between fat- and cholesterol-laden foods and atherosclerosis—to be able, for example, to follow a molecule of cholesterol from its origin in an egg yolk to its final destination as part of an obstruction in a coronary artery. It would be highly satisfying, too, to have a very long-term study—one in which, starting in childhood, thousands of individuals ate a low-fat, low-cholesterol diet—and to compare what happened to them in terms of atherosclerosis with what happened to others on a typical diet over half a century or longer. But we may not have the yolk-to-artery trail laid out for many years, and half a century is a long time to wait for results of any study from childhood on. Besides, such a study would be very complicated and expensive—perhaps too much so to make it possible.

Short of such proof, however, we do have mounting evidence that a prudent diet—one with reduced amounts of saturated fats and cholesterol—can be helpful.

In the opinion of Executive Health Examiners—as well as the American Heart Association, more than a dozen other organizations concerned with nutrition and health, and the U.S. Department of Agriculture and the Department of Health and Human Services—the magnitude and gravity of the problem of atherosclerosis does not permit indefinite temporizing while we await definitive proof.

Eating to Keep Cholesterol Levels Healthy

Dietary control of cholesterol levels in the blood is based on several principles.

The first is that foods differ markedly in their cholesterol content and cholesterol intake can be reduced by proper food selection. Among foods especially high in cholesterol are egg yolk (with 250 to 275 milligrams in a single yolk), butter (250 milligrams per 100-gram, or 3½-ounce, portion), kidneys (375 milligrams per 100-gram portion), and sweetbreads (250 milligrams per 100-gram portion).

On the other hand, some foods have very little cholesterol content. Among them are fruits, vegetables, egg whites, cereals, vegetable oils, vegetable margarine, and peanut butter. Skim milk and milk powder are also low in cholesterol.

The second principle is based on the finding that the ratio between saturated and unsaturated fats in the diet is important in determining the blood cholesterol level. The lower the ratio, the lower the cholesterol level is likely to be.

When the association between high blood cholesterol levels and atherosclerosis was first noted, attempts were made to bring down cholesterol levels by reducing the dietary intake of cholesterol, but it turned out that reduced intake was not enough to bring the levels down to any marked extent.

Then it was found that the amount of *fat* in the diet matters. People placed on low-cholesterol diets but with fat intake still high continued to have elevated blood cholesterol levels. After considerable research it was found that fat in the diet seemed to facilitate the body's absorption of cholesterol in food.

However, it was determined that even low-cholesterol, low-fat diets do not invariably lead to blood cholesterol reduction. It took further research to establish that the *type* of fat consumed also counts.

There are, you may recall from an earlier chapter, three distinctive types of fats.

Saturated fats, which tend to increase blood cholesterol levels, are fats that harden at room temperature, such as gravy fat. Such fats are found primarily in foods of animal origin—meat and dairy products, particularly beef, lamb, pork, butter, cream, whole milk, and cheeses made from cream or whole milk. Saturated fats are also found in many solid and hydrogenated vegetable shortenings, such as coconut oil, cocoa butter, and palm oil, which are often used in commercially produced cookies, pie fillings, and nondairy milk and cream substitutes.

Polyunsaturated fats, which tend to lower blood cholesterol levels, are fats that remain liquid at room temperature. Among them are such oils as corn, cottonseed, safflower seed, sesame seed, soybean, and sunflower seed.

Monounsaturated fats, a third type of fat, seem to have little, if any, effect on blood cholesterol levels. Olive oil is an example of monounsaturated fat.

Applying the Principles of Cholesterol Control to Your Diet

You can probably apply the principles of cholesterol control to your present diet with moderate rather than drastic alterations. (See chart on page 70.)

Eggs   Because egg yolks are so rich in cholesterol, a low-cholesterol, modified-fat diet to reduce elevated cholesterol calls for a maximum of three yolks a week, including those used in prepared food. There need be no limit on use of egg whites in cooking, since they are largely composed of protein.

Milk Products   The fat in whole milk and whole milk products is saturated fat. To avoid that fat and still get the benefit of the protein, vitamins, and minerals, especially calcium, that make dairy products essential for your health, you can use skim milk and skim-milk products. Choose nonfat buttermilk, cottage cheese, and other cheeses low in fat (such as farmer and hoop) in place of high-fat cheeses (read the labels of cheese for fat—and sodium—content). In place of butter choose a margarine which indicates as its first ingredient a liquid polyunsaturated vegetable oil that is not hardened or hydrogenated.

Cream   Sour cream is high in saturated fat; low-fat plain yogurt can be used instead in many recipes calling for sour cream.

Half-and-half is high in saturated fat and so, too, are many cream substitutes such as whipped topping and most nondairy creamers. They are made with saturated fats such as coconut or palm oil, so read labels carefully—don't assume that nondairy products can be substituted for dairy products if you are on a diet that excludes the latter.

Meat   If you love steaks, chops, and roasts, you don't have to do without them entirely. But have them as entrees less often, eat smaller portions, and trim away visible fat. Dripping fat from roasts should be discarded rather than used for gravy. You can also eat less fried and more roasted, broiled, baked, and boiled meat.

Poultry and Fish   As you cut down on steaks, chops, and roasts, you can eat more chicken and turkey; however, avoid their skin, which is where their fat is largely concentrated. You can also eat more fish.

Soup   Eat soups if you like, but only those that do not contain a lot of fat. At home, much fat can be eliminated by refrigerating a soup after it is cooked and then skimming the fat off the top before reheating.

Fruits and Vegetables   Eat more vegetables, salads, and fruits. Not only are they generally low in calories and fats and high in vitamins and minerals, but they also tend to moderate your appetite through their bulk.

Shortening   When buying margarine, shortening, and prepared foods, check labels carefully. Beware of coconut and palm oils. Avoid items that list "hydrogenated" or "partially hardened" vegetable oils among the first ingredients on the label; they are saturated fats. Look for products that list polyunsaturated or monounsaturated liquid vegetable oil first.

Triglycerides

When most people think of blood fat damaging the arteries, they think of cholesterol, but other fat components, triglycerides, are also involved.

Triglycerides are compounds of glycerine and fatty acids. Most fat found in the body exists in the form of triglycerides, both when it is stored in tissues and when it is mustered to produce energy.

Just as cholesterol is always present in the bloodstream, so is triglyceride. The role of triglycerides in producing atherosclerosis is less well defined than that of cholesterol, but there is evidence that high triglyceride levels are significant.

LOW-CHOLESTEROL, MODIFIED-FAT DIET: A LIPID-LOWERING REGIMEN

Foods to avoid	Foods to substitute
Butter, lard, most margarines Coconut oil, palm oil Hydrogenated vegetable fats and oils Salt pork, suet, bacon, and meat drippings Gravies, unless made with allowed fat Sauces, unless made with allowed fat and skim milk	Safflower oil, corn oil, and other liquid vegetable oils (polyunsaturated), and margarine made from these
Cream soups	Bouillon, clear broth, fat-free vegetable soup, cream soups made with skim milk, broth-based dehydrated soups
Salad dressings containing cheese and sour cream	Commercial mayonnaise Oil and vinegar
Whole milk, cream, sour cream	Skim milk, dried nonfat milk, yogurt made from skim milk
Most cheeses	Skim-milk cheese, cottage cheese
Fatty meats such as most cold cuts, corned beef, frankfurters, sausages, bacon, spareribs Regular hamburger (ground beef)	Lean beef, lamb, veal, tongue, pork, and ham Dried or chipped beef Chicken, turkey (without skin)

Foods to avoid	Foods to substitute
Goose, duck, and poultry skin	Fish, except as excluded (if canned, drain oil)
Shrimp, fish roe (caviar)	Egg white; no more than 3 egg yolks per week, one of
Fried meats and fish, unless fried with allowed fat	which may be replaced with 6 oz of shrimp or 3 oz of
Meats, canned or frozen, in sauces or gravies	cheddar cheese
Frozen packaged dinners	
Egg yolks (maximum 3 per week)	
Biscuits, muffins, sweet rolls, corn bread, pancakes, waffles,	Whole wheat, rye, or white bread
French toast	Saltines, graham crackers
Corn and potato chips, flavored crackers	Baked goods not containing excluded fat or egg yolk
Buttered, creamed, or fried vegetables prepared with	Any vegetable, fresh, frozen, or cooked with allowed fat
excluded fat	
Pork and beans	
Pies, cakes, cookies, other desserts containing excluded fats	Angel food cake, puddings, or frozen desserts made with
or egg yolks	skim milk, gelatin desserts
Ice cream, ice milk, whipped toppings	Water ices
Chocolate, coconut, cashews and macadamia nuts, most	Cocoa, nuts other than those excluded, hard candies, jam,
candies	jelly, peanut butter (old-fashioned type), honey, sugar
	Olives, pickles, salt, spices, herbs

In the Framingham study, triglycerides as well as cholesterol were found to contribute to the risk of atherosclerosis. The risk associated with one rose in proportion to the level of the other. Whether cholesterol was high or low, the risk rose with the level of triglycerides. The converse was equally true. People with high values for both seemed to be worse off than those with high levels of one or the other.

Like cholesterol levels, serum triglyceride levels are low in societies with a very low incidence of coronary heart disease, such as Japan.

The Normal and the Abnormal

Triglyceride levels below 150 milligrams per deciliter are in the normal range. Those between 150 and 300 milligrams per deciliter are in a gray zone, considered by many physicians to indicate mild abnormality. Levels above 300 milligrams per deciliter are considered to be definitely abnormal.

A *word of caution*: Hypertriglyceridemia (elevated triglyceride level) can be a real enough problem, but sometimes it can be a spurious one. When a blood sample is drawn to test for cholesterol, there is no need for your stomach to be empty, but for triglyceride testing, unless you have been fasting for 12 to 14 hours before blood is drawn, your triglyceride level will be falsely high. Because many patients are not aware of this, there may be unnecessary concern about spuriously elevated triglyceride levels.

Causes

In some cases, the elevation of triglycerides seems to be an inherited tendency. Much more often, however, abnormal levels are associated with excess weight. Excessive use of refined sugar and refined starches and excessive alcohol intake may also be involved.

Dietary Principles for Triglyceride Control

If your triglyceride level is abnormally elevated, it would be well to modify your diet according to three principles:

• Achieve and/or maintain your ideal weight. Quite often, in obese people, weight reduction alone brings about a substantial decrease in elevated triglyceride levels.

- Reduce your intake of carbohydrates—particularly the simple carbohydrates found in sugars and products rich in sugar, syrup, and honey.

- Avoid excessive alcohol intake. Government studies indicate that the desirable maximum for daily alcohol intake is two drinks a day (2 ounces of liquor, or its equivalent in other alcoholic beverages).

5.

Vitamins, Minerals, and Food Fads

If estimates are right, there are now 70 million Americans consuming an alphabet soup of vitamins and minerals every day. Many are taking doses of hundreds or even thousands of times greater than required for good nutrition. The total expenditure for all these vitamins and minerals runs as high as $5 billion a year.

While some look upon these supplements as adding up to a kind of nutritional insurance policy, there are those who regard them as virtual panaceas for what ails them.

On these same grounds—nutritional insurance and nutritional therapy—consumption of other dietary supplements, such as alfalfa tablets, herbs and herbal brews, and "natural" and "organic" foods, has increased.

Claims and counterclaims about the benefits of taking supplemental vitamins and minerals and of eating "health foods" have resulted in confusion and controversy.

Vitamins

Casimir Funk, a Polish biochemist working in London in 1912 at the Lister Institute, originated the term *vitamine,* which later became *vitamin*. Funk conceptualized the whole idea that there exist certain vital nutrient accessory factors, in the absence of which disease could result. No longer were the causes of disease thought to be only foreign, noxious agents; deficiencies of these necessary substances were also considered as possible causes.

The idea of unknown vital substances in foods was not without precedent. When Hippocrates prescribed liver for night blindness in ancient Greece, he was recommending, although unknowingly, vitamin A. When Quebec Indians gave the scurvy-ridden men of Jacques Cartier a leafy brew, they were dosing them with vitamin C. And when, in eighteenth-century England, cod-liver oil was regarded as a prized cure-all, it was because of its rich content of vitamins A and D that made up for dietary deficiencies.

What Vitamins Are

Vitamins are organic molecules required in the diet in tiny amounts to sustain the normal metabolic processes of life. For the most part, they cannot be made in the human body. There are, however, three exceptions. With adequate exposure to sunlight, you can produce vitamin D in your skin. The B vitamin niacin can be synthesized from the amino acid, or protein building block, tryptophan, and vitamin K is made in significant amounts by bacteria normally present in the intestines.

Vitamins function primarily as catalysts—action regulators—in body chemical reactions. As such, they are essential for the release of energy, tissue building, and controlling the body's use of food. By themselves they supply no energy and build no tissue.

Each vitamin serves one or more special functions that no other nutrient can serve. Deficiencies of vitamins have specific results; in fact, part of the definition of a vitamin is that its lack produces a specific deficiency syndrome, or set of symptoms, and supplying it cures the deficiency.

One way of classifying vitamins is by their solubility in fat or water. The fat-soluble vitamins—A, D, E, and K—are stored in the body.

Water-soluable vitamins—C, thiamine, niacin, and others—are not stored to any extent.

The amounts of vitamins required are very small and are measured in milligrams (one-thousandth of a gram) and micrograms (one-millionth of a gram; 28 grams equals 1 ounce) or in international units (IU). International units are used as a measure of the potency or ability of vitamins to promote growth, regulate metabolism or the processes of body maintenance, or cure a deficiency.

How Vitamins Work

Vitamins function as coenzymes. Once ingested, vitamins search out cells that need them and are taken into these cells. Within these cells, the vitamins combine with proteins called *apoenzymes,* which are already present there. The combination of vitamin and apoenzyme constitutes a *holoenzyme*—or *enzyme*, in short. It is the enzyme which serves the function of catalyzing or furthering specific metabolic reactions.

Why More Is Not Better

The quantity of any protein a cell can produce in a given time is limited. That limitation naturally applies to apoenzymes. Once the apoenzymes in body cells are saturated with a vitamin, no further activity can be achieved by adding more of it. The amount of a vitamin required to reach that saturation point is called the *recommended daily allowance* (RDA) of that vitamin.

The excess of a vitamin present in the body does not act as a coenzyme and therefore is not used to fulfill the positive functions of that vitamin. It may, however, become involved in other chemical processes that are harmful to the body.

Recommended Daily Allowances (RDAs)

Early in World War II, the government became concerned about safe-guarding public health by providing adequate supplies of essential nutrients. As a result, in 1941 the Food and Nutrition Board of the National Research Council of the National Academy of Sciences was established.

That same year the board, seeking a nutritional standard to use in measuring nutritional needs of groups of people, developed the first RDAs—designed, on the basis of available scientific knowledge, to meet the needs of almost every healthy person.

Periodic revisions—approximately every 4 to 6 years—have been made in the RDAs to incorporate new research findings. The RDAs are recommendations for maintaining health but do not cover specific needs due to illness.

How Well Do Foods Meet the RDAs?

Eat one medium-sized baked sweet potato, or half a cup of peas and carrots, or the same quantity of spinach to satisfy the RDA for vitamin A.

For vitamin C, eating a medium-sized stalk of broccoli (about 6 ounces), or half of a 5-inch cantaloupe, or half a cup of frozen orange juice will satisfy the RDA.

Eating 3 ounces of either pork, calf, or beef liver will supply all the riboflavin that is needed. Or drinking 2 cups a day of milk (low-fat, whole, or skim) will meet about half the RDA.

Three ounces of pork liver supplies the RDA of niacin. Three ounces of waterpacked tuna or the same amount of turkey or chicken (roast breast) will contribute about half of the RDA.

These few examples indicate why it is often said that anyone who eats a well-balanced diet usually needs no added vitamins. Such a diet includes daily at least four servings of grain and cereal products, four or more of a variety of fruits and vegetables, two servings of dairy products, and two of meat, fish, or poultry.

Who Needs Vitamin Supplements

Unfortunately, not all of us eat a well-balanced diet. Some of us eat erratically, others eat very low-calorie diets, and then there are picky eaters whose diets are quite limited. For such people, mulitvitamin pills may be indicated.

There are people with special problems who may need vitamin supplementation—those, for example, who have a disorder of absorption; others who require extra amounts of pyridoxine because of a genetically induced imbalance.

There are some people who believe in "nutritional insurance" to the extent of taking a capsule a day containing the RDAs of major vitamins. Many physicians have no quarrel with that. They consider, as one puts it, that it is "totally unnecessary, but if it makes someone feel better, he or she is out only a couple of cents a day."

Megavitamin doses, however, are another matter.

What Are Megavitamin Doses Supposed to Do, and Do They Do It?

Many claims have been made, and continue to be made, for the values of vitamins in large doses. Megadoses—particularly of vitamins C and E—are said by some to be effective for ills that the ordinary diet cannot handle. Consistently, however, the claimed benefits have failed to stand up under close scientific scrutiny.

Vitamin C   The idea that increased intake of vitamin C may be useful for the common cold has been around since the 1930s, although it gained widespread popularity only in 1970 with the publication of Dr. Linus Pauling's best-seller, *Vitamin C and the Common Cold*.

It has been suggested that large doses of vitamin C can prevent colds or can cure them once they have begun, but many carefully controlled experimental studies have failed to support these claims.

Are there any benefits at all to taking large doses of vitamin C? One of the major independent investigators, Terence W. Anderson, M.D., of the University of Toronto, has suggested that increased regular intake of vitamin C or a larger therapeutic dose (not of the order of grams but about 100 to 150 milligrams a day) at the time of illness "may have a small beneficial effect and this effect appears to be on severity rather than on frequency or total duration of colds."

Is further study warranted? Some investigators think not, arguing that although vitamin C may have a slight effect on the common cold, it is too small to be of any practical value and the subject is not worth pursuing.

Dr. Anderson is one of those who are open-minded on the subject, and he favors continued study. "It is possible," he notes, "that if we fully understood the mechanism involved in producing even a slight effect, we might be able to develop it further and produce effects that were quantitatively more worthwhile."

More recent claims that vitamin C can help cancer patients have thus far not been confirmed. In a clinical trial at the Mayo Clinic in Rochester, Minnesota, high doses of vitamin C gave no indications of prolonging or improving the lives of terminally ill cancer patients.

Vitamin E   Claims have been made that large doses of this vitamin can promote physical endurance, enhance sexual potency, treat meno-pausal disturbances, prevent heart attacks and a variety of heart and blood vessel diseases, slow down aging, and act against such disorders as muscular dystrophies, cystic fibrosis, and diabetes.

But these claims have not been substantiated.

Vitamin E supplements are valuable for a rare type of anemia in babies and in individuals with intestinal disorders in which absorption is impaired. In Baltimore, a group of investigators led by Robert S. London, M.D., reports that vitamin E may play a role in the treatment of fibro-cystic breast disease, but cautions that it must not be taken for this condition except under a physician's supervision.

What Harm Can Megadoses Do?

For some vitamins, notably A and D, the harm of overdosing has long been appreciated.

In excess, vitamin A can be poisonous. The symptoms of poisoning can be variable—restlessness, appetite loss, weight loss, hair loss, muscle pains, swelling over long bones, headache, and generalized weakness, with death as a possible result.

Too much vitamin D can lead at first to such symptoms as appetite loss, nausea, and vomiting, followed by weakness, nervousness, itch-ing, extreme thirst, and frequent urination. With continued intake of excessive amounts of the vitamin, kidney function can be impaired.

What of such vitamins as C and E? Although it has been alleged that megadoses of them are harmless, there is a growing body of evi-dence that this is not true.

You will recall that excess vitamins can become involved in chemical reactions besides those associated with their primary functions. In me-gadoses, the quantities are so great that the enzyme systems in which they are incorporated become saturated. The megadose excess is then free to become involved in other chemical reactions.

Thus excess vitamin C, for example, may raise the level of uric acid in the urine and trigger gout in predisposed people. It has been reported, as well, that in some people excess vitamin C can lead to an increased susceptibility to kidney stones.

Rebound scurvy may be another undesirable effect. It develops when the body, exposed to the chemical effects of excess vitamin C, speeds up its machinery for destroying the vitamin excess. If this happens in a pregnant woman, the fetus may acquire the same speeded-up machinery and may be born with a vitamin C–destructive capacity much greater than normal. The newborn may then develop scurvy, which could result in dangerous, even life-threatening, bleeding.

Similar but less dangerous, rebound scurvy has been reported in adults who stop megadoses of vitamin C abruptly rather than cut back slowly at a rate of about 10 percent a day. They may develop bleeding of the gums and under the skin, loosening of the teeth, and roughening of the skin.

For some people—about 13 percent of American blacks and as many as 20 percent of Sephardic Jews, Orientals, and some other ethnic groups—megadoses of vitamin C may present another danger. These people have a genetic abnormality—a deficiency in the enzyme glucose-6-phosphate dehydrogenase (G6PD). Ordinarily the deficiency produces no symptoms whatever and causes no problems, except under circumstances involving the use of certain drugs or in the presence of severe infection. Then it may cause the destruction of many red blood cells and anemia.

Some years ago there was a mystery about an anemia that developed in some members of the armed forces who were under treatment with drugs to overcome or prevent malaria. The anemia was being caused by the drugs, which helped many others but were harmful to these men because they had a G6PD deficiency. When this was discovered, the antimalarial drug dosage was adjusted so it produced only mild red-cell destruction in the susceptible individuals.

Subsequently, it became known that in the presence of G6PD deficiency, anemia may be produced by other drugs such as aspirin, sulfa compounds, phenacetin (which is found in some headache remedies), and nitrofurantoin (an antibacterial agent used in treating some urinary tract infections). Still more recently, there have been reports that megadoses of vitamin C may lead to severe anemia in susceptible individuals with G6PD deficiency, and at least one death has been reported.

These are not the only undesirable effects that megadoses of vitamin C may have.

At the Bronx Veterans Administration Medical Center studies indicate that megadoses of vitamin C can destroy half or more of the vitamin B_{12} in a typical VA Hospital diet.

"VITAMIN B_{15},"—WHATEVER IT IS, IT WON'T HELP

A so-called vitamin sold in health food stores may be giving users cancer rather than prolonging their lives, according to a report in the *Journal of the American Medical Association.*

One of the components of vitamin B_{15}, also known as calcium pangamate or pangamic acid, has been found by Neville Colman, M.D., of the Bronx Veterans Administration Medical Center, New York, to be mutagenic (capable of causing mutations) in a widely used laboratory test. A chemical that is mutagenic in this test has a 90 percent probability of being able to cause cancer, Dr. Colman notes.

Vitamin B_{15} is promoted as a dietary supplement as well as a drug. According to the Food and Drug Administration, it has been alleged to help heart disease, aging, diabetes, gangrene, hypertension, glaucoma, alcoholism, hepatitis, jaundice, allergies, dermatitis, neuralgia, and neuritis.

After mixing 6-demethyl griseofulvin (DMG), a compound found in the largest selling formulation of vitamin B_{15}, with a chemical to simulate exposure to saliva and incubating the mixture under conditions similar to those in the human stomach, Colman and his colleagues concluded that the compound is capable of reacting to form a potential carcinogen under conditions simulating those found in the human digestive tract.

The discovery of pangamic acid was announced in 1943 by Ernst Krebs, Sr., and Ernst Krebs, Jr. (who gave the world laetrile). They applied for a patent and said they had isolated the material from apricot kernals. After the patent was granted in 1949, the material was heavily promoted as a cure-all under the trade name vitamin B_{15}.

Journal of the American Medical Association 243:2473, 1980.

Diabetics checking their urine may get false negative results from one test (Testape) and false positive results from another (Clinitest) because of the effects of large doses of vitamin C, thus increasing the risk of either diabetic ketoacidosis or insulin shock.

Recent reports also indicate that megadoses of vitamin C can cause false negative results of tests for blood in the stool—a means of detecting cancer of the colon.

What are the undesirable effects of vitamin E megadoses? Those reported so far include headaches, nausea, fatigue, and dizziness. Blurring of vision also has been reported, and there is some suspicion that this may occur because large doses of vitamin E antagonize vitamin A.

Megadoses of vitamin E also have been reported to cause inflammation of the mouth, chapping of the lips, muscle weakness, low blood sugar, gastrointestinal disturbances, and increased bleeding.

Minerals

Among the 40-odd nutrients known to be essential to man—including carbohydrates, fats, amino acids, and vitamins—are more than a dozen minerals. Two essential minerals alone, calcium and phosphorus, represent 3 percent of total body weight.

Minerals are elements found in water and food that are required as structural components and as participants in many of the body's vital processes. Those minerals which are needed by the body are often classified, in terms of the relative quantities required, as either *macro*nutrients (required in large amounts) or *micro*nutrients (required in small amounts). Micronutrients, in fact, are often called *trace elements* because they are needed in such small amounts.

Better from a Pill? An Example of Why Not

Zinc supplementation recently has become popular. Certainly, it is an important mineral. Recent research indicates that it is a constituent of more than 80 enzymes involved in many metabolic processes, such as growth, reproduction, and disease resistance. Along with other trace elements, it is believed by some to have a protective effect against heart disease.

The adult RDA of zinc, as set by the Food and Nutrition Board of the National Academy of Sciences, is 15 milligrams a day. The board has advised that supplements should not exceed that amount by more than 15 milligrams a day; however, zinc supplements found in health food stores and elsewhere include dosages of 10, 22, 30, 50, and 100 milligrams!

Is there a potential danger from excessive amounts of zinc?

At a recent New York Academy of Sciences symposium, Dr. Walter Mertz of the U.S. Department of Agriculture Nutrition Institute, noted: "At a certain level, not overly high, zinc can interact with other essential trace elements, notably copper. You can produce a relative copper deficiency."

At the same symposium, Leslie Klevay, M.D., a medical researcher at a Department of Agriculture human nutrition laboratory, told of experiments with rats which showed that high blood cholesterol levels could be produced by increasing the amount of dietary zinc relative to copper. Subsequently, when the zinc/copper ratio was decreased, cholesterol levels fell, as did the death rate among the animals.

By producing a relative deficiency of copper, could excessive intake of zinc be a threat to human beings?

Dr. Klevay reported:

> There are many similarities between people with atherosclerosis and ischemic heart disease and animals deficient in copper. A member of either group is likely to die suddenly, to be hypercholesterolemic [have high blood cholesterol levels] and hyperuricemic [have high urinary uric acid levels], to have arteries with abnormal connective tissue and to have fibrotic, hypertrophied [abnormally large] hearts low in copper, with abnormal electrocardiograms.

The zinc-copper interaction is just one example of how it is possible, through indiscriminate supplementation, to actually cause a mineral deficiency.

Another reason for care in supplementation, where it may be indicated, is that an excess of a particular mineral can sometimes have a direct, hazardous effect.

Calcium and Phosphorus

These two minerals often work together. Both are involved in the formation of bones and teeth, and both are needed for normal functioning of the nervous system. Phosphorus goes into the making of the chemical adenosine triphosphate (ATP), which is sometimes referred to as a kind of "body spark plug" because, in effect, it sparks the release of energy from glucose for such activities as muscle movement.

Calcium is needed for normal blood clotting, and phosphorus is required for the metabolism of some carbohydrates.

A persistent deficiency of calcium can lead to bone deterioration, including osteoporosis, a thinning of bone structure that affects some men and as many as one-fourth of postmenopausal women.

Milk and dairy products are especially good sources of calcium, not only because of their high content of this mineral but also because milk sugar, lactose, enhances calcium absorption from the intestine. The RDA for calcium for adults is 800 milligrams a day, and 2 cups of milk (either skim or whole) can supply about two-thirds of this requirement. Sardines with bones are another rich source of calcium.

Vitamin D—produced in the skin by sunlight and contained in fortified margarine and milk products—is needed for calcium absorption, too.

The ratio of calcium to phosphorus is also important.

The RDA for phosphorus is the same as for calcium—800 milligrams. Phosphorus is available in many foods, especially protein foods. Cheddar cheese, beef, pork, sardines, tuna, peanut butter, Brazil nuts, cottage cheese, milk, and peas are rich in it.

Calcium utilization can be impaired by an excess of phosphorus. Hence, there is some concern about the high level of phosphorus consumed in soft drinks and meats in the United States.

It is possible for the body to have an excess of calcium (hypercalcemia). Too much vitamin D can increase calcium absorption beyond normal. Some peptic ulcer patients become hypercalcemic after prolonged use of large amounts of milk and antacids. The consequences can include appetite loss and constipation, proceeding to nausea, vomiting, and abdominal pain and, sometimes, muscle weakness, emotional disturbances, confusion, and even psychosis.

Calcium deficiency is much more common. A U.S. Department of Agriculture survey in 1965 found infants, young children, and most men getting the daily requirement of calcium, but almost all women and girls over the age of 8 and many young and adolescent boys and older men were getting inadequate amounts.

A deficiency of phosphorus is rare.

THE CALCIUM-TO-PHOSPHORUS RATIO

The ideal ratio of dietary calcium to phosphorus is considered to be 1.5 to 1 in infants up to 6 months of age, 1.35 to 1 in infants between 6 months and 1 year in age, and 1 to 1 in older children and adults. Phosphorus intake is much higher than that of calcium for most Americans because phosphorus is more abundant than calcium in most foods.

Calcium and phosphorus content of 100-gram portions of selected food items and their calcium/phosphorus ratio

Food item	Calcium, mg	Phosphorus, mg	Ca/P ratio
Beef liver	8	352	1:44
Gatorade	0.2	7	1:35
Pork loin	12	234	1:20
Chicken breast	11	214	1:19
Bologna	32	581	1:18
Fish (flounder, sole)	12	195	1:16
Flour, whole wheat	41	372	1:9.1
Potatoes	7	53	1:7.6
Peanuts	69	401	1:5.8
Coca-Cola	3	16	1:5.3
Peas, green	26	116	1:4.5
Rice, white	24	94	1:3.9
Eggs	54	205	1:3.8
Beans, white	144	425	1:3
Almonds	234	504	1:2.2
Cottage cheese	94	152	1:1.6
Processed cheese	697	771	1:1.1
Milk, cow's	118	93	1:0.8
Beans, green	56	44	1:0.8
Cheddar cheese	750	478	1:0.6
Spinach, fresh	93	51	1:0.5

In the United States, the average intake of phosphorus is about 1.5 grams a day; the average calcium intake is about 0.7 grams a day. This results in a calcium/phosphorus ratio of 1 to 2. If you consume as little as 400 milligrams of calcium a day, the ratio drops to about 1 to 4.

Adapted from *Nutrition & Health*
1(3): 4, 1979.

Magnesium

Magnesium once was listed in nutrition books as a trace mineral, needed in only minute amounts. This is no longer the case. In recent years, the Food and Nutrition Board has established an RDA of 350 milligrams for men and 300 milligrams for women, which takes it out of the trace mineral class.

Magnesium is now known to be involved in many aspects of body chemistry. It is needed for activating a number of enzyme systems involved in the use of other minerals, some vitamins, and proteins. It is required for both nerve and muscle activity.

Severe deficiency of magnesium is manifested by muscular irritability or twitching, muscle cramps and spasms, weakness, forgetfulness, irritability, depression, mental confusion, and convulsions.

Magnesium is plentiful in seafood, meats, nuts, whole grains, and wheat bran, and it is moderately available in leafy green vegetables, fruits, and dairy foods.

Potassium

Among its many functions, potassium regulates the water content of cells. It participates in the transmission of nerve impulses and the release of energy from carbohydrates, protein, and fats and plays a part in the activity of muscles, including the heart.

Potassium depletion manifests itself by muscle weakness, cramps, diarrhea, vomiting, loss of appetite, apathy, and listlessness and, in severe cases, by irregular heartbeat and heart muscle weakness.

Depletion—which can follow severe diarrhea or the use of certain diuretics for high blood pressure or other purposes—requires the intake of foods rich in potassium and, in some cases, supplementation. Potassium compounds are sold over the counter in health food stores, but self-supplementation is dangerous. Potassium supplements should only be taken at the advice of a physician.

Potassium is widely distributed in foods, especially in meats, milk, vegetables, and fruits. Oranges, tomatoes, and bananas are particularly good sources.

Trace Minerals

Although they are needed only in tiny amounts, trace minerals are essential for health. The importance of some, such as iodine and iron, has long been recognized. The influence of others has been understood only relatively recently.

Iodine   Although needed only in extremely tiny amounts—on the order of 150 micrograms (millionths of a gram) a day—iodine is crucial to the functioning of the thyroid, the small, butterfly-shaped gland in the neck that controls metabolism. Thyroid hormone secretions—less than a teaspoonful a year—are responsible for much of the body's heat production. They help maintain the circulatory system, are needed for muscle health, heighten the sensitivity of nerves, and affect every organ, tissue, and cell of the body. Iodized salt has helped tremendously to solve the problem of iodine deficiency.

Iron   Iron is an essential element of hemoglobin, the pigment in red blood cells that transports oxygen from the lungs to all the cells of the body. Inadequate iron intake can lead to anemia, with any or many of a wide variety of symptoms: pallor, weakness, fatigability, irritability, flatulence, vague abdominal pains, neuralgic pains, and heart palpitations. Iron deficiency is common. It can occur as the result of inadequate iron intake and also because of loss of blood (and hence of hemoglobin with its iron content).

According to some estimates, as many as 60 percent of menstruating women in the United States have some degree of iron deficiency. Women require more iron than men: the RDA for women is 18 milligrams, for men 10 milligrams. A good diet can help prevent iron deficiency. Meat is a good source of iron; most meats provide 2 to 3 milligrams of iron per 3-ounce serving. Beef liver provides 5 milligrams in a 2-ounce serving, calves' liver is half again as rich in iron as beef liver, and pork liver has twice the iron of calves' liver. An egg contains 1 milligram of iron. Oysters, sardines, and shrimp provide 2½ to 5 milligrams per 3-ounce serving. Most green vegetables provide 1 to 4 milligrams per cup. Other good sources of iron include dry beans, nuts, prunes, dates, and raisins, each containing about 5 milligrams per cup.

Chromium   Chromium aids the action of insulin and is essential for the body's proper handling of glucose. The earliest symptom of chromium deficiency is impaired glucose tolerance; chromium deficiency may be related to the onset of diabetes, especially in later life. The estimated maximum need for chromium is only 0.2 milligrams per day. It is found in meats and other animal proteins, whole grains, and brewer's yeast.

Copper   A part of many enzyme systems, copper is involved in the normal development of bone and muscle and in the functioning of the nervous system. It is also essential to the formation of hemoglobin from iron. Copper deficiency can cause anemia and may also lead to taste distortion. There is some suspicion that copper deficiency may increase the risk of heart disease. It is estimated by experts that only about 3 milligrams of copper are needed daily. Good sources include shellfish, organ meats, nuts, legumes, and raisins. Excessive amounts are toxic.

Fluorine   Not only does fluorine have a role in making teeth more decay-resistant, but there is evidence it may also help to protect against osteoporosis, the bone-thinning and -weakening disease of older people, especially postmenopausal women. Fluorine occurs naturally in some drinking water, but in many communities it is added to fluorine-deficient water.

Manganese   Part of many enzyme systems, manganese is needed for normal bone formation, for normal functioning of the nervous system, and for reproduction. In animal studies, a deficiency of manganese has been found to retard growth, impair lactation, and produce seizures. The maximum daily need is estimated to be 5 milligrams. Good sources of manganese include nuts, legumes, whole grains, and tea.

Molybdenum   A component of some enzyme systems, molybdenum appears to be involved in the proper utilization of iron. Some iron deficiency anemias unresponsive to iron alone have been corrected with the addition of molybdenum. The maximum estimated daily need of molybdenum is only 0.5 milligrams. Good sources include cereals, legumes, and beef kidney.

Selenium   Selenium is believed to protect membranes and other fragile structures from oxygen damage. The maximum estimated daily need is 0.2 milligrams. Grains and onions are good sources of selenium.

Zinc   A component of many vital enzymes, zinc is needed for growth and sexual maturation. A deficiency may be related to growth failure, reproductive difficulties, impaired wound healing, some skin disorders, impaired appetite, and abnormalities of taste and smell. The RDA for zinc is 15 milligrams a day for both men and women. Good sources of zinc include seafood, nuts, meat, eggs, and green leafy vegetables.

Food Additives

More and more foods, from bread to peanut butter to potato chips, have been turning up recently on supermarket shelves in packages marked "No preservatives added," in recognition of the increasing concern, among not only health cultists but also large numbers of citizens, about the safety of chemical additives in foods.

Some of the product changes are somewhat less than rational. Some bread manufacturers have stopped adding the mold inhibitor calcium propionate to their products in order to be able to promote them as preservative-free, yet calcium propionate can hardly be considered a hazard. On the contrary, it is safe, incorporates the nutrient calcium, occurs naturally in substantial amounts in Swiss cheese, and stops the growth of molds that may produce toxins.

There is nothing simple about the question of food additives.

The Arguments

Since the 1969 cyclamate ban, additives have had a bad press.

To their defenders, the reaction against additives has worrisome economic, medical, and nutritional implications and is based on false premises. Defenders of additives assert that, for one thing, the idea that foods are free of chemicals except for additives is absurd. Consider, for example, a breakfast of eggs, melon, and coffee. Among other things, it contains such naturally present chemicals as methanol, acetaldehyde, ovomucoid, anisyl propionate, and malic acid.

Defenders also argue that:

- Many foods, if free of preservatives, may develop hazardous growths—as, for example, the mold (aflotoxins) that may develop on peanuts and on wheat and rye products. Aflotoxins are known to be carcinogenic in animals and are suspected of having some role in human liver cancer.

- Many foods naturally contain chemicals which, if consumed in large quantities, can be dangerous. Potatoes, for example, contain solanine, which in excessive amounts can inhibit the functioning of the nervous system. Lima beans contain hydrogen cyanide, which can be deadly in excess. But when these chemicals are ingested as part of a balanced, varied diet, they are not harmful.

- We know more about the additives to foods than about the chemicals naturally present in foods.

- Additives have kept our food supply plentiful, pleasing, nutritious, and relatively inexpensive; they have reduced food loss due to spoilage, making it possible to enjoy food from many geographic areas; and they have helped to virtually eliminate scurvy, rickets, goiter, and botulism.

On the other hand, critics of additives reply that while such arguments offer all the favorable factors, they are silent about the dangers. They point to such things as artificial food colorings made from coal tar, indicted long ago for inducing cancer but still used, without ever having been subjected to long-term tests for carcinogenicity. Critics of additives argue that we have had a history in this country of assuming that chemicals added to foods are harmless unless it is proved otherwise, so that cyclamates, for example, were absorbed by consumers for 20 years before being removed from the market.

Critics also are concerned that although many additives may be safe individually, the combination of them—the scores that an individual may consume in a single day—may add up to a hazardous burden, because just how the various chemicals interact is unknown and untested. It should be noted here, however, that possible interactions between chemicals naturally present in foods have had little study either.

Common Additives

There are more than 2000 substances which are added to foods for one or another of four different reasons: to maintain or improve nutritional value, to maintain freshness, to help in processing or preparation, or to make food more appealing.

Nutrients Additives intended to maintain nutritional value, replace nutrients lost in processing, or provide nutrients that may be lacking in the diet include such vitamins as thiamine, riboflavin, and vitamin C. These additives may be found in flour, bread, cereal, rice, beverages, and processed fruit.

Preservatives These include antimicrobials to prevent spoilage from bacteria, molds, and other organisms and to extend shelf life and antioxidants to prevent or delay changes in texture, flavor, or color. Frequently used antimicrobials include vitamin C, citric acid, and calcium propionate. Vitamin C and citric acid also function as antioxidants. Two other frequently used antioxidants are butylated hydroxyanisole (BHA) and butylated hydroxytoluene (BHT). Antioxidants are found in processed foods, baked goods, cereals, snack foods, fats, and oils.

Additives Used to Make Foods More Appealing   There are four classes of these: coloring agents, flavoring agents, flavor enhancers, and sweeteners.

Coloring agents are among the most controversial additives because they are used solely for appearance and contribute nothing to nutrition, taste, safety, or ease of processing. There are now thirty-five permitted coloring agents, and they are used in virtually all processed foods. Nearly half are synthetic (now derived from petroleum rather than from coal tar).

In the past 6 years, the Food and Drug Administration has banned four coloring agents from use in foods: a violet dye used to stamp meats; red dye no. 2, a suspected carcinogen; red dye no. 4, used in maraschino cherries and shown to cause bladder lesions and adrenal gland damage in animals; and carbon black, used in candies. The FDA also proposed to ban orange B, used in sausage and hot dog casings, because of possible contamination with a carcinogen, but the maker voluntarily stopped producing it in 1978.

The two most widely used coloring agents, red dye no. 40 and yellow dye no. 5, are under fire because of possible health risks. Red dye no. 40 is suspected of producing malignant lymph node tumors when fed in large amounts to mice; yellow dye no. 5 causes allergic reactions—mainly rashes and sniffles—in an estimated 50,000 to 90,000 Americans.

Flavoring agents—of which there are some 1700, mostly synthetic—constitute the largest single category of food additives.

If a product contains any added flavoring, natural or synthetic, the label must indicate it. For example, "strawberry yogurt" on a label means all natural strawberry flavor; "strawberry-flavored yogurt" means natural strawberry flavor plus other natural flavorings; "artificially flavored strawberry yogurt" means the product contains only artificial flavorings or a combination of artificial and natural flavorings.

A few flavorings have been prohibited in recent years because of possible health hazards. Safrole, a derivative of sassafras root, once commonly used in root beer, was banned by the FDA after testing indicated it caused liver cancer in rats. Coumarin, often used as an anticoagulant medication, was once present in imitation vanilla extract and other flavorings, but it has been banned from use in food because large amounts could cause hemorrhaging.

Flavor enhancers intensify or modify food flavor without adding any flavor of their own. Some work by briefly inhibiting certain nerves—such as those responsible for bitterness perception—so that perception of other tastes increases.

Among the best-known enhancers is monosodium glutamate (MSG), an amino acid, or building block of protein, commonly found in prepared foods and restaurant dishes. Baby food manufacturers who once used MSG in their products stopped doing so voluntarily after studies indicated that large quantities could destroy brain cells in young mice. MSG also produces "Chinese restaurant syndrome"—with such symptoms as headache, chest tightness, and burning sensations—in some sensitive people after consumption of the large amounts often found in Chinese-style foods.

Sweeteners, of course, are commonly used additives. The nutritive types, which are used by the body to produce energy, include natural sugars such as sucrose (table sugar), glucose, and fructose, as well as sugar alcohols such as sorbitol and mannitol. Nonnutritive types, which are not metabolized by the body and so contribute no calories, include cyclamate (currently prohibited) and saccharin.

The addition of sugar to foods is opposed by many on the grounds that it provides only empty calories and contributes to tooth decay, obesity, and other problems.

The sugar alcohols, which are chemical variants of natural sugars, have been promoted as low-calorie alternatives to natural sugars, but they are not actually low in calories. New FDA regulations require manufacturers to indicate that their use in a product does not mean that the product is "low-calorie."

Sorbitol, the most widely used sugar alcohol, appears in chewing gum, mints, candies, and dietetic ice cream. Although safe, it can have a laxative effect in large quantities. Mannitol, used in some chewing gums, can cause diarrhea in small amounts.

The nonnutritive sweeteners cyclamate and saccharin have been controversial for a long time. Cyclamate was banned in 1969 on the basis of its causing cancer in animals. Saccharin is under a cloud on the basis of possible health hazards; a Canadian government study showed that it caused bladder tumors in rats.

Additives Used in Preparing and Processing Foods These are the least controversial food additives. There are seven major groups: emulsifiers, stabilizers and thickeners, pH control agents, leavening agents, maturing and bleaching agents, anticaking agents, and humectants.

Emulsifiers are used to allow some liquids to mix which otherwise would not. These compounds keep ice cream and other frozen desserts from separating and in baking serve several purposes, including making batter and dough easier to handle.

Many emulsifiers are of natural origin. Lecithin occurs in milk. Mono- and diglycerides come from vegetables and animal tallow.

One emulsifier which has aroused some concern is brominated vegetable oil (BVO), which is used in citrus-flavored drinks to keep oils in suspension. Residues from this additive are said to accumulate in body fat.

Stabilizers and thickeners, which work by absorbing water, help to keep ice crystals from forming in frozen desserts and prevent evaporation and deterioration of flavor oils used in cakes, puddings, and gelatin mixes. Most are natural carbohydrates such as gelatin (from animal bones and other parts) and pectin (from citrus rind). Vegetable gums (from trees, seaweed, and other plants) are highly effective thickeners, but some, such as tragacanth gum and gum arabic, produce allergic reactions in susceptible persons.

pH control agents affect the safety, taste, or texture of foods by regulating acidity or alkalinity. For example, low-acid canned foods, such as beets, require longer cooking at higher heat than acidic foods if they are to be sterilized; the addition of acids eliminates the need for extra heat which could lower quality. Natural organic acids—such as citric, fumaric, tartaric, and malic acids—are commonly used for canned foods. In some other foods, alkalizers are used to neutralize acids.

Leavening agents, which include yeast, baking soda (sodium bicarbonate), and baking powder (sodium bicarbonate and acid salts), are used to produce carbon dioxide to allow baked goods to rise properly.

Maturing and bleaching agents speed the process by which flour becomes useful for baking—a process which otherwise would require several months of costly storage. Bleaching agents such as benzoyl peroxide also are used to whiten milk for use in some cheeses, such as blue and gorgonzola, known for their whitish curd.

Anticaking agents such as calcium silicate, iron ammonium citrate, and silicon dioxide are used to keep table salt, baking powder, confectioner's sugar, and other powdered food ingredients free-flowing.

Humectants are substances, such as glycerine and sorbitol, which cause moisture to be retained in soft candies, shredded coconut, marshmallows, and other confections.

Practical Answers

The problem of chemicals in our foods—all chemicals, those naturally present as well as added—is extremely complicated.

The fact is that people have learned by experience, over many millennia, what natural products they can eat with apparent safety—including products now known to contain naturally many chemical substances with potential for toxicity, such as arsenic, lead, cadmium, copper, nitrates, and estrogenic materials. Eating foods with normal levels of these substances has never been known to cause injury, even though some are present at levels closer to known toxic levels than would be allowed today for additives.

Although most of our natural food materials have been accepted as safe on the basis of a long history of use without causing obvious harm, they have never been studied and evaluated scientifically. Therefore, there is always the question, recognized by many scientists, about whether any of the natural dietary components such as estrogens, arsenic and cadmium could possibly contribute in any way to degenerative diseases.

It would seem that the best insurance against getting toxic amounts of any single food component is to eat a variety of foods rather than limiting one's diet to a favorite few foods. This would hold for additives as well as for naturally present components.

Additionally, in the case of additives, it makes sense to adopt two guidelines:

• Minimize as much as possible the use of canned, bottled, or packaged food; rather, concentrate on fresh fruits and vegetables and on foods prepared and cooked at home.

• If you must eat canned, bottled, or packaged food, check the ingredients on labels. Avoid those with the longest lists of chemical additives.

Health Foods: "Organic" and "Natural"

Upon taking a hard look recently at a product offered as "natural lemon-flavored cream pie," a prominent consumer testing organization discovered that it contains no cream. It does, however, contain sodium propionate, certified food colors, sodium benzoate, and vegetable gum.

That's natural?

"Of course," avowed the also-prominent baker. "Natural," the firm pointed out patiently, modifies "lemon-flavored." The pie contains oil from lemon rinds, so "the lemon flavor comes from natural flavor as opposed to artificial lemon flavor, assuming there is such a thing as artificial lemon flavor."

"Welcome," the testing organization told its subscribers, "to the world of natural foods." It can be a confusing world. It is certainly a controversial one.

Is health food—considered by many to be synonymous with "organic" and "natural" food—more nutritious than the conventional food found in supermarkets? The idea that it is, in the view of many scientists, is fantasy, not fact.

Writing in a Food and Drug Administration publication, an FDA Bureau of Foods dietician and nutritionist, Marilyn Stephenson, put it this way:

> Advocates of "health," "organic," and "natural" foods—terms for which there is little agreement as to their exact meaning—frequently proclaim that such products are safer and more nutritious than conventionally grown and marketed foods. Although most of these claims are not supported by scientific evidence, it is difficult for the public to evaluate truth from fancy—particularly in regard to use of the term "natural" for everything from whole grain flour or bread to potato chips. Claims or suggestions that certain health foods or diets prevent or cure disease or provide other special health benefits are, for the most part, folklore, and sometimes fabrication.

Health food enthusiasts respond that eating food untouched by additives and preservatives and grown without herbicides, pesticides, and manufactured fertilizers makes sense.

If it does make sense, it is at a price. Health food products sell at a premium; the prices are sometimes staggering, as in the case of a 1-pound loaf of whole wheat bread, which may cost almost twice as much in a health food store as in a supermarket.

According to an article by Myron Winick, M.D., in *Medical World News*, there is nothing objectionable in health foods aside from cost and the need for greater care in preservation, "so long as people are not duped by the health food industry into expecting advantages that are not there. If they want to pay more for the possibility that this is more healthful, fine."

It would seem, however, that in the health food industry, as in any other, what is offered is not always what it is claimed to be.

Organic—What Does It Mean?

In chemistry, the word *organic* refers to compounds containing carbon in their molecules—a vast array of them, ranging from animal and plant products to petrochemicals and pesticides.

Organic as applied to health foods, however, means foods grown without use of pesticides, synthetic fertilizers, and other chemicals, relying instead on natural fertilizers such as manure and compost.

How Much Difference Does Organic Growth Make?

If there is any difference between the nutrient content of plants grown organically and of those grown with the help of chemicals, it has yet to be scientifically established.

Dr. Emil M. Mrak, a renowned authority on agriculture, has pointed to scientific experiments conducted for 25 years at Cornell University and elsewhere in this country and in England, which have found no differences between organic foods and those treated with manufactured fertilizers. It appears that once removed from the garden, organically grown foods cannot be distinguished from those that have been commercially fertilized.

Plants produce some of their own nutrients and derive others from the soil through their roots. Regardless of the source, roots absorb nutrients in inorganic form, and any organic matter has to be broken down by soil bacteria to release inorganic elements before there can be absorption. Since only the nutrients themselves are absorbed, plants are not concerned about the nature of the source. As far as plants are concerned, needed nutrients can come from any fertilizer, synthetic or natural.

If a soil is known to be deficient in a particular mineral, the mineral can be incorporated in a synthetic fertilizer or it may be obtainable from the decomposition of organic wastes.

Organic wastes—natural fertilizers—are not necessarily perfect fertilizers. Manure, for example, has plentiful phosphate but much less nitrogen, which may not be ideal for some plants. Manure also may contain pests, such as insects, worms, and disease-carrying bacteria.

Free of Pesticides?

A claimed advantage of organically grown foods is the absence of pesticides, which, supposedly, should make the produce free of pesticide traces or residues. But, as an FDA Consumer Report has pointed out:

> The fact is that many of these foods do contain pesticide residues. Even if no pesticides are used on a particular crop, some chemical residues often remain in the soil for years after the last application of a pesticide on a previous crop. In addition, fresh residues may be deposited from drifting sprays and dusts or from rainfall runoff from nearby farms. Traces of pesticides may be found in both organic and conventional foods, but these residues normally are within federal tolerance levels, which are set low enough to protect the consumers.

Tests by various agencies and laboratories of organic-labeled foods purchased from health food stores and comparable nonorganic foods bought at supermarkets have shown little difference in pesticide-residue levels.

For example, in 1972, the New York State Department of Agriculture and Markets analyzed 55 food products labeled "organically grown" and found that 30 percent contained pesticide residues. At the time, the department was sampling about 2000 nonorganic foods annually and finding pesticide residues in about 20 percent.

In 1978, an analysis by Wayne State University and Michigan State University investigators of five brands of bread from health food stores and five from supermarkets showed that all ten had traces of pesticide residues.

In 1979, when KNXT-TV in Los Angeles was doing a series of programs on organic foods, it had a Los Angeles laboratory—one that does pesticide testing for both government agencies and private companies—test 28 samples of fruits and vegetables from health food stores, labeled "organically grown," and 14 samples of similar nonorganic produce from supermarkets. The laboratory could find no overall difference in pesticide levels. Only 2 samples contained no residues at all, and one of those was from a supermarket.

Also in 1979, in connection with a *New West* magazine article, another California laboratory that tests for pesticides for the U.S. Department of the Interior analyzed organic lettuce from six San Francisco health food stores and nonorganic lettuce from a supermarket. It found pesticide residues in five of the six organic lettuces as well as in the supermarket lettuce. The supermarket lettuce contained 0.01 parts per million of phosdrin, an aphid-killing spray, but the tests also found six times that much in one and eight times as much in another organic lettuce. A third organic lettuce also contained residues of phosdrin and two other pesticides.

Natural—What Does It Mean?

Natural, as applied to foods, is supposed to mean that the products contain no preservatives or artificial additives and have undergone minimal processing. Certainly, there is nothing undesirable in that.

But beware.

A Federal Trade Commission staff report issued in 1978 told of nationally advertised cereals and processed frozen foods labeled "natural" that contained chemical preservatives. Some foods labeled "natural" also contain heavy amounts of added salt and sugar, the report noted. It went on to add: "The term 'natural' has been applied to foods which run the gamut on extent of processing."

Once largely limited to health food stores, products labeled "natural" today are flowing in ever-increasing quantities onto supermarket shelves.

What Passes for Natural

A recent survey in *Consumer Reports* has turned up an interesting series of examples of questionable application of the word *natural* to food products.

Consumer Reports points, for instance, to two 15-ounce cans of tomato sauce, available side by side in one store. One sauce claimed on its label to have "no citric acid, no sugars, no preservatives, no artificial colors or flavors." There were no such ingredients in the other sauce either, a house brand, "but their absence was hardly worth noting on the label, since canned tomato sauce almost never contains artificial colors or flavors and doesn't need preservatives after being heated in the canning process." There was one clear difference between the two products: price. The house brand was selling for 29 cents, the other for 85 cents.

Some other examples:

- A brand of "natural chocolate-flavored chocolate chip cookies" with fine print on the label indicating the cookies contain both artificial flavor and the chemical antioxidant BHA.

- A "whole grain date-filled fruit and oatmeal bar" whose label proclaimed "naturally good flavor" but whose ingredients include "artificial flavor."

- A well-known brand of crackers red-labeled as a natural product with no preservatives, but with an ingredient list including calcium propionate "to retard spoilage."

- A well-known brand of "high-protein cereal" which implies that it is "natural" through much material on the package about "nature," with that word used four times and the word "natural" once but never to describe the product inside, which, among other things, contains artificial color and BHA.

- The increasing presence of the claim "no artificial preservatives" on labels of jars of jam and jelly—as if this has not always been true, since sugar is all the preservative needed for such products.

- A prominent brand of so-called natural margarine, which, in fact, has been highly processed from its original vegetable oil state.

6.

Other Nutritional Considerations

Dietary Fiber

Dietary fiber is, very literally, the indigestible part of food. You eat it—and excrete it.

It was largely ignored until recently by nutritionists, who are used to thinking in terms of digestion of foods and the subsequent absorption and use by the body of nutrients.

Now supermarket shelves are stocked with a variety of new "high-fiber" foods. More than a dozen cereals directed at adults contain the word *bran* in their names or mention fiber prominently on the front of the box.

When the Surgeon General's Report on Health Promotion and Disease Prevention called for efforts to produce a "public health revolution," one recommendation was more consumption by Americans of foods rich in fiber—whole grains, cereals, fruits, and vegetables.

Shortly afterward, in testimony before the U.S. Senate's Nutrition Subcommittee, Arthur Upton, M.D., then director of the National Cancer Institute, also urged "generous" intake of dietary fiber as a measure that might help reduce the risk of one of our most common and deadly malignancies, cancer of the colon.

The New Interest

Fiber itself is nothing new. Our grandparents called it "bulk" and "roughage," and until relatively recently it was very much a part of the ordinary diet.

About the turn of the century, however, the invention of modern roller mills made it possible economically to remove the outer husk of cereal grain kernels, and with it the fiber to produce refined white flour. Quickly thereafter, fiber intake plummeted—to the point where, until quite recently, cereal fiber intake in the United States and much of western industrialized society stood at only one-tenth of what it used to be.

Even as fiber consumption was falling markedly, the incidence of many diseases was shooting up. Appendicitis, for example, became noticeably common only in the twentieth century; coronary heart disease was considered rare 50 years ago.

Yet nothing comparable was occurring among rural Africans living, as they always had, on their native unrefined diets. They certainly were subject to infections; they sometimes went hungry; but eating unrefined cereal as a staple, getting about 25 grams (almost an ounce) of fiber daily—many times as much as the average westerner—they rarely experienced the chronic western diseases.

Only recently was any of this recognized—as the result of the epidemiologic detective work of a group of British physicians led by Denis Burkitt, a surgeon famed for his discovery and cure of a childhood cancer named after him (Burkitt's lymphoma). Many of these men, including Burkitt, had worked for years as mission and government physicians in Africa. For years they, too, were unaware of the possible significance of the local diet. Then, gradually, they were struck by a series of facts.

Although cancer of the colon has become a scourge of western nations, ranking as the second most common cause of cancer death after lung cancer, it is rare in east Africa. In the United States it now strikes 100,000 persons a year, but in Kampala, Uganda, the rate is only one-fifteenth as great. Annually, 300,000 American appendixes are removed, but in African villagers, appendicitis is virtually nonexistent. Diverticulitis (abnormal outpouchings of the colon that can cause severe pain and may require surgery) is present in over one-third of Americans and other westerners over the age of 40. Dr. Burkitt reported that in 20 years in Africa he had not seen a single case.

Moreover, as some Africans moved from native villages to cities and adopted western low-fiber diets, the incidence of western diseases began to rise sharply. At one hospital in Uganda, for example, the appendectomy rate increased more than 20 times between 1952 and 1969. In 1956 came the first case of coronary heart disease reported in east Africa—in a 48-year-old high court judge who had lived for 20 years on a western diet.

AN OLD CONCERN: OVER-PROCESSED FOODS

Contrary to common belief, the concern about overprocessed food is not a twentieth-century revelation.

Hippocrates, the father of medicine, recommended eating unbolted wheatmeal bread (made from flour still containing bran) for its "salutary effects upon the bowels."

In the nineteenth century, Sylvester Graham (called by some the father of food reform in the United States) claimed that indigestion was caused by too refined a diet, and that putting bran back in wheat flour would correct it. Even today, his name has been immortalized in that common staple, the graham cracker.

The physician attending Graham at his death was Dr. J. H. Kellogg, who later, in 1985, introduced the first ready-to-eat cereal to our nation in the form of toasted wheat flakes.

Peter G. Lindner, M.D.
Obesity/Bariatric Medicine 7(4):134,
1978.

How Fiber Works

Fiber adds bulk. Upon reaching the intestinal tract, it absorbs water and swells. That leads to bulkier but soft, well-formed stools, and that in turn prevents constipation, with its characteristically small, hard, pebbly, slow-moving stools.

Native African stools weigh as much as four times those of westerners, and transit time—the interval between a meal being eaten and the remains being excreted—averages only 35 hours for African villagers, compared to 90 hours for many westerners.

Constipation—extremely common in westerners but rare in rural Africans—is more than a nuisance. It leads to straining, which may be responsible for a series of problems. It has been proposed that straining raises pressure in the colon, which may cause the outpouchings of the colon wall in diverticular disease. With straining, pressure within the abdomen also rises and may cause the stomach to push up through the diaphragm, producing hiatus hernia, with its possible heartburn, regurgitation of stomach acid back up into the esophagus, and burning pain in back of the breastbone.

Raised pressure in the abdomen can be transmitted elsewhere—to the leg veins and to the veins in the anal region—and so, it has been proposed, such pressure from constipation-induced straining may be responsible for varicose veins and hemorrhoids (which are also varicose, or unnaturally swollen veins).

Evidence is accumulating that restoring fiber to the diet can achieve some highly desirable effects. In one study, for example, the substitution of 2 slices of fiber-rich wholemeal bread and the addition of 2 teaspoonfuls of fiber-rich bran daily led, within 3 weeks, to marked increases in stool weight and speedup of transit time, with an end to constipation. There have been reports as well of relief for hemorrhoid sufferers as stools soften and straining is eliminated.

Until quite recently, fiber, or roughage, was banned for people with diverticular disease in the mistaken belief that it was too irritating. Now there have been many reports that adding fiber to the diet produces striking improvement. In one large study, 88.6 percent of patients improved, and many who had been scheduled for surgery no longer required it.

Other Possible Benefits

In addition to such benefits as overcoming constipation and helping in diverticular disease, dietary fiber may have other benefits. The evidence for this comes from varied studies—some from direct human research, others from animal experimentation. Some are epidemiologic, attempting to relate various disease statistics to local dietary customs. Still other projected benefits are based on what are essentially theoretical hypotheses, taking into account both the physical characteristics of foods and physiology.

Cancer of the Colon   Epidemiologic studies of various populations, comparing disease incidence with dietary fiber intake, have suggested that dietary fiber may provide protection from cancer of the colon and rectum.

To account for the protection, the following hypothesis has been offered: Cancer of the colon and rectum results from cancer-causing chemicals (carcinogens) produced by bacteria in the bowels. When stools are small, hard, and slow-moving, the bacteria in them have more time to act and the carcinogens they produce are more concentrated in the stools, are retained longer, and thus can act for longer periods on the lining of the colon.

Some investigators suggest, the extra water, bile acids, salts, and fat bound by added fiber may serve as solvents to remove many chemical factors that might be carcinogenic.

It has also been suggested that a high-fiber diet may alter the types and numbers of bacteria in the bowel and possibly inhibit their production of carcinogens. One study, which supports this possibility, showed that one class of microorganisms that produce compounds convertible to carcinogens is present in western stools in much greater amounts than in stools from populations in underdeveloped countries.

Although fiber may well be protective against cancer of the colon, many investigators caution that more definitive evidence is needed. Theories based on epidemiologic findings may be misleading. For example, some recent studies indicate that the incidence of colon cancer in various areas correlates even better with the amount of fat in the diet than with the amount of fiber.

Heart and Blood Vessel Disease   Fiber may help reduce elevated cholesterol levels, which are believed to be involved in atherosclerotic artery disease, heart attacks, and strokes.

In one study, for example, fiber-rich rolled oats reduced cholesterol levels in 3 weeks. In another, when high-fat diets were fed to healthy men, their cholesterol levels shot up; when one form of fiber, chickpea, was added to these diets, cholesterol increase was inhibited. In other studies, guar gum and pectin—other forms of fiber—have reduced cholesterol levels. Bran, however, does not appear to change blood cholesterol levels.

Diabetes   In one of the first studies of the possible effects of fiber on diabetes, a decline in insulin requirements was noted in patients who ate increased amounts of fiber-rich foods. Another found blood glucose levels of patients taking insulin to be significantly higher on a low-fiber than on a high-fiber diet. Since then, several other preliminary studies have shown a drop in blood glucose levels and in the need for insulin (or for oral antidiabetes drugs) after the institution of high-complex-carbohydrate and high-fiber diets—in some patients within a few weeks. Diabetic patients should have the advice of a physician before changing to this diet.

Gallstones   Stones in the gallbladder may form from excess cholesterol in the bile. Recent studies suggest that a fiber-rich diet reduces bile cholesterol. A study at the University of Bristol, England, found bile cholesterol reduced in 80 percent of patients.

Weight loss   Preliminary investigations indicate that a high-fiber diet may help promote weight loss, and further studies are certainly indicated.

At the University of Bristol, Kenneth Heaton, M.D., a pioneer fiber investigator, noted that when he, his wife, and several colleagues increased fiber in their diets by eating wholemeal bread instead of refined white bread, they lost weight—not dramatically, but gradually and smoothly. The losses went as high as 15 pounds—and without any attention to calories or attempts to restrict the amount eaten.

Wholemeal breads, pound for pound, frequently contain fewer calories than conventional white breads, and they may also reduce food consumption because they increase the feeling of satiation.

In a study in Denmark, 25 healthy nurses took a little less than 1 ounce (24 grams) of wheat bran a day for 5 weeks. Their food intake remained constant, yet they lost weight. One possibility is that fiber, by shortening transit time through the intestines, may decrease absorption of nutrients.

Fiber—More than Just a Single Substance

For a long time, all fiber was considered to be "crude fiber," which is what is left after a food sample is treated in the laboratory with a solvent, hot acid, and hot alkali. Chemically inert, this residue consists mostly of the lignin and cellulose in the food being analyzed.

Dietary fiber is different, however. It is defined as including all the components of a food that are not broken down in the digestive tract to produce small compounds which can be absorbed into the bloodstream.

Dietary fiber includes hemicelluloses, pectic substances, gums, mucilages, and other carbohydrates, as well as lignin and cellulose. These compounds occur mainly in the cell wall of plant tissue, and their total greatly exceeds the total of crude fiber.

The various fiber components have different properties and effects; thus, the fiber composition of food is significant in discussing its effect on the body. For example, pectin, lignin, guar gum, oat hulls, and barley have been found to have some cholesterol-lowering effect, but bran and cellulose have none.

Food Sources of Dietary Fiber

Many varied foods supply significant amounts of dietary fiber and its components. As the Institute of Food Technologists points out, the total dietary fiber in both fresh vegetables and fruits may appear to be relatively low, but that is because of their high water content. The fiber actually represents a substantial proportion of the solids content.

Potatoes and starchy vegetables supply significant amounts of fiber if eaten in fairly large quantities. The lignin content of most vegetables is low, while that of fruits is highest in those containing lignified seeds, such as the strawberry, or lignified cells in the flesh, such as the pear. The noncellulosic polysaccharides in these foods are usually rich in pectic substances (uronic acids) and in pentoses.

Use of wholemeal flour instead of white flour increases the lignin in the diet and provides as well a threefold increase in total dietary fiber from that source.

HIGH- AND LOW-FIBER MENUS

Low-fiber and high-fat	High-fiber and low-fat

BREAKFAST
Instant powdered orange drink | 1 orange
1 slice white bread | 1 slice whole wheat bread
1 tsp butter | 1 tbsp apple butter
6 oz whole milk | 6 oz skim milk
½ cup canned peaches | 1 tbsp almonds and 1 tbsp raisins
1 cup cornflakes | 1 cup 40% bran flakes

SNACK
10 potato chips | 1½ cup popcorn (plain)
12 oz carbonated beverage | 12 oz apple juice

LUNCH
3 oz roast beef on white bread | 3 oz turkey (white meat) on whole
1½ tbsp mayonnaise | wheat bread, mustard and lettuce
20 french fries | Tossed salad with lemon juice
6 oz instant onion soup | 1 cup vegetable soup
Cola | 8 oz apricot nectar
Gelatin dessert and topping | 1 apple, medium

SNACK
Snack pie | ½ cup dried fruit and nut mix
Coffee and cream | 6 oz vegetable juice

DINNER
4 oz fried chicken | 4 oz broiled fish
½ cup macaroni and cheese | 1 cup gumbo (corn, tomatoes, okra)
¼ cup cole slaw | 1 cup brown rice
½ cup buttered peas | 1 cup fresh relish (radishes, celery,
2 dinner rolls | green peppers, carrot curls)
2 tsp butter | ¼ cantaloupe wedge
¾ cup ice cream |

TOTAL
45 g fat | 27 g fat
4.7 g fiber | 17.23 g fiber

What is a Good High-Fiber Diet?

Fiber is bran and bran is fiber—or so it seems to many. But that is not the case at all.

Certainly, wheat bran—composed of the outer layers of wheat, which are removed in the preparation of white flour—is a rich source of fiber. It can be bought as miller's bran—preferably as coarse flakes, rather than fine, because it is more effective in the coarse form. Two tablespoons provide about 7 grams, or ¼ ounce, of dietary fiber, which is usually adequate to benefit bowel behavior.

However, there are other sources of fiber, and to get maximum benefit from dietary fiber and its various components, selections should be made from a variety of whole-grain products, fruits, and vegetables, including:

- Cereals such as old-fashioned, slow-cooking (not instant) oatmeal; shredded wheat; cereals labeled as being all-bran or largely made up of bran.

- Breads and other bakery products made with wholemeal flour (whole wheat or whole rye).

- Seeds, including whole sesame seeds and sunflower seeds, and seed-filled berries such as raspberries and blackberries.

- Other fruits and vegetables, such as mangoes, carrots, apples, brussels sprouts, eggplant, spring cabbage, corn, oranges, pears, green beans, lettuce, winter cabbage, peas, onions, celery, cucumbers, broad beans, tomatoes, broccoli, cauliflower, bananas, rhubarb, potatoes, turnips.

Can You Have Too Much Fiber?

There is a tendency when some important nutritional finding is reported as the result of research, for it to be applied to an extreme. Eating as much as 10 tablespoons of bran a day has been urged in some popular regimens—with no evidence whatever that such large amounts are necessary or valuable. In fact, a sudden, excessive increase in the amount of fiber eaten can cause painful intestinal bloating and diarrhea. It is even possible that very large amounts of fiber could cause enlargement and twisting of the colon.

It has been suggested that too much of the pectin form of fiber may cause decreased absorption of vitamin B_{12}. There is also a possibility that excessive fiber intake could lead to loss of minerals such as zinc, iron, calcium, copper, and magnesium because of the binding of these minerals by phytic acid, which is present in some plant-based foods.

Alcohol

Alcohol—its use is two-pronged.

Does it relax tension? It may, but it can also impair reason and judgment. Does it heighten sexual desire? Perhaps it does, but it can have the opposite effect on performance.

Clearly, alcohol in excess can be hazardous to one's health, even deadly. It is toxic to many body tissues. Now, however, there is evidence that it may be, in moderation, a life extender through an apparently beneficial effect on the heart.

New Evidence: Alcohol and Heart Attacks

Recent research findings from epidemiologic (or population) studies and from clinical and laboratory studies suggest that alcohol in moderate amounts is associated with fewer heart attacks, possibly because it reduces the formation of fatty deposits inside the coronary arteries supplying the heart muscle. Several epidemiologic studies have shown that moderate drinkers are less likely to die from heart attacks than are abstainers. Clinical studies using coronary arteriography (special X-ray techniques for examining the coronary arteries) have reported that heavy alcohol users have relatively low plaque buildup in their arteries. Autopsy studies, too, have found that heavy drinkers generally tend to show little atherosclerosis. Their deaths are usually from other diseases or other causes, such as accidents.

There has been other suggestive evidence, as well, from cross-cultural studies that moderate alcohol consumption may be beneficial. Countries such as Spain, Portugal, France, and Italy, which have relatively high per capita rates of alcohol consumption, have comparatively low death rates from coronary heart disease.

Further confirmation has come from a large-scale California study.

The California Findings

Recently, Arthur L. Klatsky, M.D., of the Kaiser Foundation Hospital in Oakland, California, reported the results of a massive study at Kaiser-Permanente system facilities throughout northern California. He and fellow investigators analyzed the hospitalization of 87,926 adults, between 1971 and 1976, whose drinking patterns had been recorded routinely a decade earlier. Since 2,105 testees had reported taking six or more drinks a day, the investigating team selected three comparison groups of the same number—abstainers, persons taking no more than two drinks a day, and those taking three to five drinks regularly. All together, the study covered more than 8000 adults.

It was not surprising at all when the heaviest drinkers turned out to be the likeliest to be hospitalized for accidents, cirrhosis of the liver, other digestive diseases, alcoholism, and mental disorders, as well as for cancer, respiratory problems, high blood pressure, and stroke.

But it was surprising when the people with the fewest hospitalizations proved to be not the abstainers but those taking one or two drinks daily.

When it came to hospitalization rates for coronary heart disease and heart attacks, they were significantly higher among nondrinkers. Of nondrinkers, 8 percent were hospitalized for coronary disease, compared with 5.9 percent of less-than-two-a-day drinkers.

What Does Alcohol Do?

Alcohol appears to increase the level of protective high-density lipoproteins (HDLs) in the blood.

At the Arteriosclerosis Research Center at Wake Forest University, Thomas Clarkson, M.D., has recently carried out studies with monkeys which indicate that the severity of coronary artery atherosclerosis, as it developed in animals fed a high cholesterol diet with or without alcohol, was largely determined by the inclusion or exclusion of alcohol. Alcohol increased HDL concentration. It also decreased the molecular weight of low-density lipoproteins (LDLs). Heavier LDLs in the blood were found to be strongly associated with atherosclerosis in the animal studies.

Still more evidence of alcohol's beneficial effects on HDL levels has come recently from human studies. A particularly noteworthy one was carried out by W. Willett, M.D., and a group of investigators in the

Department of Preventive Medicine at Harvard Medical School and in the Framingham Heart Study.

Aware that physical activity, body weight, and other variables may affect HDL levels, the investigators wanted to determine whether alcohol itself could be responsible for increasing HDL or whether in fact the benefits attributed to alcohol might have been due to activity and other variables.

Using a study group of ninety male physicians, 29 to 60 years of age, who had participated in the 1979 Doctors' Marathon, they measured HDL levels and correlated the results with each man's quantitative alcohol intake.

By well-established statistical procedures (multiple regression analysis), the investigators were able to assess independently the effects of alcohol, physical activity, weight, and other variables. They found that the level of HDL was higher in those men whose rate of alcohol consumption was higher. The statistical analyses showed that alcohol itself, not the physical activity, caused the elevated HDL levels, even though each of the subjects was a marathon runner.

Drawbacks

If moderate use of alcohol may offer some benefit, it is important to put this in perspective. It has been established that alcohol in excess is harmful. Ten million adult Americans—7 percent of those 18 years old or older—are estimated to be alcoholics or problem drinkers. According to the 1979 U.S. Surgeon General's Report, *Healthy People*, "Of all adults who drink, more than a third have been classified as either current or potential problem drinkers, with women making up one-fourth to one-third of the latter."

The Surgeon General's Report underscores these facts:

- Alcohol misuse is a factor in more than 10 percent of all deaths in the United States, about 200,000 a year.

- It is associated with half of all traffic deaths.

- Cirrhosis, which ranks among the ten leading causes of death, is largely attributable to alcohol consumption. (We should add that the liver, the only body organ which can metabolize alcohol, is a main target for other alcohol damage. When forced to use alcohol as an energy source, instead of fatty acids, which are its normal source, the liver becomes fatty as the fatty acids accumulate there. Alcoholic hepatitis, a liver inflammation, may be triggered by heavy drinking bouts. Also, an alcohol-damaged liver may be unable to detoxify poisons and carcinogens that get into the body.)

- Alcohol use is associated with cancer, particularly of the liver, esophagus, and mouth. Primary liver cancer—malignancy originating in the liver—is often attributed to alcohol consumption. People who drink and also smoke cigarettes have an ever greater risk of developing esophageal cancer.

- Excessive drinking during pregnancy can produce infants with severe abnormalities, including mental retardation.

What Do You Do?

Clearly, the recent findings about possible benefits from moderate alcohol intake in terms of heart disease are encouraging—to a point—and for some, but not all, people.

What is moderate intake?

Pending further studies of what might constitute an ideal intake for the heart without other risk, it appears to be about two bottles of beer, or two 4-ounce glasses of wine, or 2 ounces of whiskey daily. At least, for now, this seems to be the level at which, for most healthy people, benefits may outweigh risks.

For people with certain medical problems, however, even moderate levels of alcohol may be too much, and abstinence in some cases may be best. These problems include, of course, alcohol-related conditions such as fatty liver and cirrhosis. They also include epilepsy and diabetes. And it goes without saying that continued abstinence may be best for anyone who has had to give up drinking before because of problem drinking or alcoholism.

Caffeine

Americans are hardly in a class with Voltaire, a king of coffee lovers, who drank more than 50 cups a day. But we do well enough as consumers of the brew, averaging about 16 pounds worth per person per year and drinking up to half of the world production.

We also take in huge amounts of caffeine in addition to what we get in coffee. Most people know there is caffeine in coffee and tea, but not as many realize it is also present in some soft drinks. Even fewer may know that they are consuming caffeine when they sip a cup of cocoa, munch on a chocolate bar, or take some pills for a headache or cold. It is even used in some foods.

Coffee: Friend or Enemy?

For a time, not so long ago, a cloud hung over coffee. One of the first reports suggesting a possible association between coffee and coronary heart disease appeared in 1963 to the consternation of lovers of the beverage.

To make matters worse, in 1972 and again in 1973 came other reports suggesting that people who drink more than 5 cups a day have about twice as great a risk of having a heart attack as people who do not drink coffee.

In 1974 there were sighs of relief when two important studies were published contradicting the findings of the earlier ones.

One was an analysis of health checkup questionnaires which had been completed by 197 men, 40 to 79 years of age, some time before they died suddenly. Comparison with data on other men of comparable age and characteristics obtained from 250,000 computerized health checkup questionnaires revealed no significant increase in the incidence of sudden death from heart attacks among those who drank even more than 6 cups of coffee a day.

The other report came from the Framingham Heart Study in which, over a 12-year period, careful records of daily coffee consumption were kept for the thousands of participating men and women. No significant differences could be found between coffee drinkers and non-coffee drinkers for onset of coronary heart disease or development of such heart disease indications as chest pain (angina pectoris) or heart attacks.

The Framingham report also found no significant relationship between coffee consumption and development of stroke and other heart and blood vessel problems not related to coronary heart disease. The data also showed no significant effect on high blood pressure or blood cholesterol levels, although this had been suggested in some earlier studies.

More recently, because smoking had been shown to adversely affect blood cholesterol levels and there remained some belief that coffee might do the same, Siegfried Heyden, M.D., and other investigators at Duke University Medical Center carried out a study of 361 people. As we noted earlier, high LDL cholesterol levels can be harmful, and the Duke study found LDL levels to be significantly higher among those who smoked and consumed 5 or more cups of coffee daily than among nonsmokers who abstained from coffee. However, although smoking and coffee drinking interacted to increase LDL levels and total blood cholesterol, coffee drinking alone had no apparent effect on cholesterol.

Other Caffeine Effects

Caffeine, which qualifies as a drug, has several effects on the body. It acts as a diuretic, promoting urination, and as a stimulant for the central nervous system. Although it does not affect everyone in the same way, if consumed in large enough doses, it can cause insomnia, nervousness, irritability, anxiety, and disturbances of heart rate and rhythm.

Some people, whether they realize it or not, become addicted to the stimulant effect of caffeine and may experience withdrawal symptoms—typically, headache—when they do not get their usual amount.

Ulcers? Caffeine in coffee and other drinks does tend to stimulate stomach acid secretion. The stimulation appears to be mild and transitory in healthy people but may be sustained in those with ulcers, suggesting that ulcer-disposed people may be more sensitive to caffeine and should moderate their intake.

At various times, caffeine has been suspected of being linked to other diseases, such as diabetes and bladder cancer—but to date no firm evidence has been found to prove a cause-and-effect relationship.

Caffeinism Syndrome

In sensitive people, large amounts of caffeine can produce a syndrome, or set of symptoms, mimicking the psychiatric disorder of chronic anxiety. While tranquilizers and other drugs then may be used, the need is not for new drugs but simply for a reduction in the intake of caffeine.

Among the symptoms of the caffeinism syndrome are restlessness, irritability, insomnia, headache, muscle twitching, racing pulse, flushing, lethargy, nausea, vomiting, diarrhea, and chest pain.

Individual sensitivity varies. For some people 250 milligrams of caffeine a day may be enough to provoke a reaction. That amount is considered sizable, yet many people exceed it almost daily. For example, if you drink 3 cups of coffee and a cola and take two caffeine-containing headache tablets, your total intake of caffeine is about 500 milligrams.

Caffeinism was first brought to light at an American Psychiatric Association meeting several years ago by John Greden, M.D. Greden noted several dramatic cases of people who had benefited when their caffeine problem was recognized and their caffeine intake was reduced.

The Final Word

For some people—those very sensitive to its effects—caffeine, obviously, is best avoided. But for many, if not most, people, caffeine—in moderation—has its value. Coffee, for example, smells good, tastes good, and produces mild euphoria, reduced fatigue, and increased alertness. Tea lovers and appreciators of other caffeine-containing beverages may feel the same about their favorites.

For most people, moderation is the key. Avoiding excess, they can enjoy these pleasures with little, if any, likelihood of harm.

Vegetarianism

Vegetarianism is no longer looked upon as a faddish way of eating. For those who follow it, it can be an alternative way of eating a healthy diet.

Currently an estimated 7 million Americans—three times as many as just a generation ago—consider themselves vegetarians. Some avoid meat simply because it is too expensive, some believe it is wrong to kill animals for food, and for others it is a religious matter not to eat meat.

In 1974, when the National Research Council of the National Academy of Sciences evaluated vegetarian diets, it found that all but the most restricted are nutritionally safe. "The most important safeguard for average vegetarian consumers," its report declared, "is great variety in the diet"—a safeguard equally applicable to meat eaters.

What Vegetarians Eat

Vegans, vegetarians who eat no animal products in any form, are relatively rare in the United States. Those who do eat dairy products and eggs are known as *lactovovegetarians*, and those who eat milk products but no eggs are known as *lactovegetarians*.

Lactovovegetarians have access to all four basic food groups: dairy products (milk, cheese, yogurt, ice cream, and other dairy products); vegetables and fruit; grain products (bread, pasta, cereals, rice, and other grains); and protein sources (eggs, dried beans and peas, peanut butter, lentils, soybeans, nuts, and seeds). Although lactovegetarians do not use eggs, there are protein-rich foods in the meat group that they can eat, and protein can be found in the other food groups.

For lacto- and lactovovegetarians, the greater diversity of vegetables, fruits, cereals, legumes, nuts, and seeds added to the dairy products in the diet, the better the nourishment. They can improve the quality of protein by combining dairy products with grain products—for example, cereal with milk, and macaroni with cheese.

Vegans need to select foods with great care to get adequate nutrients, with special attention to protein. Only proteins from animal muscle, milk, and eggs contain the amino acids needed for protein synthesis in the body in approximately the proportions the body needs. Proteins from vegetables, grains, and nuts provide significant amounts of many amino acids, but they do not supply as much protein as animal sources.

Vegans can improve the protein content of their diet by including plenty of legumes such as soybeans and chickpeas, which have protein of almost as high quality as animal protein.

Combining foods from different groups also improves the quality of protein from nonanimal sources. For example, legumes complement grains; the combinations of beans with rice provides a good source of vitamin B_{12}. One such product, tempeh (an Indonesian bean cake sold in this country), is reported to be a particularly reliable source.

Is a Vegetarian Diet More Healthful?

Many claims have been made that vegetarian diets are more healthful, that vegetarians live longer and that vegetarianism protects against such degenerative diseases as cancer, high blood pressure, coronary heart disease, and diabetes. But there has been little evidence up to now to support the claims.

A vegetarian diet, however, may help with some health problems. For one thing, it is often lower in calories, and vegetarians have been found in some studies to weigh less for their height than nonvegetarians. Because of the amount of fiber in their diet, vegetarians are also less likely to have problems with constipation.

It is a fact, too, that a typical vegetarian diet is closer than the typical American nonvegetarian diet to some of the guidelines in the recent government publication, *Dietary Guidelines for Americans*. It is lower in saturated fats, higher in fiber, and has more complex carbohydrates.

7.

Ideal Diet

Balance and Variety

It must be obvious that nutrition plays not only a vital role in health, but also a complex role. There is no one predominant nutrient or group of nutrients. There are dozens of them, including amino acids (in proteins), carbohydrates, fats, vitamins, and minerals. All are essential and interrelated. Let one be either deficient or present in excess, and others are affected. For example, without enough vitamin C in the diet, you may not absorb all the iron you need; with too much calcium in the diet, you may become zinc-deficient.

The more we know about nutritional complexities, the more one fact stands out: Except for certain specific problems—disease states for which special diets have been established as clearly helpful—the healthiest diet is balanced and varied.

Finding the Correct Balance

This is simply a matter of getting, in suitable servings each day, foods from each of the *basic four food groups* (see table on page 119). A

THE BASIC FOUR FOOD GROUPS

The four groups	Nutrients supplied	Daily adult servings	One serving equals
Meat and meat substitutes: Beef, pork, lamb, veal, fish, poultry, eggs, organ meats, cheese, dry beans, lentils, peas, nuts	Protein, fat, iron, niacin, thiamine, vitamins B_{12} and E, copper, phosphorus	2	2 oz cooked lean meat, fish, or poultry; 2 eggs; 1 cup cooked dry beans, peas, or lentils; ½ cup nuts or 4 tbsp peanut butter; 2 oz hard cheese; ½ cup cottage cheese
Dairy products Milk, yogurt, natural and processed cheeses, ice cream, ice milk, food products made with whole or skim milk	Protein, fat, calcium, riboflavin, vitamins A and D, zinc, magnesium	2	1 cup milk or yogurt; 1 oz cheese; ½ cup cottage cheese, ½ cup ice cream; 1 cup milk-based food (pudding, soup, or beverage)
Fruit and vegetables: All fruits and vegetables (fresh, frozen, canned, dried, and juices)	Carbohydrates, water, vitamins A and C, iron, magnesium	4	1 cup cut-up raw fruit or vegetable; 1 medium apple, banana, orange, tomato, or potato; ½ melon or grapefruit; ½ cup cooked vegetable or fruit; ½ cup fruit or vegetable juice
Grains: Whole-grain or enriched flour, pasta, rice, cereal products	Carbohydrates, fat, protein, thiamine, niacin, vitamin E, calcium, iron, phosphorus, magnesium, zinc, copper	4	1 slice bread; 1 oz dry cereal; 1 roll or muffin; 1 pancake or waffle; ½ cup rice, pasta, or cooked cereal

balanced diet requires two servings each from the meat and meat substitutes group and the dairy products group and four servings each from
the fruit and vegetables group and the grains group. By varying our
choices within each group from day to day, we can have a healthy,
balanced variety of foods, with neither too much nor too little of any
valuable nutrient, either currently known or still to be identified.

Shopping for Food

In the Meat Department   Choose more fish and poultry. Both are as
rich in protein as red meat, but they have less total fat and some
polyunsaturated fat. If possible, eat fish at least twice a week. With
whole wheat bread and tea or coffee, smoked fish—salmon, whitefish,
haddock, cod, or herring—can make a nutritious and enjoyable breakfast, but eat it no more than once a week in order to keep your salt
intake low. For dinner, grilled steaks of salmon, swordfish, or other
fish, or baked whole fish, can provide nourishing protein with relatively
little saturated fat and only a moderate amount of calories.

Choose veal before other meats. It is beef, but it has much less fat
than other beef products. In buying beef, lamb, or pork, choose the
leanest cuts possible (leg of lamb; less-marbled cuts of beef, which are
often cheaper than other cuts).

Keep to a minimum the purchase of such fatty meats as sausage,
bacon, pastrami, corned beef, and many cold cuts. Buy instead cold
sliced chicken or turkey.

In the Dairy Department   Switch to skim or low-fat milk in place of
whole milk. They contain the same amount of calcium, protein, and
vitamins as whole milk, but much less butterfat (usually 3.5 percent,
or none at all). Both can be used in coffee, although you can also use
evaporated skim milk or a dried skim-milk powder. You should know
that many of the preparations sold as coffee lighteners are made from
one vegetable oil, coconut oil, which is a saturated fat.

Switch from cheeses made with cream or whole milk to skim-milk
cheeses. Also, avoid butter and shortenings in foods; choose foods—
and recipes, if you cook yourself—that substitute polyunsaturated margarine and vegetable oils. (Polyunsaturated margarine can be substituted
for butter in *any* recipe.) An acceptable margarine would be one that
lists liquid corn oil as its first ingredient.

Breads and Cereals   Buy whole wheat or other whole-grain breads—which are rich in fiber—rather than white bread. Avoid butter rolls and commercial cakes, doughnuts, and muffins, which are usually baked with saturated fats. It is preferable that homemade bread, pastries, cakes, and biscuits be made with whole wheat, rather than white, flour. Choose unsugared cereals, preferably, those high in fiber, many of which are labeled as including "bran" or "oats."

Fruits and Vegetables   Keep some fresh fruit and cleaned vegetables ready to eat as low-calorie snacks. Buy fresh fruit for dessert, to be eaten by itself or as a topping on frozen yogurt or sugarless gelatin.

Food Preparation

Vegetables and Fruits   Handle them as little as possible and don't prepare them far ahead of time. Wash them quickly; don't soak them. Don't overdo peeling, because there are nutrients and fiber in the skin, too; cook them whole, with skins on, whenever possible. Peeling and slicing can cause as much as a 50 percent loss of vitamin C.

Avoid thawing frozen vegetables and fruits until immediately before you are ready to cook or eat them; they can lose much of their nutrients otherwise.

Don't drain the liquid from canned vegetables. It contains as much as 40 percent of the vitamin C and one-third of the thiamine and riboflavin. Cook with it and save what is left for soups and sauces.

Avoid trimming such leafy vegetables as lettuce and cabbage; nutrient concentration tends to be greatest in the outer leaves.

Don't overcook frozen or canned vegetables; they have already been parboiled.

In cooking a fresh vegetable or fruit, drop it into already boiling water. (At high temperatures, because of the effect of an enzyme system in the foods, there is less destruction of vitamin C.) Cover the pot, bring the water to a boil again, and cook until tender but still firm. Better yet, cook vegetables and fruit in a steamer, because they retain even more of their vitamins when they're steamed than when they're boiled.

Don't use baking soda in cooking yellow or green vegetables; it destroys vitamins.

Don't leave vegetables in water or over heat once they are cooked.

The cooking should be timed so that they can be served as soon as they are done. Continued heating speeds the destruction of vitamins.

Serve leftover vegetables such as asparagus, beets, peas, and beans in a salad the next day instead of reheating them, which causes more loss of nutrients.

Keep fruit at room temperature until ripe; then refrigerate it to conserve nutrients.

Orange juice is good for you, but remember that a whole orange provides more vitamins and fiber than juice; even the core and peel are high in valuable nutrients.

Meats   The higher the cooking temperature, the greater the shrinking and drying—and also the loss of nutrients. Cook meat at moderate temperatures, 300 to 350°F, and don't overcook it. That also applies to pork, which, because of the possibility of trichinosis, many people "cook to death." Trichinae are destroyed at 140°F, so pork cooked at 325°F for 30 minutes a pound is safe—and more nutritious.

Roasting and broiling are the best ways of cooking meat from the standpoint of nutrient retention. During broiling, moreover, much of the fat drips off and can be discarded. Frying may actually double the calorie count.

When roasting, it is advisable to use a rack so the meat does not sit in the drippings while cooking. Low-temperature (325 to 350°F) roasting is best for flavor and also allows more fat to come out of the meat; higher temperatures tend to seal the fat in. Instead of basting with drippings (which contain fat) during roasting, try using wine, fruit juice, or broth to keep the meat moist and add an interesting flavor besides.

Roast turkey or chicken with a few onions, carrots, or other vegetables in the cavity to add flavor, and bake stuffings separately, using fat-free broth to flavor them. Stuffing in poultry absorbs a lot of fat.

Fish   Broil or bake fish at 400°F, leaving the skin on to prevent loss of juices and nutrients.

Poaching can produce a mild-flavored fish with the smallest amount of fat. For the poaching liquid, use a small amount of water, white wine, and some onions and herbs. Simmer the fish; don't let the poaching liquid boil or it may cause the fish to break up.

Cook fish only until it flakes easily; further cooking will make it dry and tough.

Steam lobsters and crabs in their shells to preserve nutrients. Shrimp can be shelled with little nutrient loss, since their cooking time is only 3 to 5 minutes.

A Quick Course in Reading Food Labels

With few exceptions, food product labels include a list of ingredients. This shows the ingredients in descending order of quantity in the recipe, main ingredient first. If the list for a frozen turkey dinner, for example, reads "potatoes, carrots, turkey," you are getting more vegetables than meat.

You can also figure that when sugar or some other sweetener is one of the first two or three ingredients of a product, there could be more sugar present than is nutritionally desirable. Note, too, that different kinds of sugars are listed separately, so you should look through the list for all such ingredients as honey, dextrose, corn syrup, corn sweetener, invert sugar, molasses, etc.

Ingredient lists give other useful information, too. Here, for example, is a list for a chocolate-chip cookie product:

> INGREDIENTS: Flour, chocolate, sugar, blend of partially hydrogenated vegetable shortening (may contain partially hydrogenated soybean, cottonseed and/or palm oils), eggs, corn syrup, molasses, water, salt, sodium bicarbonate, natural and artificial flavors.

You can see that the major nutrients are carbohydrates (starches from flour, and sugars from corn syrup and molasses as well as common sugar) and fats (from chocolate, shortening, and eggs).

The flour is unenriched (without added B vitamins or iron), and the oils have been partially hydrogenated to improve their shortening properties, which means that the level of saturated fat has been somewhat increased and the level of polyunsaturated fat decreased.

Because of the salt and sodium bicarbonate content, such cookies— the recipe is a typical one for chocolate-chip cookies—should be eaten very sparingly by anyone on a low-sodium diet and also by anyone on a cholesterol-fat-controlled diet, because of the chocolate, shortening, and eggs.

Particular attention should be paid to whether an ingredient list includes coconut or palm oil, both of which are more saturated than animal fats, or whether the list simply lists vegetable oil without indicating the kind, in which case it is likely to be coconut or palm oil.

A Final Word

Nutrition is still a very young science, and there is much yet to be learned about it. What we are counseling encompasses what is known and leaves room for what is still to be discovered.

If what we are counseling had to be summed up in just one word, the word would be *moderation*. Until everything there is to be known about nutrition is, in fact, known (and quite possibly even then) moderation, with all that it means, is a fine practical guide to good nutrition.

Everything we know indicates that nutritional deficiencies, excesses, and imbalances play significant roles in many conditions, especially degenerative diseases. All the evidence points to the importance of sound nutrition in maintaining both mental and physical health.

Good nutrition, desirable for all, can be highly critical for executives who are under stress, lead extremely busy lives, need their wits about them at all times, and obviously need to maintain their health in order to advance in their careers.

Use our "Concise Reference Guide to Prudent Eating" for important information on the calorie and cholesterol contents of numerous foods.

If you are really well nourished now, you probably already know the benefits—or, if you have only suspected them before, you should realize what they are now from what you've read here. If you have been less than well nourished, we are confident that the information in this book will have been a revelation to you and will have shown you the direction to a healthier—and happier—life.

There can be no guarantees, of course, that you will live longer because of improved nutrition, although it is certainly a possibility. We are sure, however, that you will take well-justified pride—and pleasure—in feeling more fit and vigorous as the result of good nutrition.

Part II

Executive Fitness

Introduction

Let us face it—executives are sitting for most of their workdays, and in the evenings and on weekends as well. Think about your own daily schedule. Does it go something like this? Up at 6:30 A.M., with time only for a shower and a cup of coffee before you are off to work. Then a frustrating 45-minute drive through rush-hour traffic to work. You park in a garage and take the elevator up to the office. Then comes an 8-hour day or more, stuck for the most part behind a desk, and then another drive home. After supper you sit down in your favorite easy chair in front of the television set.

The routine is the same for 5 or even 6 days a week. Sometimes on the weekend you work in the yard, raking leaves, cutting the grass, and so on. You play tennis occasionally. You travel regularly, spending most of that time on airplanes, in meetings, and in hotel rooms.

A growing number of medical authorities now believe that exercise can be an antidote to the sedentary lifestyle. In fact, Executive Health Examiners sees exercise as a form of preventive medicine that almost always leads to better physical and mental health. We have found that a complete, balanced exercise program, when combined with a healthy diet and lifestyle, can contribute to the prevention of many diseases, including the most prevalent and dangerous physical problem facing executives: cardiovascular disease.

Executive Health Examiners has found that no one—not even the most deskbound executive—has to suffer the consequences of the sedentary lifestyle. We have devised a preventive medicine prescription that almost any executive can follow.

8.

Every Executive
Needs to Exercise

Richard O. Keelor, the longtime director of program development for the President's Council on Physical Fitness and Sports, has a cogent description for the typical sedentary executive lifestyle. He calls it "habitual inactivity." Keelor has identified two of the most serious health hazards in the American workplace. They are not asbestos and coal dust but the desk and the swivel chair, which deprive working men and women of the opportunity to exercise. Today's typical office job, Keelor says, requires "less exertion than a hot shower."

The consequences of habitual inactivity are not pleasant to contemplate; they include degeneration of the muscular, respiratory, and cardiovascular systems.

Many scientists now believe that sedentary work and living habits are not compatible with the design of the human body. They contend that the body's muscular, respiratory, and circulatory systems not only need, but were designed specifically for, participation in regular vigorous movements. Depriving the body of regular vigorous exercise can therefore cause these systems to degenerate.

James Nora, M.D., director of preventive cardiology at the University of Colorado School of Medicine, calls the sedentary life the "nonphysical lifestyle." Dr. Nora describes the effects of this lifestyle on the body in the following manner: "The less physical work you do, the less physical work your body becomes capable of doing. And the converse is also true: The more physical work you do (up to defined limits), the more you become able to do. . . . Demand little and you get little. Demand a lot and you get a lot. That's the homeostatic wisdom of the body."

Demanding little of the body can lead to degeneration, which in turn can cause heart disease, stroke, hypertension, and premature aging. In short, depriving the body of regular exercise also deprives it of health and vitality. As Keelor says:

> Experiments have shown that prolonged bed rest, or chair rest, can transform a robust young man into a feeble fellow with weak muscles and the unsteady gait of an old man. Sedentary work and living habits have the same of debilitative effects, though they are slower to develop—and more insidious because they are so often mistaken for the normal ravages of time.

As the Blue Cross/Blue Shield publication "A Very Simple Guide to Help You Feel Better" (1980) puts it, "We are not only beneficiaries of the industrial, technological, scientific and electronic revolution: we are victims of it."

Exercise as an Antidote to the Sedentary Lifestyle

Although science has yet to prove beyond doubt that exercise is 100 percent effective in prolonging life and preventing heart problems, the evidence is overwhelming that this is so. For the vast majority of executives, exercise is a prudent and beneficial undertaking. Even medical scientists who do not believe that exercise programs can reduce the risk of cardiovascular disease still recommend that most people take part in regular exercise regimens.

Here are the conclusions of an American College of Cardiology-sponsored task force in the Prevention of Coronary Heart Disease, chaired by Robert S. Eliot, M.D., director of the University of Nebraska Medical Center's Cardiovascular Center:

> Although exercise programs have received a great deal of publicity, their benefits in reducing cardiovascular disease are still uncertain. Scientific evidence from many sources suggests that people who are vigorously active have less heart disease, have an increased sense of well-being and are less depressed and anxious than are people who are sedentary. If people entering an exercise program also stop smoking cigarettes, alter their diet, lower their body weight, reduce serum lipids [cholesterol-like fatty deposits in the bloodstream] and bring levels of arterial blood pressure to ideal values, then they probably lower their risk for cardiovascular disease.

There may be some equivocation in that statement, but the message is clear. Exercise can do most people no harm, and there is a very real possibility that it will help prevent a heart attack. At the very least, exercise will help you look and feel better physically and feel better mentally.

Getting the Right Kind of Exercise

One of the first questions EHE doctors ask a patient about to take a physical examination is, "Do you get any exercise?" About 75 percent of the executives we examine say, "Yes, but I don't think I get enough." They are usually right. Not only do they not get enough exercise, they usually do not get the right kind. Consider these two examples:

The vice president of a New Jersey savings and loan association, on days when he feels especially chipper, will do his exercise routine in the morning before showering. The routine, which he has been doing on and off (mostly off) since high school, consists of situps and pushups. On a good day he can do 35 pushups and 100 situps. When he is through with the routine, he is panting and sweating but happy. The situps flatten his stomach, and the pushups build his arm and chest muscles.

A female executive of a sporting goods chain climbs the stairs at work instead of using the elevator, walks several blocks to and from her commuter train, and works around the house on weekends. That is the extent of her regular exercising.

These two executives know they are not getting enough exercise; they told EHE doctors that they were not feeling exactly "right." One of the most common complaints we hear is that an executive feels tired in the late afternoon and evening or even in the morning after awakening. One 39-year-old vice president of a men's clothing chain put it this way: "My back's been bothering me lately. I'm lethargic, and I wake up in the morning still tired. I don't quite know how to put my finger on it. Eating, sleeping, and so on are all okay. I'm not having any trouble with the family. The job's all right. I just don't particularly feel quite right. I guess I'm getting older."

That man may be getting older, but he does not necessarily have to feel the aging process so acutely. His lack of energy, as with the other two executives who complained that they did not quite feel right, is due to the fact that he does not get the correct type of exercise. The irregular, unbalanced types of exercise that all three executives take part in do not compensate for the habitual inactivity involved in their everyday lives. In spite of the sporadic exercising, their bodies are stagnating. They need to get involved in regular, balanced exercise programs.

Building Reserve Strength

There is also the important factor of building reserve strength. A balanced exercise program provides cardiovascular conditioning and helps strengthen and tone the muscles, thus building bodily strength. This can prove very beneficial when the unexpected happens and you need to call on your reserves. If you break a leg, for instance, and are forced to get around on crutches, you will be able to handle that physically demanding task more easily if you have reserve strength, which will allow you to function at a relatively normal level. Or you might have to dash from one end of a large airport terminal to the other, carrying a heavy suitcase. Reserve strength from exercise (plus that surge of adrenaline) will go a long way toward getting you through the physical emergency without placing undue strain on your heart, and you might well catch that plane.

Being physically fit also can help you cope with disease more effectively. We have found that our well-conditioned patients who experience unexpected illnesses seem to have a significantly easier time tolerating disease. Whether it is a cold or the flu, the physically fit individual will usually recover faster than the out-of-shape person.

In summary, we believe that every executive can benefit from a program of exercise, provided that a physician gives him or her the green light. This is true especially for those who have one or more of the cardiovascular risk factors, but it also applies to those with no detectable risks. Experience has taught us that if executives exercise regularly, they become much more adept at performing their usual daily activities at work and at home, and this includes sex. Sexual activity involves vigorous movement. The better the physical shape you are in, the more you will be able to engage in strenuous sexual activity without risking fatigue.

Senator Strom Thurmond of South Carolina provides a good example of the effects of regular exercise. Thurmond is an avid runner. He has been taking a daily run of 2 to 4 miles for longer than he cares to remember. He married a woman in her thirties in 1968 when he was 65 years old. They now have four children.

9.

The Proper
Exercise Program

A recent European visitor to the United States remarked that the first thing he noticed in the large cities he visited was "a lot of people running around in their underwear." He was talking about the ubiquitous urban jogger, of course, the most visible manifestation of a physical fitness explosion that began in the early 1970s in this country. By the end of the decade, opinion polls showed that for the first time more than half of all Americans aged 18 and over were participating in some form of daily physical exercise. Nearly 60 percent of the adults questioned in the 1978 Harris Poll, for example, said they took part in a regular exercise program that lasted 2½ hours or more a week. About 15 percent said they exercised more than 5 hours a week. In comparison, only about 24 percent of those questioned in 1961 reported that they exercised regularly. Jogging, however, is only one of many forms of exercise now being practiced regularly that offer the same physical and psychological benefits.

Aerobics, Stretching, and Strength Building

Jogging/running is classified as an aerobic exercise, or one that is maintained in a continuous, rhythmic manner. The aerobic exercises are named for the Greek word for *air* because they stimulate increases in oxygen-bearing blood flow, inducing the heart to work harder and thereby expanding the blood vessels.

Medical research strongly indicates that aerobic exercises—which include running/jogging, walking, swimming, bicycling, rope skipping, and cross-country skiing—develop and maintain cardiovascular fitness and body strength. Doctors believe that a regular exercise program that includes as its basis an aerobic program probably will aid in the prevention of coronary disease and could prolong one's life. It is known for certain that aerobic exercises can help you lose weight and keep it off. Moreover, most people who continue an aerobic program for at least 6 months find that they look healthier and feel stronger and more confident.

Stretching Exercises

While aerobics should be the basis of a balanced exercise program, no such program is complete without the incorporation of a series of stretching exercises. These routines are designed to make the muscles more flexible and relaxed and to mitigate the effects of stress. They help extend and maintain the range of movement in specific joints and series of joints. All the major muscle groups should be stretched regularly. Many doctors recommend paying special attention to the lower back, which is particularly susceptible to soreness and pain. Joggers, runners, walkers, and cyclists should also pay close attention to the thigh and leg muscles. These muscles should be well stretched before one takes part in aerobic exercises. For more details on stretching exercises, see Chapter 11.

Strength-Building Exercises

The third component of a balanced exercise program consists of muscular strength exercises. Think back to the executive described earlier whose exercise regimen consisted only of situps and pushups. These two strength-building exercises helped him build up his stomach, back, arm, and chest muscles, but the man's exercise program was incomplete since it did not include any aerobic or flexibility exercises. We consider the program incomplete because strength-building exercises have only the most minute effect on the cardiovascular system and do not help stretch or relax the muscles. A body builder with rippling muscles may look like the healthiest person in the world, but underneath the bulging muscles could be a rapidly aging cardiovascular system. It does little good to build up the muscles without simultaneously building up the cardiovascular system.

The two basic kinds of strength-building exercises are isometrics and isotonics. Both systems involve overloading the muscles so that they are forced to work increasingly harder to lift progressively heavier loads. In isometric exercises, the muscle pushes against an immovable object such as a wall. This forces the muscle to contract and eventually to build up strength. Isotonic strength building involves lifting weights or using the body's movements, as in situps and pushups. Both isometric and isotonic exercises, if done properly, can be valuable parts of a total exercise program. You will not be totally healthy without strength, but strong muscles alone do not mean that you are totally healthy.

Who Needs a Stress Test?

A New England advertising executive, after hearing about the three-part balanced exercise regimen recommended by Executive Health Examiners, was ready to go home and work out a self-prescribed program. "Well, I've got the basics," he said, "and I can't wait to start my program." We asked him to wait and listen to a few other things about exercise first. We told him that some people can easily and safely prescribe their own balanced exercise programs by choosing one of the aerobic exercises, one of the flexibility exercises, and one of the strength-building exercises. If they practice each exercise for a given amount of time for a certain number of days a week, they soon will reap the physiological and psychological benefits.

We also told this man that since he was 39 years old, there was at least one very important thing he needed to do before starting his exercise program: take a stress test. At Executive Health Examiners we do *not* automatically give every executive embarking on an exercise program a stress test, but we do advise every executive starting an exercise program who is over 35 years old to take one. According to the American Heart Association, as many as 10 percent of men over 35 with no overt symptoms have some form of hidden heart disease, whereas only about 1 percent of those under 35 with no symptoms do. A stress test can uncover hidden heart disease.

Executive Health Examiners follows the advice given by the American College of Sports Medicine in recommending what type of physical examination should be given before the start of an exercise program.

To summarize briefly, if you are under 35 and are physically active, you have little to worry about as you embark on an exercise program. But if you are physically inactive, regardless of your age, it's best to be prudent and have a physical examination before you begin exercising. The physical should include tests of your cardiovascular system and blood pressure and an examination of your muscles and joints. Your cholesterol and triglyceride levels should be determined, and you should be given a resting electrocardiograph (EKG) test.

The most important part of the physical examination is the exercise stress test, which we recommend for everyone over 35. The stress test is usually given on a stationary bicycle or a treadmill. The individual being tested pedals or jogs at increasing rates of speed until his or her ultimate capacity is reached. While this is going on, the following measurements are taken: pulse rate, electrocardiogram, blood pressure, and muscle fatigue. As the load is intensified, the body's responses are evaluated, and the stress test can pick up signs of previously hidden heart problems.

It should be pointed out that stress tests are not always accurate. On occasion a stress test will indicate that the patient has some sort of heart problem, but more extensive tests will show that there is nothing amiss. Conversely, a stress test sometimes will show that a patient has no heart irregularities when, in fact, they may exist. The medical terms for these two circumstances are false positives and false negatives, respectively. The stress test, then, is not perfect, but it is the best indicator doctors now have of how the body responds to exercise.

The Exercise Regimen: Type, Frequency, Duration, and Intensity

The four basic components of the EHE exercise regimen are the type, frequency, duration, and intensity of the exercises chosen for the program.

Type   As we have seen, there are three basic types of exercise in the balanced program: aerobic, stretching, and strength building. Among the aerobic exercises, Executive Health Examiners recommends any one of the following: walking, jogging or running, bicycling (indoors on a stationary machine or outdoors on a regular bike), swimming, and rope skipping. There are other aerobic exercises, including skating, rowing, cross-country skiing, and strenuous games such as basketball, but we do not recommend them. Our experience working with hundreds of executives in exercise programs has shown that walking, running, cycling, swimming, and rope skipping are particularly suited to the executive lifestyle.

Another factor: Once you have chosen an aerobic exercise, stick with it. Do not switch from cycling one week to swimming the next and jogging the next and so on. Think about what you like, what you do not like, and what you do well. If you choose an aerobic exercise you cannot abide by, leave it and go on to another, but choose the next one carefully so that you can stick with it, become proficient at it, and receive the maximum benefit from it.

For the stretching component of your balanced exercise program you may use any type of flexibility movements that are performed slowly and aid you in gradually progressing to a greater range of motion. You may choose several yoga stretching positions, for example, making sure that you take the time to stretch all the large muscle groups of the body.

We recommend a number of different types of muscular strength-building exercises. You can practice isometric exercises, using immovable objects. These require extremely strenuous but very brief expenditures of strength. You also can lift weights in the isotonic method. You can buy a chinup bar and work out on it, or you can use the old standbys, pushups and situps. The thing to keep in mind here is to work on building up strength equally in the arms, back, and legs.

Frequency   There can be no real benefit in an exercise program if it is not performed regularly. We therefore recommend that you exercise at least three times a week and that you do not allow more than 2 days to go by between sessions, but you can gain even more from exercising five times a week. A good habit to get into is to exercise each weekday at a set time, either before or after work or during the lunch hour. The minimum of three sessions and the maximum of five hold true for all three components of the exercise program. It also is a good idea to do all three during the same session.

Duration   This brings us to the all-important question of time. In order to gain the minimum benefit from an aerobic program, you need to spend at least 20 minutes with your heart working at about three-quarters of its maximum capacity, in the so-called target zone. You should not reach this plateau immediately after you start exercising, nor should you stop exercising immediately after you have been at this plateau for 20 minutes. You need both a warmup period and a cooling-down period.

The good news for time-conscious executives is that you can use warmup and cooling-down time to do your stretching and strength-building exercises. If you spend 10 to 15 minutes warming up with stretches and some situps, pushups, and other calisthenics and another 10 to 15 minutes cooling down with more stretching, your total daily exercise period should last about 45 to 60 minutes, or nearly an hour a session. This is the absolute minimum, and it bears repeating. The minimal exercise session should consist of about 10 to 15 minutes of stretching, 20 to 30 minutes of aerobic activity, and 10 to 15 minutes of strength building. That amounts to a 40- to 60-minute session, and you should do at least three, and preferably five, of these sessions a week.

Intensity   The intensity of an exercise program is the most subjective and personal component. Just how far you should push yourself requires an individualized exercise prescription, preferably formulated after reviewing the results of a stress test. Remember, the most important rule for anyone starting an exercise program is to begin *slowly*. The temptation, of course, is to set high goals and try to attain them quickly. No one wants to admit that at age 41, for example, he or she no longer has the physical capacity to run cross-country races. This is very hard to explain to ex-athletes. Many executives we work with at Executive Health Examiners have in their younger days been active in organized sports. When they make the decision to try to get back into shape, they often forget that it has taken them many years, and sometimes decades, to put their bodies out of shape. The tendency is to try to get back to where they once were in a matter of days.

Dr. Kenneth H. Cooper, the former Air Force physician who developed the theory of aerobics, says that the "cardinal rule" of aerobics is "safely, slowly and progressively," and that goes for the other parts of your exercise program as well. "More speed or intensity too soon," Cooper writes, "is like taking a whole bottle of medicine instead of just the recommended dosage—an invitation to trouble, in this case from tendons, muscles, joints, and your heart."

Time Constraints

"I know I should take part in an exercise program," a 36-year-old vice president of a publishing firm told an EHE doctor at a recent checkup. "But I just don't have the time." We have found that there is no lack of interest in exercise among executives, but there is a lack of time, or at least a perceived lack. The publishing executive told us that she has to catch a 6:40 A.M. train to get to work in New York City. When she gets off the train, she has just enough time to hop aboard the subway that takes her to work. She usually is tied up nearly every day in business lunches and therefore cannot exercise during the day. When she gets home from work, it's time for dinner. "I sit down and eat, and then the evening is gone," she told us. "Where do I fit in exercise?"

We told this woman what we tell all executives with this complaint. Believe it or not, you can fit a complete, balanced exercise program into a busy executive schedule without sacrificing anything, either on the job or at home. We believe that you should not fit that hour of exercise into your schedule—you should instead fit your schedule around that hour of exercise.

Dr. Nora puts it this way: If your "schedule is already so full that there's no way you can fit another hour a day into it . . . then it becomes even more imperative that you do just that. Take an hour away from the hassle and invest it in saving your life. This hour absolutely must not be looked on as just another hour to add to your other conflicting demands. You must not think of it that way or approach it that way. This hour is yours. It's for you and your life and your well-being. It's first priority. There's nothing you have to do that's more important."

Here is how we solved the publishing executive's time dilemma. When we explained how important we believed that hour to be, she sat down with us, and we reexamined her daily schedule. Before long we were able to help her find the time for an exercise regimen. She followed our suggestion and was able to fulfill the aerobic component of her exercise program easily. She had been taking the subway from the train station in the city to her office a mile and a half away. Instead of riding the subway, she began walking that distance at a brisk enough pace— about 5 miles an hour—to get aerobic benefits. She even made it to work on time.

The publishing executive also discovered another beneficial side effect of her morning walk. When she finished the brisk 15-minute walk, she was not dripping with sweat or exhausted. In fact, she was ready for the morning's work, feeling freshly invigorated and mentally alert. She soon stopped eating heavy breakfasts before leaving for work, because they did not sit well during her morning walk. Instead, she ate a light breakfast and was not at all hungry when she got to the office.

The Right Time to Exercise

As this example illustrates, with proper motivation a way can be found to carve out an exercise routine that does not disrupt a regimented, time-filled daily work routine. One way to find that time is to look at three periods during the day: in the morning before work, in the evening after work, and in the afternoon during lunch hour. The way for an executive to find out which of these periods is best is to examine his or her schedule. If, for instance, your one-way commute between home and the office is between 1.5 and 4 miles, think about getting your aerobic exercise by either walking or jogging to work. You may eventually also want to walk or jog home as well. You do not have to do this every day of the week—3 days is sufficient—but once you get in the habit, you may discover you enjoy walking or jogging to work, and you may want to do it each weekday, except perhaps for days when there is particularly inclement weather.

If you live 3 to 10 miles from the office, you might consider riding a bicycle to and from work. You can easily get aerobic benefits in this manner. Or, like the publishing executive, you can take public trans-

portation part of the way to work and walk briskly for the last 1.5 to
2 miles. Another option is to drive your car within a few miles of where
you work, carrying your bicycle on a rack. You can then park the car
and ride the bike the last 3 to 10 miles. A 37-year-old EHE client who
lives 25 miles from work has used this method for 6 years. He says the
commute takes only 10 minutes longer than normal using the car-bike
method, and he avoids the nerve-wracking (and stress-building) experience of fighting city rush-hour traffic, not to mention rates for a parking
space in the city.

If for some reason you cannot work your exercise routine into your
daily commute, try setting aside three to five lunch hours a week for
exercise. Many companies have installed gymnasiums in their office
complexes. If your office does not have one, you have other options.
You can join the many other lunch-hour joggers out in the streets and
parks, or you can take a brisk 30- to 45-minute walk and window-shop
your way to better health. You also can go to a health club, gym, or
yoga class during lunch.

Whatever time period you choose, experiment to see what suits your
schedule. If you cannot fit in an exercise regimen in the morning, try
the evening hours after you get home from work, or try getting up a
bit earlier. You might just stumble into a perfect time, but you will
never know until you experiment and try.

There are other times of the day during which you can exercise. We
have learned from many of our patients that it is possible to work all
the exercises into a daily executive schedule. Some of them eschew
elevators during the day at work; instead they walk briskly up and down
stairwells. Just bolting up a staircase for a few seconds does not provide
aerobic benefit; this is classified as an anaerobic exercise, or one that
provides no cardiovascular benefit. But there are physiologic benefits,
including helping the leg muscles become stronger, to be gained by
moving out from behind your desk and hitting the stairs. Above all,
the activity keeps you from stagnating, both mentally and physically,
in your sedentary job.

Two EHE doctors have devised a walking routine which they undertake while waiting for the commuter train on the way home from the
office each evening. During the wait, which sometimes lasts up to 30
minutes, they walk briskly from one end of the platform to the other.
Fifteen minutes of walking provides them with aerobic exercise for the
day. A number of EHE patients make it a practice to walk to all their

appointments in the city during working days. Some executives get off the bus several stops before work and walk rapidly for the last mile or two to the office.

There are many stretching and isometric exercises you can do while driving to work or while sitting as a passenger in a car, train, or airplane. In fact, there is a book, *Autocize*, by Jay David, that explains exactly how to do these sorts of exercises. David suggests one stretching program for men and women who spend at least a half hour a day in a car. It's a 4-day program with each day set aside to exercise a different muscle group. One day you concentrate on the head and neck, the next day on the arms, then the waist and buttocks, and finally the legs and feet. The exercises range from full body stretching while standing outside the car before you begin to drive and isometrics using the car's fenders, to neck stretches and leg raises while you are driving.

Exercising on a Business Trip

For the executive on a business trip, there are many chances to exercise. Some hotels offer out-of-town guest maps of the surrounding area's best running paths, and some have swimming pools and gyms. If possible, it's a good idea to stay at a hotel that caters to executives with regular exercise schedules.

10.

Choosing an Aerobic Program

When biologists talk about *aerobes*, they are referring to organisms that can live only in the presence of oxygen. When physicians refer to *aerobics*, they are talking about exercises that impel the human body to use oxygen more efficiently. Aerobic exercises increase the flow of blood to the heart, and this blood supplies life-giving oxygen to all of the body's muscles and organs. The body's ability to deliver oxygen to the heart and skeletal muscles is the prime determinant of physical fitness. The more efficiently oxygen is supplied to the heart and muscles, the better the level of physical fitness, because an efficient flow of oxygen allows a person to exercise vigorously without undue fatigue.

The way to determine the efficiency of your flow of oxygen is to notice your condition after vigorous activity such as running. If running for 10 minutes causes you to gasp for breath, your cardiovascular system is not pumping blood efficiently. As your heart pounds and you try to catch your breath, your lungs are trying desperately to pump more oxygen-bearing blood throughout your body, and they are failing.

You may have noticed that long-distance runners do not gasp for breath after a race. This is because their cardiovascular systems are operating at peak efficiency, delivering large volumes of blood through-out their bodies quickly as they call on their muscles to perform.

If you practice an aerobic exercise routine faithfully for several months, you will begin to notice that you are feeling less tired throughout the day; your cardiovascular system will be working, like the long-distance runner's, at peak efficiency. You may not be able to run a mile in under 4 minutes, but at 4 P.M. on a hectic Friday you should have sufficient reserve energy to be mentally alert and physically strong enough to perform any task at hand.

Your Pulse and the Target Zone

The main object of aerobic exercise is to get your heart beating at between 70 and 85 percent of its maximal attainable rate. This level is called the *target zone*. Anything lower than that does not stimulate the heart enough. Anything higher, and you may hit a danger point that can overstress the heart. The best way to determine your own target zone is to locate your age on the accompanying chart. Your target zone is the shaded area that indicates the heart rate in beats per minute (BPM) that is between 70 and 85 percent of your age group's maximal heart rate.

The way to find out if you are in the target zone (and getting maximal aerobic benefit from your exercise) is to check your pulse during and after an exercise period. As a measure of the heartbeat, the pulse is 98 percent accurate. To take your own pulse, the best point to use is a carotid artery located on either side of the throat. You can feel your pulse by placing your thumb on your chin and your four fingers on the side of your neck and gently pressing into the throat. Use a watch while you count the number of beats for 10 seconds and then multiply that number by 6 to determine your pulse rate.

Beginners should check the pulse several times during the exercise period. Take the first pulse after your warmup. At this point, before you begin aerobic activity, your pulse should be below the target zone. Then, 3 to 5 minutes into your aerobic activity, take the pulse again to make sure you have reached the lower limits of your target zone. (If you are below the target zone, step on it; you need to increase your intensity. If you are over the target zone and into the danger zone, *slow down*.) Finally, take your pulse immediately upon finishing aerobic exercise. Waiting a few seconds will not give an accurate measure, because the heartbeat decreases rapidly when you stop exercising. After a few months of steady aerobic activity, you will not need to check your pulse often. After 6 months, you will know your body's reaction well enough to tell intuitively when you are in the target zone.

Achieving the Target Zone

Your warmup period should serve as a gradual transition from inactivity to aerobic activity. Take it easy for the first few minutes and then gradually increase the intensity of your stretching and calisthenics. When you begin aerobic activity, do not try to get your heart into the target zone immediately. This is akin to revving up the engine of a sports car and shifting directly from first to fifth gear; the car is not designed to be used in this fashion. If you do not go through all five gears in the sequence, you can wreck the engine. The same dangers are present when you push your body too strenuously in too short a period of time. The aim is to stay in the target zone for at least 20 minutes per aerobic session. It's perfectly all right to be under the target zone for 5 minutes or so as you begin doing aerobic exercises.

If you stay within the target zone, you will soon be rewarded. The prime benefit of sustained aerobic exercise is the improvement of cardiovascular capacity, or what is called the training effect. When this happens, you will be able to run, walk, cycle, swim, or skip rope for longer periods of time without feeling overly tired. This is due to the physiological changes that occur in the heart after a few weeks of aerobic training. In essence, you are building up your heart muscle and making your heart stronger and more efficient. A strong heart pumps an increased volume of blood with each beat, which allows oxygen to be transported more rapidly throughout the entire body. With this enhanced circulation comes a toning of the body's muscles and a lowering of the blood pressure.

Then comes what is perhaps the most dramatic evidence that your cardiovascular system is in good shape. Your resting heartbeat decreases. Of course, it will not go as low as Frank Shorter's. The 1972 Olympic marathon champion has a resting heartbeat of 34 beats per minute. But then again, he runs 17 miles a day when he is in training. With continued aerobic exercising, your resting heartbeat can drop from the average 70 to 80 per minute to 55 to 65 after a year of aerobic

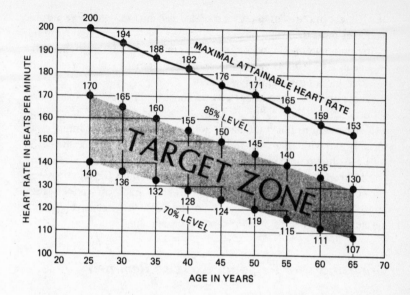

training. When your resting heartbeat lowers, your heat beats thousands of times fewer each day. Although it has not been proved that humans are built with a finite number of heartbeats, it makes sense that the fewer times your heart beats each day, the less you are demanding of that vital organ.

What Type Is Best For You

There are at least twenty different aerobic exercises to choose from, including walking, jogging/running, cycling, swimming, cross-country skiing, roller skating/ice skating, rope jumping, running in place, chair stepping, stationary bicycling, rowing machine, treadmill, jumping jacks, dancing, handball/squash, soccer, basketball, sculling/canoeing, and just about any other activity you can imagine that stimulates the heart and lungs for 20 to 30 minutes so that the heart rate is elevated to 70 to 85 percent of maximum capacity.

Executive Health Examiners does not recommend the majority of these exercises for two basic reasons. They may be impractical for most executives to practice on a regular, year-round basis, or they may not be efficient in terms of energy expended per minute. Only five aerobic exercises meet these and other EHE criteria: walking, running/jogging, swimming, cycling (indoors or outdoors), and rope skipping. These five regimens also require very little special equipment and can easily be worked into a crowded daily schedule.

These exercises also offer two additional benefits. Along with cross-country skiing, they cause the body to expend a level of energy that will allow you to reach the target zone and stay within its limits comfortably and without undue strain. These exercises, moreover, are easily suited to precise, uncomplicated measurement of performance, allowing you to keep track of your progress in terms of miles (or laps) covered per session. It's much more difficult to keep track of week-to-week improvement in programs which do not lend themselves to precise measurement, such as aerobic dancing or canoeing.

Choosing Your Personal Exercise Regimen

Now that we have narrowed the list to five exercises, how do you choose among them? The most important thing—really the only important thing, since they all provide the same benefits—is making sure that the exercise you choose suits you. One client of Executive Health Examiners, the president of a New York City accounting firm, provides an example of what can happen if you choose an exercise that does not suit you.

Our client took up jogging after we pointed out the benefits of aerobic exercise. He told us that he had never liked running, but he was willing to give it a try because he knew that it would help him. He later told us he had hated every minute of every run he took during the 6 months he stuck with the program. "The only thing I think about when I'm running is how soon it will be before I stop," he said. Obviously, this man was not suited for running, and it took a bit of persuading before he was ready to try another aerobic routine. He was pleasantly surprised to learn that he actually enjoyed his second aerobic choice, bicycling, and he has continued to cycle three times a week.

Another way to choose an aerobic exercise is to determine which one suits your physical capacities. If you have especially strong legs, try running or cycling. If you are an accomplished recreational swimmer, look no further than swimming. If you have always been well coordinated and quick on your feet, try rope skipping. If you are overweight, try walking. Walking is the least strenuous of the recommended aerobic exercises and is especially suited to the sedentary executive who has been inactive for many years. Many executives start their aerobic programs with walking and then go on to running or cycling after a few months. Many others find that they enjoy walking and stay with it.

For running and walking, all you need is a good pair of running shoes—you can run or walk just about anywhere. Cycling, of course, does entail buying a sturdy indoor stationary bicycle or a decent ten-speed bike, but we feel that the benefits of cycling—especially the fact that it brings the heart to the target zone quickly—far outweigh the investment in equipment.

The same thing is true for swimming. An aerobic swimming program requires ready access to a swimming pool with lanes set up for exercising. For some executives finding such a pool might be as complicated as renting a canoe, making arrangements to store it in a boathouse, and paddling down a river on a 3-day-a-week basis. But if there is a swimming pool near where you work or live—and for most executives who live in or near a metropolitan area this should be no problem—we recommend swimming over exercises that require the use of outside facilities.

Exercises We Do Not Recommend

Here are some of the exercises we regard as causing problems: cross-country skiing, roller and ice skating, sculling, canoeing, dancing and using a rowing machine. Exercises such as these can have drawbacks because they require an investment in too much equipment and usually also require ready access to facilities such as health clubs or special classes that are not available everywhere. Contrast this with running and walking, which require only one piece of special equipment.

We do not recommend basketball, squash, or handball for most executives, especially those who have been inactive for many years. These sports are simply too strenuous for the average executive starting an aerobic program. In addition to that, they are competitive, and one of the objectives of the exercise prescription for executives is to provide a chance to escape from the competitive lifestyle of the office. Exercise is meant to help you relax, and a competitive sport often has the opposite effect. We therefore strongly suggest that only executives in top cardiovascular shape take up basketball, squash, and handball for aerobic exercise.

Chair stepping, running in place, and jumping jacks are on our reject list for one basic reason: they can easily become exceedingly boring. All aerobic exercises are repetitive, but at least the scenery changes when you run, walk, or cycle outdoors, and the indoor rope-skipping routine requires dexterity and coordination. Chair stepping, running in place, and jumping jacks, however, are so monotonously repetitive that there is a very real possibility you will be so bored after a few weeks that you will quit exercising and never go back to it.

But, you might object, Executive Health Examiners recommends the exercise bicycle. What could be more boring than sitting on an indoor stationary bike and staring at a wall for 20 minutes at a time three days a week? Several of our clients have provided a solution to that problem. One 32-year-old publishing executive told us she moved her exercise cycle in front of the television soon after she took up the exercise. She gets on the cycle early in the morning and watches the network news while pedaling her way to cardiovascular health.

Golf and Tennis

A large number of executives play golf or tennis, and we are often asked whether these sports are good "exercises." The answer usually disappoints the golfers and does not exactly cheer the tennis players.

Golf provides no aerobic benefit and is not much use as a strength-building exercise. The only physiological benefit it gives is flexibility for the leg, arm, and chest muscles. But the golfer's routine of walking (if you are not riding a motorized cart), stopping, and hitting a ball does little to improve cardiovascular conditioning. However, there is an offbeat way to get aerobic benefit out of golfing. Lenore R. Zohman, M.D., and her colleagues describe it in their book *The Cardiologists' Guide to Fitness and Health through Exercise*:

> It's possible for a golfer to run in place between shots, run to and from the course or jog alongside the golf cart. However, the combination of golf shoes (not designed for running), loss of concentration on the golf game itself and the reaction of other players tend to make the prospect of such activity rather questionable.

Executive Health Examiners recommends that if golf helps you relax, go out and play a round or two each week. But you still will have to take up a three-part exercise regimen of stretching, strength building, and aerobics in addition to your golf game.

The disappointing news for tennis players is that you may not be able to meet your exercise needs on the court. Tennis is a strenuous sport, and many executives who play it feel that it keeps them in good shape. As one corporate vice president who plays tennis twice a week told us, "I don't think I need anything else for exercise. I run around a lot on the court, my strokes make my arm and chest muscles work, and I work up a good sweat. It's great exercise."

When you look more closely at the body's physiological response to tennis, you can see that tennis is not an ideal aerobic exercise. Tennis, like volleyball, racketball, handball, and badminton, is a sport that consists of bursts of energy interspersed with brief rest periods. This takes away much of the aerobic benefit of the game, even though the heartbeat may be in the target zone for 20 to 30 minutes in the course of an hour on the court. The brief rest periods between serves, games, and sets negate much of the aerobic benefit. Dr. Cooper explains it this way: "You dash about the court chasing the ball, and the heart rate goes up to 150 or more. A point is scored and the action stops. The heart rate comes down to 120 or less. After a few games like this, the average heart rate is less than the 150 produced by non-stop aerobics."

This is why Executive Health Examiners recommends to our clients who want to play tennis, and play it safely, that they get in shape first by practicing a fitness regimen. Tennis should not be the basis for fitness programing. We classify it as a beneficial side effect of a good overall exercise program. If you want to play tennis, you should not go out and play a vigorous singles game three times a week. You should work up to it gradually by building up your cardiovascular fitness through a balanced exercise regimen that stresses aerobics. You can improve your tennis through a half hour a day of other exercises. That way, when you do play tennis, you will be in better shape, be in better control, and play a more effective game.

Scientific evidence that tennis and golf do not provide high cardiovascular fitness was given in 1978 by Rudolph H. Dressendorfer of the Department of Physical Education at the University of California, Davis. Dressendorfer, a certified American College of Sports Medicine program director, undertook a study at the John A. Burns School of Medicine at the University of Hawaii to measure the cardiovascular fitness of a group of healthy men, 25 to 38 years old, whose major source of exercise was 3 to 6 hours a week of skin diving, golf, surfing, or tennis. The three golfers tested played two or three rounds (36 to 45 holes) a week and did not use motorized carts on the course; they walked. The two tennis players in the study played one or two sets of singles three times a week. All had been active for 2 years at their sports.

Dressendorfer found that golf and tennis "appeared to be no more effective in developing satisfactory cardiorespiratory fitness than the normal physical activity of men entering an adult fitness program." Dressendorfer also tested these same men after they began a 3-day-a-week aerobic jogging program. After 3 months, all showed marked improvement in cardiovascular conditioning and aerobic capacity. Those who stayed in the jogging program an additional 3 months showed even more improvement.

"Our results indicate that these men had not attained high cardio-respiratory fitness through their recreational sports," Dressendorfer concluded, "and that jogging stimulated noteworthy improvement in oxygen consumption without significant changes in body weight or percentage of body fat."

Walking

Walking is by far the easiest and least complicated aerobic exercise. You do not have to learn how to walk, of course, and all you need in the way of equipment is a good pair of shoes.

We recommend walking either as a continuing aerobic exercise or as a transitional exercise before you move on to running or cycling. The basic walking rules are the same as those for all aerobic training.

- After a 10- to 15-minute warmup, start walking slowly.

- Make sure you spend 20 to 30 minutes with your heartbeat in the target zone.

- Spend another 10 to 15 minutes cooling down.

We recommend walking for executives of all ages and in all stages of physical condition, but several types of executives are especially good candidates for walking programs. Since walking, unlike running and cycling, presents few problems to people with leg injuries, we recommend it for those who are prone to shin splints or heel, ankle, knee, or other running-induced leg problems. We also recommend walking for executives 55 years of age or older for the same reason. Walking will not present a problem to older executives' more vulnerable hips, ankles, and other lower-body joints.

Executive Health Examiners recommends walking for overweight executives mainly because walking is the least strenuous aerobic exercise. We often recommend walking for executives who have arthritis. Some arthritis sufferers have found that walking helps the symptoms of the disease and also improves muscular flexibility. Some emphysema patients have also been helped by walking routines, and, of course, walking is now *de rigueur* for recuperating heart patients. Cardiologists have found that walking is the perfect exercise to stimulate the flow of blood throughout the body without putting undue strain on a heart patient's recovering cardiovascular system.

If you cannot believe that such an "easy" routine can actually improve cardiovascular conditioning, consider the results of a recent medical experiment in Israel. A series of tests conducted by doctors at the Heller Institute of Medical Research at Tel Aviv University Medical School measured the aerobic capacity of forty-four men aged 18 to 23. These young men walked about 3 miles per hour for 30 minutes a day, five days a week, carrying backpacks that weighed from 3 to 6 kilograms. Thirty-two men stayed with this program for 3 weeks; twelve stayed with it for 4 weeks. The doctors found that it is "possible to improve substantially aerobic physical fitness in three weeks by walking daily with a light backpack load." They also found that the walking regimen was "most useful for people who have low initial aerobic work." They recommended walking "as a gradual and safe method for improving physical fitness, mainly for people who have a low initial work capacity. Walking can easily be adapted as a way of life: everyone can use a briefcase or shopping bag instead of a backpack load."

The Optimum Walking Pace

Executive Health Examiners has found that the best walking pace is about 4 miles per hour. This is a brisk pace, amounting to about 15 minutes per mile. If you walk 3 miles at this pace, you should have 45 minutes in the target zone. Remember, most sedentary executives will not be able to keep up this pace without becoming exhausted. Begin your walking routine at a lower pace and work up to 4 miles per hour gradually.

Find a 1-mile stretch of street (you can use your car's odometer to measure it) and time yourself as you walk the distance at a brisk yet comfortable pace. You may be unable to walk that mile in 15 minutes, but that is perfectly all right. Just keep at it. If you do, you will find that after a few weeks you will be able to get to 4 miles per hour. You should also be checking your pulse to make sure your heartbeat is in the target zone.

As you begin to close in on a pace of 15 minutes per mile, your pulse should be reaching the target zone rapidly, and you should have little trouble keeping in the target zone for most of your walk. If your heartbeat is below your target zone level, you will need to build to a higher intensity. One way to do this is to increase your speed to a pace of five miles per hour (12 minutes per mile). Or as the Israeli study showed, you can carry a backpack or a briefcase. It usually takes from 4 to 6 weeks of walking for a previously inactive executive to reach the target zone rapidly.

Charles T. Kuntzleman, author of *The Complete Book of Walking*, offers three more rules to follow to make sure you are walking at the proper intensity. First, you should be walking at a speed that will enable you to hold a conversation with someone beside you as you go. Second, you should have no pain while you walk. If you experience any sort of constant pain, see a doctor. Third, you should not be excessively tired after your walk. If you are, the walk was too strenuous, and you need to slow down. "All three points," Kuntzleman writes, "emphasize 'listening to your body.' This listening is something you'll have to learn. But you'll probably find it fun. You'll enjoy your body more. It will let you know when to slow down and when to speed up. You are the best judge of your exercise."

Running/Jogging

The first thing to remember about running or jogging (we use the words interchangeably because there is no clear distinction between the two) is that it can be hazardous to your health. Running is a strenuous form of exercise and demands a great deal from the body. If you are not in good shape, running can be a punishing activity, but it does not have to be. If you use common sense and take the proper precautions, you will find that running can be an exhilarating, stress-reducing, safe, and pleasurable experience.

With your doctor's consent, you can map out a running strategy. The first thing to do is to go out and spend a few dollars on a good sturdy pair of running shoes. We will give fuller details on the specifications for running shoes in Chapter 15. The most important thing to remember as you begin is to start *gradually*, especially if you have been living a sedentary life. Running is such a jarring shock to the out-of-shape body that Executive Health Examiners urges all beginners to combine walking and running at first and then to work gradually up to a total running regimen.

A Beginner's Jogging Program

We recommend a 12-week beginner's jogging program of the American Running and Fitness Association (see box). The system suggests distances for jogging and walking expressed not in miles but in minutes. These are guidelines; you may vary the distances to your taste, but try to stay within the general area. You should take an extra day of rest any time your body tells you to and feel free to substitute brisk walking for jogging at any point. Remember, after the first week or so, your primary objective is to get the heartbeat into the target zone for 20 to 30 minutes every time you run. Beginning in the second week, start checking your pulse frequently: before you start your run, 5 minutes or so after you have started running, and finally after you have finished. If you are below the target zone, increase the speed of your run or jog, but do not go over the target zone. If you feel yourself getting dizzy or if you have trouble catching your breath, slow down and then stop. Do not forget that the walking/jogging routine should be preceded by 10 to 15 minutes of warming up and followed by 10 to 15 minutes of cooling down.

After you have completed the 12-week course, stay at the twelfth week's level for 4 more weeks. You will be ready to increase your distance when you feel no excessive fatigue or injury after your exercise. Move up about 10 percent at a time and stay at the new distance for at least 2 weeks before you go on.

WHEN YOU BEGIN TO JOG

First Week

Days 1, 3, and 5. Walk 15 minutes. Vary your pace. Try not to stop.
Days 2, 4, and 6. Walk 5 minutes, jog 1 minute, walk 5 minutes, jog 1 minute, walk 5 minutes. (Total time: 17 minutes)
Day 7. Rest.

Second Week

Days 1, 3, and 5. Walk 15 minutes, jog 1 minute.
Days 2, 4, and 6. Walk 5 minutes, jog 3 minutes, walk 5 minutes, jog 3 minutes, walk 5 minutes. (Total time: 21 minutes)
Day 7. Rest.

Third Week

Days 1, 3, and 5. Walk 15 minutes, jog 1 minute.
Days 2, 4, and 6. Walk 6 minutes, jog 4 minutes, walk 6 minutes, jog 4 minutes, walk 6 minutes. (Total time: 26 minutes)
Day 7. Rest.

Fourth Week

Days 1, 3, and 5. Walk 15 minutes, jog 2 minutes.
Days 2, 4, and 6. Walk 3 minutes, jog 2 minutes. Repeat five more times. (Total time: 30 minutes)
Day 7. Rest.

Fifth Week

Days 1, 3, and 5. Walk 15 minutes, jog 2 minutes.
Days 2, 4, and 6. Walk 5 minutes, jog 5 minutes; repeat three times, ending with a 5-minute walk. (Total time: 35 minutes)
Day 7. Rest.

Sixth Week

Days 1, 3, and 5. Walk 30 minutes.
Days 2, 4, and 6. Walk 4 minutes, jog 6 minutes; repeat twice more, ending with a 5-minute walk. (Total time: 35 minutes)
Day 7. Rest.

Seventh Week

Day 1. Walk for 30 minutes.
Days 2, 4, and 6. Walk 4 minutes, jog 6 minutes; repeat twice
   more, ending with a 5-minute walk. (Total time: 35 minutes)
Days 3 and 5. Walk 5 minutes, jog 10 minutes, walk 5 minutes.
Day 7. Rest.

Eighth Week

Day 1. Walk for 30 minutes.
Days 2, 4, and 6. Walk 2 minutes, jog 1 minute; repeat nine times,
   ending with a 5-minute walk. (Total time: 32 minutes)
Day 7. Rest.

Ninth Week

Days 1, 3, and 5. Walk 5 minutes, jog 1 minute, walk 1 minute.
   Repeat with 1 minute of each for 20 minutes. End with a 5-
   minute walk. (Total time: 30 minutes)
Day 7. Rest.

Tenth Week

Days 1, 3, and 5. Walk 5 minutes, jog 20 minutes, walk 5 minutes.
Days 2, 4, and 6. Walk 5 minutes, jog 10 minutes, walk 5 minutes.
Day 7. Rest.

Eleventh Week

Days 1, 3, and 5. Walk 5 minutes, jog 25 minutes, walk 5 minutes
   (always walk as needed).
Days 2, 4, and 6. Walk 5 minutes, jog 10 minutes, walk 5 minutes.
Day 7. Rest.

Twelfth Week

Days 1, 3, and 5. Walk 5 minutes, jog 30 minutes, walk 5 minutes.
Days 2, 4, and 6. Walk 5 minutes, jog 15 minutes, walk 5 minutes.
Day 7. Rest.

Cycling

Cycling is one of our recommended aerobic exercises that calls for the use of a major piece of equipment. For indoor cycling, you need a stationary bicycle; for outdoor riding, you need a simple three-speed bike. There are pluses and minuses involved in both indoor and outdoor cycling. By examining both routines, you can choose the one that suits you.

Outdoor Cycling

One prime advantage of cycling outdoors is that you can use your bike to commute to and from work. You can also take scenic rides and get aerobic exercise at the same time. But you cannot bicycle year-round in most climates, and bad weather at any time of the year can interrupt your cycling routine. You have to watch out for traffic if you ride in the streets. Pollution can be a problem in hot summer months, especially in large, congested cities. You must always keep in mind that bicycling can be dangerous; one spill and you can injure yourself seriously. You also have to plan your route carefully to keep your heart in the target zone. Downhills and long flat stretches can cause you to ease up and fall below the target zone.

If after all those cautionary words you are still considering using an outdoor bicycling routine as your aerobic component, there is one more thing to keep in mind. We recommend that you have access to a bicycle path. If there is a bike path stretching from your house to near where you work, it's practically an invitation to pedal to and from work for aerobic exercise. You do not have to live within a few miles of the office to bicycle there and back.

Indoor Cycling

If you do not have a bike path readily available and want to cycle for aerobic exercise, consider purchasing a stationary bike. There are two big pluses with the indoor bike. First, you can cycle at any time of the year; weather is no inhibiting factor. Second, you can adjust the pedal resistance to a level at which your heartbeat will stay continuously in the target zone. The biggest drawback with the indoor cycle is that sitting and pedaling in the living room can be very boring.

Buying the Right Bicycle

If you decide to go with an outdoor cycling program, we recommend that you purchase a solid three-speed bicycle. If you prefer a five- or ten-speed bicycle, these have a range of low gears to enable you to flatten out hills without straining too much. Choose any major brand of bike from a reputable dealer. Before you leave the shop, make sure the salesperson adjusts the bicycle to fit your body. This is very important. The seat should be adjusted carefully for height so that when your leg is fully extended with your toe on the pedal, there will be a very slight bend in the knee. If the seat is too high or too low, you run the risk of injuring your knees. The seat also should be adjusted properly for distance from the handlebars. To do this, measure your arm's length to the handlebars with your elbow resting in front of the seat. A properly adjusted seat enables you to ride in a relaxed and comfortable position.

The same basic rules apply when you are purchasing an indoor bike. There are dozens of types of indoor cycles on the market, from the simplest no-frills stationary bike to fancy ones that come with mini-computers to tell you what your pulse is each second, keep track of how much time you spent in the target zone, and automatically adjust the level of resistance of the pedals. The important thing to keep in mind is that you can get the same aerobic benefit from the most simple bike that you get from the most complicated.

It's up to you to decide what type of stationary bike to buy. The only mandatory criteria are that the seat be adjustable so that the fit is perfect for your body, that the bike be sturdy and not wobble or make excessive noise, and that it be equipped with an easily adjustable device to vary pedal resistance. It also helps to have a speedometer.

The routine for both indoor and outdoor bicycling is the same as in all other aerobic exercises. Before you start, spend about 5 minutes warming up with stretches and calisthenics. Pay particular attention to the leg muscles; make sure they are well stretched out before you get on the bike. Unlike running, cycling causes no harsh jolting to the legs. You do need strong leg muscles to cycle steadily for long distances, but you can build up those muscles through a combination of isometric and isotonic exercises and your aerobic cycling regimen.

Once you get on the bike, take it easy for the first 5 minutes or so. This is considered a warmup time. When you have loosened up, start pedaling harder for 5 minutes and then check your pulse. If you are not up to the target zone, try pedaling a bit faster. After 20 minutes in the target zone, begin gearing down and pedal lightly for 5 to 10 minutes to cool off. When you get off the bike, stretch out again for a final cooling-off minute.

If you have been sedentary for a long time, it is wise to proceed extremely cautiously for the first few weeks of cycling. You can even forget about the target zone for the first 2 weeks. Just concentrate on pedaling up to a speed that feels comfortable without overexerting yourself. After you are used to the feel of the bike, begin checking your pulse and adjusting your speed and intensity to get in the target zone for 20 to 30 minutes per session.

In *The Complete Book of Bicycling*, Eugene A. Sloan gives the outline of a recommended routine on an outdoor bike for the sedentary executive:

> Keep your bicycle in the lowest, or next to lowest gear and ride slowly, without strain, three or four miles a day for two or three weeks. Build up your cycling stamina gradually by increasing your daily rides by two or three miles each week. If you are in good health . . . you will probably find that ten miles or so a day will keep you fit and trim.

Swimming

Swimming is the only aerobic activity recommended by Executive Health Examiners that requires facilities not available in most homes. If you decide to choose swimming as your aerobic exercise, you are going to have to make arrangements to travel to and from a swimming pool that has time set aside for lap swimming. This does not necessarily have to take up large amounts of your time. Many executives find that swimming is a perfect lunch-hour activity. The research director of a hospital in New York City, for example, lives thirty blocks from his YMCA swimming pool, but the pool is only two blocks from his office. He takes a 5-minute walk to the Y at noontime three days a week, depending on his schedule, and thereby receives an aerobic workout without interrupting his everyday routine.

Swimming, of course, fulfills the aerobic component of your exercise regimen. But swimming, unlike walking, running, or cycling, also exercises all the body's muscle groups, including the arms, trunk, and legs. Another attribute of swimming is that it is the only one of the recommended aerobic programs that is not weight-bearing. In walking, cycling, and especially running, the legs bear the brunt of the exercise. However, in swimming the water holds you up, and very little strain is put on the ankles and knees. This is why we especially recommend swimming for those with ankle or knee injuries and for older persons. It is not uncommon to see men and women in their sixties and seventies and older slowly but steadily swimming laps at many pools.

There is one final aspect of swimming that should help you decide whether it is the right aerobic exercise for you. If you are not comfortable in the water, if you do not like water sports, or if you can swim but are not very good at it (if you flail around, expending a lot of energy but getting nowhere fast), we suggest that you consider another aerobic activity. This is not to say that only polished swimmers should take up swimming as an aerobic exercise, but it certainly bodes well for your future happiness in the water if you already have a modicum of swimming ability.

A Swimming Regimen

The routine for your swimming exercise has the same basic outline as the routine for other aerobic programs. You need a warmup, 20 to 30 minutes of aerobic activity, and then a cooling-down period. As with cycling, most of your warmup and cooling-down time can come during the beginning and end of aerobic activity.

Begin with a few minutes of stretching exercises before you get in the pool. Then swim a lap and check your pulse. Most pools have a large swim clock on hand so that you will not need to wear your watch in the pool. After another warmup lap or two, check your pulse again. Take a few more laps and recheck your pulse. Here's the advice of Dr. Lenore Zohman about pulse taking and the beginning swimming regimen: "Your carotid pulse rate and your feeling of tiredness can tell you whether you are doing too little or too much and, over the next few days and weeks, whether you are making progress. If you can cover more laps at the same pulse rate, you are getting there."

We recommend that beginners use just one stroke. Try the overhand crawl, the least demanding stroke. As in all types of exercise, you should start with the least demanding routine and then progress slowly. You probably will be exhausted after a few laps at first. Therefore, take your time and do not push yourself. If you keep at it steadily, you will find that your cardiovascular capacity will increase within a few weeks. Remember to progress slowly and gradually and to listen to your body for warning signs. If you hear them, slow down and then stop.

You can experiment with other strokes after you have built up your cardiovascular capacity. The least vigorous strokes after the crawl are the breaststroke, the backstroke, and the butterfly. Once you attain proficiency and feel confident in the pool, it's best to stay with one stroke. That way you will know what it takes to reach your target zone and will not have to stop and check your pulse. You will be able to feel intuitively when you are there.

Cooling down is easier in a pool than in any other aerobic activity. All you have to do is slow down for the last 5 to 10 minutes of your program. Before you leave the pool, paddle about for a bit to finish your cooling-down period. There is no problem with getting overheated, because the water cools your body and also prevents problems with sweat evaporation.

Rope Skipping

The main advantage of rope skipping is that it is extremely vigorous and gets your heart to the target zone very rapidly. In addition, rope skipping helps increase strength in the legs and arm muscles.

Rope skipping is not for everyone. In fact, it is so strenuous that some doctors do not recommend it for the average sedentary person. Recent studies have indicated that people with low fitness levels should approach rope skipping with extreme caution, since it taxes the body so enormously in a brief period of time.

It was once thought that 10 minutes of rope skipping provided the same cardiovascular benefits as 30 minutes of running, but a recent study found that the claim is "exaggerated and unfounded" and that "the energy requirement imposed by skipping rope is not reasonable for the average sedentary person."

Because rope skipping is so easy to do, takes only one piece of equipment, and can be done just about anywhere, we recommend it. But there is an important caveat: Undertake rope skipping only after a physical examination by a doctor that includes a stress test, and make sure you specifically ask the doctor for permission to set out on a rope-skipping exercise program.

If you have your doctor's permission, remember that the same rules of warmup, 20 to 30 minutes in the target zone, and a period of cooling down apply in rope skipping. When you start, begin extremely gradually and be cautious at all times for signs of exhaustion. Do not overstrain. At the first sign of fatigue, stop.

11.

Strength Building and Stretching—Complements to Aerobics

There are two other components that round out the EHE total fitness program: strength-building and stretching exercises. As we pointed out previously, aerobic exercises should be the key element of your exercise regimen, but for total fitness you must also build up strength and at the same time keep your muscles stretched out and flexible.

You will have to work on the muscles three to five times a week, spending 10 to 15 minutes per session on the stretching exercises and another 10 to 15 minutes on the strength-building routines. You have the option of doing these exercises separately or integrating them into your aerobic sessions during the warmup and cooling-down periods. These exercises complement each other, and they also complement the aerobic exercises, since strong and flexible muscles enable you to walk, run, cycle, swim, or skip rope without putting undue strain on your musculoskeletal system. Well-stretched-out muscles provide an extra bonus by helping to reduce the possibility of injury and easing physical tension. In so doing, they can help you soothe the stress of mental tension as well.

Strength-Building Exercises

Just as aerobic exercises in effect build up the heart muscles, strength-building exercises build up another set of muscles, the skeletal muscles. The strength-building exercises have almost no direct effect on the cardiovascular system, but they are important in an overall fitness regimen for two reasons. First, they help you perform aerobic routines more easily. Second, strong muscles help in everyday activities such as moving, lifting, and holding weight. By building strength in the 400-odd skeletal muscles you will be able to perform any number of tasks—from lifting a suitcase off a baggage rack to pushing your lawn mower—without strain or discomfort. Having strong muscles also gives you a subtle but palpable feeling of confidence in your physical capabilities.

The strength-building exercises are in some ways similar to the aerobic exercises; both involve pushing muscles to perform beyond their normal capacity. Then, between exercise sessions, the resting muscles increase in strength. However, there is also a fundamental difference between aerobic and strength-building exercises.

In aerobics you push the cardiovascular system to work at a level of 70 to 85 percent of maximal heart capacity (the target zone), but strength-building exercises require you to push your muscles to their maximum. In other words, in strength building you can overload the muscles to force them to work as hard as they can. In both types of exercises the muscles reset themselves between sessions so that they can perform more demanding tasks.

The Risk of Injury

As you might expect, pushing muscles to their limit involves some risk of injury, especially for sedentary individuals. Thus, common sense dictates that when you begin a strength-building program, you should start gradually, progress slowly, and be alert for signs of danger.

The main danger for a sedentary executive embarking on a program of weight lifting, situps, pushups, chinups, or other strength-building activities involves blood pressure. These exercises increase blood pressure, making the heart work harder as its need for oxygen increases. When this happens, the blood flow to the heart and brain can be reduced, and the cardiovascular system can be endangered. Therefore, if you think you have any of the risk factors associated with coronary disease (obesity, high blood pressure, high cholesterol, or cigarette smoking), or if you have been sedentary for a long time, it is wise to consult a doctor before beginning a program of strength-building exercises. This also holds true for anyone with known heart disease.

After securing your physician's permission, it still is best to proceed extremely cautiously. One important thing to keep in mind is not to hold your breath when you lift, push, and strain. You should breathe freely and deeply, concentrating on exhaling forcefully when you are putting out the most effort, like the karate experts who let out loud screams as they smash bricks with their hands.

Isometrics

Isometrics refers to a type of strength-building exercise that gained some popularity in the 1950s and 1960s. In isometric exercises you build up muscles by exerting pressure against an immovable object. This high-intensity exercise builds strength and muscle tone when the muscle contracts as you exert considerable force for only 6 to 10 seconds. These exercises include pushing against a wall, doorjamb, chair, or desk. After several weeks of steady practice, you can make substantial improvement in muscle strength and tone.

But isometric exercises have significant drawbacks, and Executive Health Examiners recommends them only to those very few persons who cannot spare 10 to 15 minutes three times a week to do other strength-building exercises. One problem with isometric exercise is that each exercise benefits only one muscle. This makes it nearly impossible to devise a balanced isometric strength-building program. You would need dozens of individual isometric exercises to build strength in all the leg, arm, back, and shoulder muscles. Moreover, isometric exercises require such concentrated intensity that we do not recommend them for people with cardiovascular risk factors. Executive Health Examiners agrees with the American College of Sports Medicine, which discourages isometrics both for sedentary persons and for those with cardiac disease risk factors.

The bottom line on isometric exercises is that if you feel you must do them, check with your doctor, especially if you are leading a sedentary life. Then proceed slowly and cautiously. You should also devise a routine in which many different muscles from all the major muscle groups are involved.

Since isometric exercises can be performed almost anywhere and at any time, you can do them on the train or bus as you commute to and from the office. You can even do them in your office whenever you need a short break during the day.

There is no set order for isometric exercises, and you do not have to do an entire routine in one session. You can therefore spice up different parts of the day by taking 2- or 3-minute isometric breaks.

Isometric exercises require concentrated effort, but you should not hold any one contraction longer than 8 seconds; 6 seconds is all that is necessary. When you first begin isometric exercises, it's best to take it easy and hold off giving your maximum effort for about 3 or 4 weeks. During that initial time, expend only about half your maximum force. During the first 3 or 4 seconds of each exercise, build up to your maximal effort—or half maximum when you are just starting out—and for the final 3 or 4 seconds, maintain that intensity. You should gradually increase your effort in the fourth and fifth weeks so that by the sixth week you can give maximum effort for the full 6 to 8 seconds you do each isometric exercise.

Here are eight isometric exercise routines that strengthen the neck, upper body, arms, chest, abdomen, lower back, buttocks, thighs, and legs. Remember to relax and breathe deeply between exercises and at the first sign of pain, immediately stop and forget about doing that exercise for a while.

The Neck

Isometric exercises for the neck are done in a sitting or standing position with the fingers interlaced on the forehead. The idea is to push your head forward while at the same time pushing back equally hard with the hands. The counterexercise is done with the fingers interlaced behind the head. You push the head back and the hands forward. To exercise the sides of the neck, place the palm of the left hand on the left side of the head and push with the hand while resisting with the head and the neck. Do the same with the right hand on the right side of the head.

The Upper Body

The first isometric exercise for the upper body is done in a standing position with your back to the wall. Put your hands at your sides, palms against the wall, and press your hands backward against the wall. Keep your arms straight. Then face the wall with your hands at your sides, palms against the wall, and press forward, keeping your arms straight. Finally, stand in a doorway or with your side against a wall and your right palm facing your right leg. Press your right hand outward against the wall or doorframe, keeping the arm straight. Repeat with the left arm.

The Arms

For the arms, stand with your feet about 12 inches apart. First flex your right elbow close to your body with the palm up. Then put your left hand on top of your right hand in front of you and forcibly try to curl your right arm up while pushing down with the left hand. Then repeat with the left arm and the right hand.

The Chest

To strengthen the arms and chest at the same time, stand with your feet a shoulder length apart and your knees slightly bent. Clasp your hands with the palms together close to your chest; then press the hands together. Hold for 6 to 8 seconds. Now grip your fingers together with your arms in the same position and pull hard.

The Abdomen

For the abdominal muscles, stand with your knees slightly bent and your hands resting on the tops of your knees. Forcibly contract your abdominal muscles for the required 6 to 8 seconds.

The Lower Back, Buttocks, and Thighs

To strengthen the lower back, buttocks, and the backs of the thighs, lie face down on the floor with your arms at your sides, palms down. Maneuver your legs under a table, chair, desk, or other heavy object. With the hips flat on the floor raise one leg, keeping the knee straight.

Make sure the heel is pushing hard against the table or chair. Hold for 6 to 8 seconds, and then repeat with the opposite leg.

The Legs

The best isometric exercises for the leg muscles are done sitting in a chair. Cross the left ankle over the right with your feet on the floor and your legs bent at a 90 degree angle. Try with all your might to straighten your right leg while resisting the push with your left. Repeat with the opposite legs.

The inner thigh muscles can be strengthened isometrically by sitting in a chair and extending your legs with each ankle pressed against the outside of another chair's legs. Make sure the second chair is sturdy. Keep the legs straight and pull one toward the other. To exercise the outer thighs, put your ankles inside the chair legs and exert pressure outward.

Isotonics—a Beginner's Calisthenics Routine

A much better all-around program for strengthening muscles is provided by isotonic exercises. Isotonic exercises include weight lifting as well as calisthenics such as pushups and situps. It's quite easy to incorporate a few isotonic exercises into your regular aerobic routine during the 10- to 15-minute warmup and cooling-down periods.

Here is a calisthenics routine to use for either warming up or cooling down in conjunction with aerobic exercise. If you use these calisthenics for cooling down, give yourself a few minutes of rest after completing your run, walk, swim, or cycling. The last part of your aerobic routine should be done in slow motion; that is, if you have just finished running, walk slowly but steadily for about 5 minutes. Spend the last few minutes of cycling or swimming taking it very easy and then gradually slow to a halt. Then take some deep breaths and stretch your arms and legs gradually. Limber up a bit before beginning, swinging your arms from side to side, shaking out your legs and arms, and rolling your head and neck in circles.

Now you are ready to do calisthenics. We recommend starting with side stretches to tone your midsection. Stand with your feet a shoulder length apart and your hands clasped behind your head. Bend to the left as far as possible, hold that position for a second, and then return to the starting point. Bend to the right and repeat left and right fifteen to twenty times.

Situps

The next exercises are situps. There are many ways to do situps, which strengthen the abdominal and back muscles. You can keep your knees bent or extend them out straight. You can sit on a slant board or raise your legs up on a chair. You can touch your right elbow to your left knee and then your left elbow to your right knee. You can clasp your hands behind your head, keep them at your sides, or stretch them over your head. You can come halfway up, sit up just enough to see your toes, or come all the way up and touch the toes. Choose the routine that is right for you, one you can do without undue strain but one that also requires some effort. It is recommended that individuals with low back disorders perform situps with knees bent, since this technique places less strain on the back.

Each different type of situp strengthens the abdominal and back muscles.

If you are really out of shape, start with ten situps and then add one or two a week until you hit thirty. If you can do thirty situps easily, try for fifty.

Pushups

After your situps, take a minute to stretch out. Take some deep breaths. Now you are ready for the pushup routine, an excellent strength builder for the shoulders, chest, and back of the arms. Pushups are hard work. You may have trouble doing even one or two, but keep at it. If you practice regularly, you will see dramatic improvement in weeks. Try for a maximum of thirty pushups at one time. When you reach thirty— and this may take 6 months or longer—stay with it.

A good pushup goes like this: Keep the body straight; do not sag and do not arch your back. Keep the legs together. Put your palms on the floor and keep them a couple of inches outside your shoulders. Your weight should be distributed evenly between your hands and toes. Keeping your body in a straight line, push up until the elbows are straight. Then let yourself down to the point where your nose or forehead brushes the floor. Do not let your stomach or chest hit the floor. Then push up again.

If you cannot do one regular pushup, try modified pushups, in which you keep the knees on the floor and push with your hands. If you keep at this for a few weeks, you will soon develop the strength to do regular pushups.

If thirty regular pushups a day are easy for you, there are ways to make them a bit more challenging. Try fingertip, or "Marine," pushups, in which you clap your hands between each push. We have found that for most executives, thirty pushups three times a week is sufficient to get good muscle strength and tone in the upper body.

Pullups

The final calisthenic is the pullup. For this you need a sturdy steel pullup bar, which can be mounted in almost any doorway, at home or in the office. There are various pullup (sometimes called chinup) methods, all of which build strong arm and shoulder muscles as you lift all your weight with the upper body.

Some executives cannot do even one pullup the first time. The secret is to keep plugging and not give up. It is simply a matter of time before the muscles gain enough strength to do the job of pulling your chin up to the bar. Once you are able to do one pullup, you will feel a sense of accomplishment, and soon you will be doing two or three. Aim for sets of six pullups. When that gets easy, go for sets of ten. Do no more than three sets per warmup or cooling-down period.

If you are interested in doing an extra abdominal muscle-building routine at the same time you do pullups, try leg lifts on the pullup bar. Pull yourself up on the bar and hang there for a moment with your chin over the bar. Then try to bring both legs up parallel with the floor without bending your knees. Hold the legs out there for a second and then let them down slowly. Do not swing the legs for momentum; make your stomach and back muscles do the work. Try for sets of six, and if you find that easy, do sets of ten.

These calisthenics provide a well-rounded strength-building routine that takes only about 15 minutes per session. If you do this routine three times a week, you will see improvements in overall body strength in a matter of months.

Weight Lifting and Calisthenics

The main difference between weight training and calisthenics is that weight lifting builds up muscular strength in a few specific muscles, while calisthenics exercises provide strength to a range of muscles. Executive Health Examiners does not recommend weight lifting for most executives. However, if you need to strengthen certain muscles that have atrophied from longtime neglect, if you need to build up leg or arm muscles to be more proficient in your aerobic routine, or if you merely want to build overall body strength, a weight-training program could be the answer.

Such a program will take up a lot of your time. You will need to spend a minimum of 30 minutes on each weight-training session. An ideal session should last about 90 minutes and should consist of ten to twenty different exercises designed to build up the muscles in all parts of the body. You should work out every other day. You can combine weight training and aerobic exercises in one session, but this would lengthen your total exercise period by at least a half hour—probably by as much as an hour—and most executives cannot spare that amount of time on a regular basis.

Stretching for Flexibility

Stretching exercises are an integral part of the EHE fitness routine. Stretching provides a kind of preventive maintenance for the muscles. It helps loosen tight muscles that can cause injuries such as cramps, strains, and pulls. Stretching exercises also help relieve tension in the muscles. In so doing, they also relieve other kinds of bodily tension, including mental stress. Stretching helps impart a feeling of calmness to the body and the mind.

Stretching exercises can make up the bulk of your warmup routine. For those who run, walk, or cycle, the leg muscles—especially the thighs, calves, and Achilles tendons—must be loose and stretched out.

The important thing to remember when stretching for flexibility is to perform the exercises very slowly and progress gradually. Stretch the muscles slowly, relax for a few seconds, and then stretch slowly again until you feel the tenseness ease.

The Art of Yoga

Some of the most beneficial stretching exercises were developed as part of the ancient Indian system of exercise called yoga, but many executives seem to have a mental block against yoga. When they hear the word, it brings visions of exoticism, although nothing could be further from the truth. As executives who have taken our advice and joined yoga classes have found, yoga is a demanding form of exercise that requires coordination, flexibility, and strength.

One EHE client, a 43-year-old Connecticut bank vice president, took his first yoga class 4 years ago at the suggestion of a friend. A yoga center near his office offered open classes at noontime five days a week, and he decided to try a class one Wednesday afternoon. The first class was torture; he could not seem to bring his stiff limbs into any of the pretzel-like postures. But this man felt very relaxed after that first session and decided to try it again the next week. He has continued going to noontime sessions nearly every week since then, and he also does yoga stretches every morning at home. On the three mornings a week when he runs, he does an abbreviated yoga routine, including a twelve-part salute to the sun. It is a perfect warmup exercise for aerobics because it stimulates nearly every muscle in the body. On days when he does not run, he does a 45-minute routine that mixes yoga with some calisthenics.

To find out about yoga, enroll in a special beginner's class or at a health club, yoga school, or adult-education class. Or, as the Connecticut banker did, you can join an open class, one that is open to beginners, intermediate, and advance yoga practitioners. After you have learned the basics, you can do an entire routine (or a few postures of your choice) at any time and place. Yoga requires no equipment or facilities not found in the home. A well-padded rug and some loose exercise clothing (or a leotard) are all you need.

Yoga can help any sedentary executive not only to stretch his or her muscles but also to relax. As your yoga instructor will no doubt tell you, relaxation is as important as exercising during a yoga routine. You make a conscious effort between postures to relax your mind and body. Taking the time to do yoga during the middle of a hectic day is a good antidote to the tensions and pressures inherent in the executive lifestyle, and a yoga class at noon can be a refreshing change from a three-martini lunch.

Suggestions for Warmup and Cooling-Down Exercises

It's best to work on stretching primarily in the warmup period for aerobics and on strength-building primarily in the cooling-down period, but you can mix the two in any way that suits you so long as you get 10 to 15 minutes of both stretching and strength building in each exercise session. You can choose any combination of stretches that focus on the lower extremities. These include:

Standing leg stretches

You put one foot on a table or chair about 3 feet in height, extend your leg, lean forward, and try to touch your toes with your fingertips. This is extremely good for stretching the hamstring muscles. All you have to do is stretch each leg for about 15 to 20 seconds two or three times.

Achilles tendon and calf muscle stretches

You stand 2 to 3 feet from a wall and lean forward until your palms touch it. Then you step backward, and as your weight is supported by your hands and you remain flat-footed, the calf muscles and Achilles tendons stretch out. Do this five to ten times, holding each stretch for about 15 seconds.

You can also try neck rolls, side stretches, and other upper-body limbering-up exercises. If you want to add calisthenics to the routine, try pushups and situps.

After you have cooled down by pedaling your bike slowly, slowing your run to a walk, or slowing your walk to a crawl, try some additional cooling down with situps, pushups, chinups (if a bar is available), and light stretching. Start these exercises in groups of six at a time; then stop, stretch out a little, and continue with another six situps, pullups, or whatever calisthenics you choose. After you get used to the routine and it becomes easy (this should take from 4 to 6 weeks), try increasing the sets of calisthenics exercises to ten each.

As we've said, swimmers do not need elaborate warmup or cooling-down sessions, because the aerobic activity itself increases strength in the arms, shoulders, and legs and also provides flexibility to the muscle groups. Before you go into the pool, though, it would not hurt to take a few minutes to gradually but fully stretch out your body. The twelve-part sun salutation will suffice, but you can also do any combination of stretches that gets the neck, shoulders, arms, trunk, and legs in motion.

Your first lap or two in the water also can serve as warmup time, just as the last few laps can count as cooling-down time. Just to make sure, you might want to take a few minutes to walk back and forth in the shallow end of the pool before you finish in the water. After you get out of the pool, spend a few minutes doing calisthenics. Those who swim in athletic clubs have equipment and space on hand to do situps, pushups, pullups, other calisthenics, and weight training.

If you think the cooling-down period is not necessary, remember these words of Dr. Cooper:

> The worst thing you can do right after a workout is to go into a steam room, a sauna, or a hot shower. Also, don't go sit down in your car, especially after a winter run. . . . When you combine a sudden stop of activity with a sudden decrease in warmth, the blood pools and the surface capillary vessels dilate, keeping an even greater percentage of blood away from the heart. So taper off gradually. You should take at least as long to cool down as you did to warm up. . . .

12.

Exercise at Work

The best way to fit an exercise regimen into your daily schedule is to exercise at the office. Does this sound funny? It should not.

Hundreds of employers have now installed on-the-premise exercise facilities, including some of the nation's largest corporations, such as Exxon, General Foods, Kimberly-Clark, Firestone, Johnson & Johnson, Prudential Insurance, and Pepsico; the list also includes smaller firms such as local banks, government offices, and various other types of businesses.

According to the American Association of Fitness Directors in Business and Industry, more than 500 companies employ full-time directors to run company-sponsored fitness facilities; tens of thousands of other business organizations have some sort of organized recreation programs. The association itself, which had only 25 members when it was formed in 1974, achieved a membership of about 1800 by 1981.

Helping Employees Stay Healthy

The main reason corporations set up in-house fitness centers, of course, is to help employees stay fit, but employers also have another, less altruistic, reason. Richard O. Keelor of the President's Council on Physical Fitness and Sports says that:

> The simple truth is that fitness pays. In boardrooms and executive suites throughout the country, top management is recognizing physical fitness as a prudent investment in the health, vigor, morale, and longevity of the men and women who are the company's most valuable asset. By preventing heart attacks, disabilities, and premature retirements, fitness saves money. For the employee, half an hour's vigorous exercise can be a refreshing, needed respite from the stress and occasional tedium of work.

Although no one knows the exact figures, the President's Council estimates that premature deaths cost American industry 132 million lost workdays and about $25 billion a year. There are also billions more dollars lost as a result of lowered productivity from sickness and other disabilities. Heart disease, the nation's number one killer, accounts for 52 million lost workdays each year. Back pain, which afflicts about 75 million adults, costs industry $1 billion a year in lowered productivity and $250 million annually in worker's compensation according to the National Safety Council. Doctors say that the prime cause of most back pain is lack of exercise of the back muscles. Finally, the American Heart Association reports that industry pays about $700 million a year just to recruit replacements for executives killed by premature heart attacks.

How to Get Your Company to Become More Fitness-Conscious

As the President's Council on Physical Fitness and Sports and its affiliate, the American Association of Fitness Directors in Business and Industry, advise, the best way to get your company on the road toward setting up a fitness center is to gain the support of top management. Executive Health Examiners has found that enthusiasm for exercise is contagious. When a company president or chairman of the board regularly takes part in fitness activities, many of the firm's executives follow suit, and the company develops some sort of employee fitness program. The reverse is also true. When we see nonexercising top management people who are out of shape, most of their executives are often in the same poor condition.

What You Can Do On Your Own at Work

If your company does not have a fitness program, or if you do not have the time or the inclination to take part in one, there are ways to exercise on your own while at the office. You can exercise individual muscles when they tense up, or you can design your own program of exercises as preventive medicine.

There is also the option of undertaking a series of isometric exercises, most of which you can do while sitting at your desk. You can do neck rolls any time during the day to prevent tension from building in your neck muscles. To tighten your stomach muscles while sitting at your desk, suck in your stomach and hold your breath for 6 seconds. To tone your buttocks, take a deep breath and tighten your stomach and buttocks. Hold it for 6 seconds, relax, take another deep breath, and then repeat the exercise.

If you feel tension in your arms, place your hands on the arms of your chair and slowly lift yourself up a few inches. Hold yourself there for 5 seconds and then let yourself down slowly. Repeat several times.

If your hands and wrists become tired from too much desk work, take time to flex them. Make tight fists, hold them for a few seconds, and then relax. Repeat several times. Let your wrists go limp and then shake your hands as if you were trying to dry them. Relax the hands and then make quick tight fists; follow this by throwing open your fingers several times. Shake out the hands again and go back to work.

If your legs are stiff from too much sitting, get up and walk around the office for a few minutes. Or stay in your chair and grab one knee with both hands. Pull the knee toward your chest. Do several rounds with each knee and finally hug both knees and pull them to your chest one last time. Hold your legs in that position for a few seconds; then stand up and raise yourself up and down on your toes (take off your shoes if you feel like it). After you have gone up and down on your toes a half dozen times, roll back and forth on your heels for a minute or so.

While you are standing, stretch your arms a bit, lean forward, and touch your toes with your knees bent slightly. Slowly come up and stretch toward the ceiling and then back to the toes.

Do some knee lifts, raising each knee as high as possible and grabbing your legs with your hands and pulling the knees alternately against your body. Be sure to keep your back straight.

You can even lift "weights" in the office without dragging in a set of barbells. Take a book in each hand and lift them slowly over your head and back down to your sides. Repeat this several times.

The stair climb, as we mentioned earlier, does not provide aerobic benefit, but it helps build leg muscles and keep you mentally alert at the office by getting you out from behind your desk and moving around. The way to get the most out of stair climbing at the office is to climb three flights of 9-inch steps at a 30- to 40-step-per-minute pace in 30 seconds or less. If you can handle it, take the steps two at a time. If you can do nine or ten of these 30-second workouts during the day, you will have accomplished a fruitful mini-exercise regimen.

Remember, as with any other exercise routine, you must begin your stair climbing slowly and progress gradually. This can be vigorous exercise; if you are in poor physical shape, you risk injury by dashing up the stairs without warming up properly.

You should also check with building management to see if it's acceptable to have you running up the stairs during the workday. Some buildings do not allow this type of activity. It's also a good idea to see if you can talk a coworker or two into venturing into the stairwell with you. It's not that misery loves company, but as in any exercise routine, you get a psychological lift when you have someone to share the exercise with.

13.

Weight Reduction: Calories and Calorie Burning

The best way to lose weight is to cut down the amount of high-caloric foods you consume every day while at the same time burning off extra calories through a balanced exercise program which emphasizes aerobics. Exercising works in two ways to burn up calories. First, during the exercise period itself the body is forced to work harder and burn extra calories. Second, studies have shown that vigorous exercise raises the basal metabolic rate (the rate at which calories are burned when the body is at rest) for as long as 15 hours after you have finished working out.

As the case of the constantly dieting furniture executive illustrates, you can lose weight by going on a drastic diet and not exercising. However, the weight usually comes back. If you want to lose weight and keep it off, all you have to do is burn more calories than you consume. Once you have reached your ideal weight, if you keep the amount of calories consumed and burned in balance, you will maintain that weight.

The validity of this arithmetic of weight control has been borne out in a number of medical experiments. Grant Gwinup, M.D., of the

University of California at Irvine, examined thirty-four chronically over-weight women whose weight ranged from 134 to 218 pounds and who were 10 to 60 percent overweight. None had ever been on a truly successful diet. Dr. Gwinup decided to see whether these women could lose weight without changing their eating habits. Each subject began an exercise program that involved a brisk daily 30-minute walk. The results were astounding. The eleven women who completed the 60-week program lost an average of 22 pounds. Every woman lost weight, but none went on a diet.

Another study, conducted by Drs. W. B. Zuti and L. A. Golding of Kent State University, came up with similar results. Zuti and Golding examined the weight-reduction progress of a group of women who did enough exercise to burn 500 calories a day but did not change their eating habits. These women, some of whom were 40 pounds overweight, chose whatever exercise they wanted as long as it burned up 500 calories a day. Without altering their diets, the women lost an average of 10.6 pounds in 16 weeks.

No Quick Results

Losing weight through diet and exercise is not easy. You have to work at it, especially in the beginning. It's hard enough for overweight people to cut back on food, and it's doubly hard to stick to an exercise regimen when you are overweight and out of shape, but the physical and mental effort is worthwhile. If you follow our exercise prescription and keep an eye on your daily caloric intake, you will soon not only be losing weight, you will be looking and feeling better.

But it will take time. You cannot lose weight quickly through exercise, because it takes a large amount of exercise to burn calories. To work off the 101 calories in just one large apple, you would have to walk for about 19 minutes, ride a bicycle for 12 minutes, swim for 9 minutes, or run for 5 minutes.

As Kenneth Cooper points out, the average person burns about 1200 calories running for 1 hour at an average pace of 6 minutes per mile. That is only about half the calories an adult consumes every day. If that sounds discouraging, it should not. If you eat a balanced, low-calorie diet and follow an aerobic exercise program, you can lose 20 pounds or more within 6 months. All you have to do is maintain a moderate level of food intake and increase your exercise activity only slightly. Cardiologist Lenore Zohman and her colleagues have written: "If you increase your activity level only modestly, in a year you will weigh less. Certainly, if you diet as well—not crash diet, but follow a sensible and nutritious program—you will lose weight faster and enjoy good health and renewed vigor."

You will lose weight gradually, but you will also lose it permanently. Not only that, you will be making permanent changes in your diet and exercise habits. This changing pattern of diet and exercise is a type of behavior modification, and in the end, behavior modification is the only answer for long-term weight control. It's a question of changing bad living habits, and you should keep in mind that habits can be made as well as broken. It will take time, because you are trying to break habits formed over many years. Some people need professional guidance to help them change their sedentary lifestyles, but Executive Health Examiners has found that most executives who learn the facts about diet, exercise, and weight control can modify their eating habits and control their weight on their own.

Psychologists have studied the characteristics of people who have lost weight by successfully modifying their behavior on their own. Their characteristics mirror those of many successful executives. They tend to be self-disciplined, dependable, and readily willing to accept the consequences of their own behavior. They also tend to be vain.

Exercise Increases Appetite: A Myth

"I can't lose weight and exercise at the same time," a chronically overweight New Jersey account executive told EHE doctors during a recent checkup. "When I do the least bit of vigorous exercise, I'm famished afterwards. Then I eat even more than I usually do. So what's the use of exercising when I immediately eat as many calories as I burn up?"

Does exercise increase appetite? For most people, no. Dr. Mayer says the idea that exercise increases appetite is a myth that

> seems to have incredible staying power. This may be because many
> people believe that an increase in physical activity always causes
> an increase in appetite and food intake which is at least as great

in calorie replacement as the calories expended in exercise. This
is not necessarily true. Actually, in a normally active person exercise often depresses the appetite for a period of time.

It is true that a well-conditioned, lean person sometimes will eat
more than usual after vigorous activity, but that person has nothing to
worry about. The extra exercise that caused him or her to eat more will
burn up the extra calories. Some obese people may get the urge to gorge
after exercising to excess, but as Dr. Mayer and other medical authorities
point out, for nearly everyone else, vigorous exercise actually *depresses*
the appetite.

When you have finished a vigorous aerobic exercise session of running, walking, cycling, swimming, or jumping rope, you will not be
famished. If, as Dr. Cooper recommends for dieters, you do your aerobic
exercise shortly before your biggest meal of the day, you will want to
eat less than you usually do. Exercise can therefore make following a
diet much, much easier.

What Type of Exercise Is Best for Weight Reduction?

You have just determined that you need to lose weight. Your next
question is, What is the best exercise for weight control? Doctors say
that nearly any type of exercise will help you lose weight. However,
the most efficient and most beneficial exercises for weight control are
the ones Executive Health Examiners recommends as the basis for the
executive's overall program: aerobic exercises. Aerobic exercises are
best for weight control for the same basic reasons they are best for
cardiovascular conditioning. They involve constant movement of the
major muscle groups, they are long in duration, and they are low in
intensity. In addition, there is an extra bonus for the overweight person
who follows the EHE exercise prescription. Not only will he or she
lose weight permanently, but along with that weight loss will come the
improvement in cardiovascular conditioning that is the basis of the
executive's exercise program.

The basics of the sound diet needed to keep you from gaining weight
are well known. The diet should include daily, moderate balanced amounts
of foods from the three food groups: meat and dairy products, fresh

AN EXERCISE SELECTOR
FOR BURNING UP
SPECIFIC AMOUNTS OF CALORIES

1   Exercises Burning up to 50 Calories

Walk ½ mile in 7:30 minutes
Walk/jog ¼ mile in 3 minutes
Swim 250 yards in 7:30 minutes
Cycle 1½ miles in 9 minutes

2   Exercises Burning 50–99 Calories

Walk 1 mile in 15 minutes
Walk/jog ¾ mile in 9 minutes
Run ¾ mile in 6 minutes
Swim 450 yards in 15 minutes
Cycle 3 miles in 18 minutes

3   Exercises Burning 100–149 Calories

Walk 1½ miles in 30 minutes
Walk/jog 1 mile in 12 minutes
Run 1 mile in 8 minutes
Swim 900 yards in 30 minutes
Cycle 3 miles in 12 minutes

4   Exercises Burning 150–199 Calories

Walk 2½ miles in 50 minutes
Walk/jog 1½ miles in 18 minutes
Run 1½ miles in 12 minutes
Swim 1500 yards in 50 minutes
Cycle 4½ miles in 18 minutes

5   Exercises Burning 200–249 Calories

Walk 3 miles in 45 minutes
Walk/jog 2 miles in 24 minutes
Run 2 miles in 16 minutes
Swim 1350 yards in 45 minutes
Cycle 6 miles in 24 minutes

6 Exercises Burning 250–299 Calories

Walk 4 miles in 1 hour and 20 minutes
Walk/jog 2¼ miles in 27 minutes
Run 2½ miles in 20 minutes
Swim 2400 yards in 1 hour and 20 minutes
Cycle 12 miles in 1 hour and 12 minutes

7 Exercises Burning 300–349 Calories

Walk 5 miles in 1 hour and 40 minutes
Walk/jog 2¾ miles in 39 minutes
Run 3 miles in 24 minutes
Swim 1350 yards in 24 minutes
Cycle 9 miles in 24 minutes

8 Exercises Burning 350–399 Calories

Walk 5½ miles in 1 hour 36 minutes
Walk/jog 3 miles in 36 minutes
Run 3½ miles in 28 minutes
Swim 1350 yards in 36 minutes
Cycle 9 miles in 36 minutes

9 Exercises Burning 400–449 Calories

Walk 6 miles in 1 hour and 45 minutes
Walk/jog 3¾ miles in 45 minutes
Run 3¾ miles in 30 minutes
Swim 1575 yards in 42 minutes
Cycle 10½ miles in 42 minutes

10 Exercises Burning 450–500 Calories

Walk 7 miles in 2 hours 20 minutes
Walk/jog 4 miles in 48 minutes
Run 4 miles in 32 minutes
Swim 1800 yards in 48 minutes
Cycle 12 miles in 48 minutes

vegetables and fruit, and grains, cereals, nuts, and seeds. The diet should contain little or no refined sugars or salt and should be low in highly refined and processed foods. Finally, it is important to keep a close watch on calories consumed to match them with the amount of calories you expend in your daily exercises.

Other Benefits: Toward a Healthier Lifestyle

Executive Health Examiners has found that many executives who enter into a weight-control program based on exercise and diet are pleasantly surprised to find themselves changing their lifestyles in other ways. It seems to happen naturally. Time and again we have seen executives involved in exercise and weight-control programs cut down and then eliminate smoking, become more conscious about their eating habits, and cut back on excessive drinking. It all starts with the commitment to lose weight through an exercise-based program.

A 47-year-old investment banker provides a good example of this evolution toward a healthier lifestyle. When he came to Executive Health Examiners for a physical examination, he was 20 pounds overweight. He smoked a pack and a half of cigarettes a day, had a high cholesterol count and a high normal blood pressure reading of 140/90, and did not exercise regularly.

The banker's wife and teenage children all were involved in exercise programs, and he asked our doctors if jogging with his wife and kids would be good for him. His stress test was normal, and we advised him to begin his exercise program on his own but to start gradually.

The banker stopped smoking soon after he embarked on an aerobic walking-jogging exercise regimen. Family pressure helped him. His wife and kids threatened and cajoled until he finally gave in. Much to his surprise, he actually lost weight after giving up smoking. He thinks that his jogging program is the reason.

When the man came back to Executive Health Examiners 12 months later for a physical exam, we found that he had lost 21 pounds, that his cholesterol level was down, and that his blood pressure had dropped to 135/85. He said he felt better about himself psychologically. He also felt more productive professionally and reported that his jogging had enhanced his family life. He was spending more time with his family on the running track where they all worked out. He looked better, felt better about himself, and felt he had more energy during the day. Best of all, he was able to eliminate smoking. It's easy to see that all these improvements were sparked by the man's decision to lose weight through diet and exercise.

14.

Exercise and the
Woman Executive

A 46-year-old vice president of an investment firm recently asked EHE doctors whether she needed to go on an exercise program. "I've heard that women are far less likely to have heart attacks than men," she said. "And I'm in fairly decent shape. Do I really need to spend time exercising?" The answer our doctors gave was, of course, a resounding yes. The pressures and demands of the executive lifestyle do not discriminate by sex. Woman executives suffer from the same job-related mental and physical ailments that plague their male counterparts. Both men and women executives need to build their cardiovascular and musculoskeletal systems through a carefully prescribed balanced exercise program.

There are significant physiological differences between men and women, but there is no essential difference in terms of the cardiovascular system, respiratory capacity, or metabolism. Women have the same capability as men of developing athletic skills such as dexterity, agility, coordination, and cardiovascular training. But only in recent years, following the nationwide exercise boom, have large numbers of women begun to participate in exercise and sports. Margaret Dunkle, a leading expert on women in athletics, explained part of the reason: "Women have not been encouraged to participate in athletics at least partly because the traits associated with athletic excellence—achievement, self-confidence, aggressiveness, leadership strength, swiftness—are often seen as being in 'contradiction' with the role of women." These traits once were reserved only for men, but today they fit the profile of most successful executives, male or female.

Physiological Differences

Of course there are significant differences between men and women, but none of the unique feminine characteristics prevents women from taking part in, and benefiting from, exercise. The most important physiological factor determining human athletic ability is the effect of hormones on the physical maturation process. All male and female bodies contain estrogen, the female hormone, and testosterone, the male hormone. Men have a much higher ratio of testosterone; women, a significantly greater amount of estrogen. Boys and girls mature nearly evenly until about age 10. Then, during the next 5 to 6 years, girls undergo rapid physical maturation. During this time boys also are maturing but not as rapidly as girls.

Men reach their maximum growth at around age 20. The longer, slower growth in men results primarily in more defined muscles, especially in the upper body and arms; it also is responsible for masculine secondary sex characteristics, including a lower voice and facial hair. The rapid female maturation process causes most women to have lower centers of gravity than men, because more weight is concentrated in women's thighs and hips. Thus, the only innate physical advantage men have over women is a stronger upper body.

The upper bodies of men have larger bone and greater articular surfaces than the upper bodies of women. This gives men a mechanical and structural advantage over women in sports such as football and baseball, which require upper body strength, but there is no advantage for men over women in aerobic or flexibility exercises. Men's "longer bones act as greater lever arms, producing more force for sports requiring striking, hitting or kicking," writes Dr. Letha Yurko Hunter, assistant professor of orthopedics at the University of Washington. Men also have more muscle mass than women: about 40 percent of total body weight compared to about 23 percent. Women have a heavier proportion of body fat: from 22 to 25 percent of body weight, compared with men, who have 14 percent. Women also have slightly lower metabolic rates than men.

The most obvious differences between men and women are seen in the reproductive systems. These differences have given rise to a number of myths involving women and exercise, all of which have been proved untrue.

Reproductive Organs and Breasts   One widely held myth is that taking part in exercise is harmful to a woman's reproductive organs and breasts. Doctors say that there is virtually no risk of harming the female sexual organs during physical activity. As Dorothy Harris, director of the Center for Women and Sport at Pennsylvania State University, says, a woman has "more natural protection for contact sports than a man; she has a subcutaneous layer of fat protecting the muscles and joints and her sex organs are internal, making them practically invulnerable to injury."

Although some women report sore or tender breasts after exercising, much of that discomfort can be relieved by wearing a specially designed sports bra. Many types are now on the market. Exercise does not contribute to sagging breasts, by the way. Many forms of exercise, especially those involving the arms, can strengthen the pectoral muscles, thus improving posture and breast contour.

Postchildbirth   Some people believe that a woman's athletic abilities decline after childbirth, but again, there is no scientific evidence to prove the allegation. "There is no need to restrict physical activity for women in any manner whatsoever," says athletic trainer Joan Gillette. "There . . . are no ill effects during pregnancy, delivery or later on. . . . Women athletes receive injuries due to the lack of proper conditioning and poor coaching."

Menstruation   Another myth holds that a woman cannot exert maximum physical strength during menstruation. However, world records have been set and Olympic gold medals won by women during all stages of the menstrual cycle, and mild menstruation should not prevent a woman from doing her everyday exercise routine.

Amenorrhea, which is a medical term for the absence of menstrual periods, and other menstrual irregularities are often blamed on exercise, but that myth has been dispelled by Mona Shangold, M.D., professor of obstetrics and gynecology at the Albert Einstein College of Medicine in New York. Dr. Shangold, an expert on the effects of exercise on the female reproductive system, wrote recently: "Despite alarming claims of menstrual irregularity in athletes, it has not been proved that exercise is responsible or harmful. For women who do experience irregular menstrual periods when they exercise heavily, it should never be assumed that the problem is exercise related—or that it is not serious." Dr. Shangold recommends that women experiencing amenorrhea or other menstrual abnormalities consult their gynecologists.

Executive Health Examiners has found that women involved in EHE-recommended exercise programs report that exercise decreases premenstrual tension and physical symptoms such as cramps and bloating. "The months when I do active physical exercise, I experience no menstrual discomfort whatsoever," said a 32-year-old advertising executive. "When I don't do any exercising, I'm in agony. I get cramps, bloating, and it's just misery. It's the best motivation I can think of to do my exercises regularly."

The bottom line on the subject of exercising and menstruation is to use common sense. If your period is particularly heavy, do not exercise; the same is true if you have a heavy cold or a sprained ankle. But remember that most women can exercise normally during normal menstruation. As Dr. Shangold sums it up:

> The beneficial effects of regular physical exercise on the heart, lungs, bones and muscles are well known. Less publicized benefits are an improved sense of well-being, weight loss, weight control, and decreased menstrual pain and discomfort. . . . These combined advantages of regular exercises far outweigh any potential reproductive hazards.

Pregnancy

Executive Health Examiners has found that pregnant women can exercise safely for nearly the entire term of pregnancy, but we strongly recommend that pregnant women consult a physician about the types of exercise they undertake. Again, common sense dictates that women should moderate their exercise regimens during the late stages of pregnancy.

According to a survey conducted by Dr. David A. Leaf of Portland, Oregon, pregnant women respond to exercise in much the same way as women who are not pregnant. There is even some evidence, Dr. Leaf reported to a Northwest Sports Medicine and Conditioning Seminar, that exercising mothers may have shorter periods of labor than mothers who do not exercise. No evidence has been found that running or other aerobic exercises harm the developing fetus. Nevertheless, it is very important that pregnant women avoid excessive fatigue and consult a doctor about their exercise routines during the entire term.

The Muscle Controversy

Perhaps the biggest myth that has kept women from exercising is the fear that they will develop large, "unfeminine" muscles, although it has been proved medically that women can greatly increase their strength through weight lifting without building large, bulky muscles. The reason is that most women do not produce male hormones in sufficient quantity to develop large muscles.

The leading expert in this field is Dr. Jack Wilmore of the Department of Physical Education at the University of Arizona. His experiments in this area involved 10-week weight-training programs with groups of untrained college-age men and women. Dr. Wilmore found that while men are able to lift heavier weights than women, the male/female ratios all but disappear when considered in relation to overall body weight. We've always been told that women are so much weaker than men, but Dr. Wilmore's experiments show that they have almost exactly the same strength.

Wilmore's experiments also showed that women's muscles, while increasing in strength, did not significantly increase in size. The studies showed that women generally developed one-tenth the muscle size of men who worked out in the same weight program. Women's biceps grew an average of only about one-fourth of an inch, while their strength improved 11 to 30 percent.

The results of a study of men and women volunteers at Oregon State University who used a special technique of weight training called power lifting correlated with Dr. Wilmore's findings. Women and men have "the same physiological ability . . . to tolerate and adapt to" the demands of power lifting, according to Oregon State professor of physical education John P. O'Shea and his assistant Julie Wegner, who oversaw the study. O'Shea and Wegner found that there is no medical or scientific basis for the myth that women "lack the physical capacity to respond to strength training." They concluded that while "it is true that women have less muscle mass than men per unit of body weight and bone density and consequently do not possess the same absolute strength potential as men, women can develop strength relative to their own physical potential."

15.

How to Avoid Injury

Injuries and exercise go together. The odds are that if you embark on an exercise program involving aerobics, stretching, and strength building, sooner or later you will suffer some sort of injury. The most common injuries are relatively minor, and there are commonsense steps you can take to greatly minimize your chances of developing serious injuries. If you feel a twinge in your knee while running, slow down. If the pain persists, slow to a walk and give your leg a rest. Most injuries are caused by overuse, by doing too much exercise with too much intensity in too short a period of time. The way to avoid the consequences of overuse injuries is to use your head. Warm up slowly and gradually for at least 10 minutes before aerobic exercises, decrease the intensity at the first sign of trouble, and stop completely if pain persists.

Another way to minimize the risk of injury is to choose equipment designed to come between your body and injuries. The most important piece of equipment in running and walking is the shoe.

Running and Walking Shoes: What to Look For

One of the prime benefits of the physical fitness explosion of the mid-1970s for American joggers and walkers has been the parallel expansion and availability of scientifically designed exercise shoes. There are at least twenty brands of excellent athletic shoes on the market today, ranging in price from under $20 to over $75, and there are many different types of special athletic shoes from which to choose. There are running shoes that are perfectly suitable for walking. There are basketball shoes, baseball shoes, track shoes, tennis shoes, golf shoes, and so on.

One question frequently asked EHE doctors by executives about to embark on jogging programs involves what type of shoe to buy. "*Running Times* magazine gives out 'gold shoe' awards to some brands that don't even make *Runner's World* magazine's 'highly recommended' list," an advertising executive complained to our doctors recently. "How am I supposed to know what brand and model to buy?"

The answer to that question is that even though buying running shoes is an individual decision, there are several things everyone should consider before selecting a pair. First, buy a shoe especially made for running; basketball or tennis shoes will not do. Any of the major brands such as Adidas, Nike, Puma, New Balance, Converse, Tiger, Patrik, and Etonic are acceptable. Executive Health Examiners recommends buying running shoes from a store that specializes in athletic footwear.

Talk to the salesperson and discuss exactly what you will be using the shoes for. Especially important is the kind of surface you will be running on and how many miles a week you will be running. Try on several pairs of shoes, because the most important criterion is how they feel on you. Remember to wear the same type of socks you will be running in. One important thing to check is how the heel fits; it should be stable and fit snugly, but not too tightly. If you are used to wearing a built-up heel, buy a pair of running shoes with that feature. If your street shoes are flat, go with running shoes with low heels. You should also make sure there is room between your toes and the tips of the shoes. The shoes also should be flexible and have well-padded soles.

Footwear for Cycling, Stretching, and Weight Lifting

Choosing the type of footwear for the other exercises in your routine is not as crucial as it is for running and walking, because your feet and legs take the most pounding in running and walking. (If you choose rope skipping, use running shoes.) For both indoor and outdoor cycling, all you need is a good pair of basketball or tennis sneakers. Do not use running shoes on rolling bicycles, because the waffle soles can get caught in the pedals, and do not wear sandals or high heels.

Bicycle specialty stores sell shoes designed to be worn while cycling, but these shoes are designed for serious race cyclists and are by no means necessary for the cyclist interested only in exercise. The same holds true for stretching and strength-building exercises. You can buy special gym shoes for these exercises, but it's perfectly all right to wear sneakers. If you are doing your stretching and strength building in the same sessions as your aerobics, you can either warm up and cool down indoors without shoes or use the same shoes you use for aerobic exercises if you work out outdoors.

Clothing

The next time you are out on the jogging path or bike path, look around. You will notice that the basic running and cycling outfits consist of T-shirts and shorts in the spring and summer and sweat suits or warmup suits in fall and winter. That is about all you have to know in the area of exercise clothing.

Executive Health Examiners recommends that you wear loose and comfortable clothing made of natural fibers to facilitate comfort. Cotton or wool shirts, shorts, and pants "breathe," whereas synthetic fabrics hold in perspiration. You will therefore be much more comfortable in cotton or wool. Nylon running shorts are best for hot weather because they are extremely lightweight.

The layered look is still fashionable for exercise in cold weather. Try a T-shirt covered by a sweat shirt or warmup jacket, but it's not necessary to worry about protecting yourself from cold weather until the temperature dips below freezing. Once you start running, walking, or cycling, your body will adapt well to temperature in the 40s and 50s; in fact, long-distance runners say that 55 degrees is about the perfect temperature for running. When the thermometer dips below freezing, you should protect your hands and head. We recommend lightweight wool or cotton gloves and caps.

Clothing for Cyclists

There are many different types of clothes made especially for cyclists. You can buy a special head-to-foot cycling outfit complete with shoes, socks, pants, shirt, cap, and gloves, but the average exercise cyclist can wear any comfortable clothing so long as the outfit does not restrict movement. The black cotton skintight cycling shorts that racers wear have a special inner lining designed to cushion road bumps, but most of those who cycle for exercise do not need these shorts. If you find yourself logging lots of miles on your bike, you might think about getting a pair. Shorts and a T-shirt are *de rigueur* for warm weather; the layered look, for cool weather. In the winter, it's best to wear a pair of gloves, because your hands bear the brunt of the cold.

There is some mandatory equipment for outdoor cyclists. A helmet is a smart investment. More than one experienced cyclist has wound up in the hospital, and some have been killed, from falling off a ten-speed bike. Something as seemingly innocuous as a wet leaf can cause a fall. If your head is not protected, you are asking for trouble. There are many types of helmets to choose from. The best ones are lightweight and have tinted adjustable visors.

There is some other equipment rolling bicyclists should not be without: a lightweight backpack or saddlepack to carry extra clothing, rain gear for an emergency, some sort of clip to keep your pants legs out of the chains, a tool bag and pump to handle road repairs, a headlight, and front, rear, and wheel reflectors to make yourself visible at night.

Clothing for Swimming, Rope Skipping, and Yoga

Swimming, of course, requires only a good swimsuit that clings to your body but does not cut off circulation. For rope skipping, loose-fitting but not billowing clothing will do. Again, you cannot go wrong with shorts and a T-shirt. The same is true for strength-building exercises. For stretching, and especially for yoga, loose and comfortable clothing is the rule; women can wear leotards.

Avoiding Injuries

There is an entire branch of medicine devoted to sports. The science of sports medicine has grown markedly in the last decade, and those of us who exercise are among the beneficiaries of the gains in knowledge about injuries and injury prevention. We now know that most injuries are caused by overuse. Thus it is vital that you warm up before beginning your aerobic, strength-building, and stretching exercises. It is equally vital to cool down afterward. It also is important to increase your times and distances gradually.

If you do not use these commonsense procedures, chances are, you will suffer an injury similar to the one that befell an EHE patient who increased his running time too quickly after beginning his program. This man, a physician in his late forties, noticed great improvement in his cardiovascular capacity after 4 weeks of running regularly. He began increasing his distances nearly every time he ran, but within a month he complained to EHE doctors that he had severe pain in his knees and that his hamstring muscles were constantly sore. When we found out how long he ran every day, we immediately advised him to refrain from running entirely for a month. After the 4-week enforced rest, we set him up on a new running program designed for gradual progress. He began to warm up slowly and gradually and stayed on the timetable. His leg problems soon disappeared.

The Most Common Sports Injuries

As you might assume, leg and foot problems are the most common injuries associated with exercise. According to a study done by a Lenox Hill Hospital clinic that treats primarily recreational athletes in New York City, the most frequent injuries involve knees, ankles, and shoulders. Knee injuries, in fact, accounted for nearly half of all problems.

Other studies of exercise-related injuries similarly indicate that the knee is one of the most vulnerable parts of the body, an extremely fragile joint commonly injured in many sports, including cycling. Extensive uphill pedaling puts tremendous pressure on the middle surface of the kneecap. This can cause what is also the most common runner's injury: inflammation of the cartilage behind the kneecap, commonly known as runner's knee. The knee "is simply not designed for most of the things people want to do with it today," says Robert Kerlan, M.D., director of the National Athletic Health Institute in Inglewood, California, and an expert on knee injuries.

Preventing Injuries

Doing special strength-building exercises, running on smooth surfaces, warming up the leg muscles well, and choosing good running shoes are the best ways to avoid not only knee but other common leg problems associated with exercise. These include stress fractures, bone bruises, shin splints (the aching of inflamed muscles or tendons in the lower legs), inflammation of the Achilles tendon, and bone spurs of the heel.

Another preventive measure involves a fairly new type of sports medicine called orthotics. A group of podiatrists now specializes in fitting runners, cyclists, and walkers with orthotic devices, which are molds designed from your foot to fit into your running shoes. The object is to balance the foot in a neutral position while you exercise. These lightweight devices are made of plastic, rubber, or leather and can be custom-made to correct many of the various leg problems. Orthotic devices, which cost as much as $150, are not recommended for everyone, but if you have recurring leg problems, consult a podiatrist or orthopedist and ask whether such a device will provide you with relief.

To repeat, for leg problems, the most important things you can do to lessen the risk of serious injury are to: Buy a well-built, comfortable pair of running shoes; run or walk on a smooth and, if possible, pliable surface; warm up slowly, progress gradually, and cool down slowly; see a podiatrist or orthopedist for an orthotic device if you have continuing problems.

There are other problems associated with running that have nothing to do with the legs but that for the most part are avoidable with some commonsense preventive techniques. Doctors have uncovered what is believed to be a benign condition in many joggers: athletic pseudonephritis, or "jogger's kidney." The symptoms are abnormal levels of

AN INJURY SURVEY
AT LENOX HILL HOSPITAL, 1975 TO 1979

Injuries to Urban Recreational Athletes			Sports in which Injuries Occurred		
Body Part	No.	%	Sport	No.	%
Knee	486	45.5	Running/ jogging	340	32.6
Ankle	105	9.8	Basketball	101	9.7
Shoulder	82	7.7	Tennis	97	9.3
Foot/heel	77	7.2	Ballet/dancing	74	7.1
Elbow	63	5.9	Football	44	4.2
Back	53	5.0	Snow skiing	37	3.5
Hip	48	4.5	Weight lifting	36	3.4
Tibia	47	4.4	Baseball/ softball	32	3.1
Femur/ hamstring	44	4.1	Martial arts	31	3.0
Fibula/calf	19	1.8	Soccer	16	1.5
Wrist	17	1.6	Gymnastics	14	1.3
Neck	9	0.8	Ice hockey	11	1.1
Pelvis	7	0.7	Miscellaneous (35 sports)	133	12.7
Groin	4	0.4	Unspecified	78	7.5
Finger	2	0.2			
Humerus	2	0.2	**Total**	1,044*	100.0
Leg (unspecified)	2	0.2			
Total	1,067	100.0			

* Some athletes did not identify any sport and some identified more than one.

Philip A. Witman, et al., "Common Problems Seen in a Metropolitan Sports Injury Clinic," *The Physician and Sportsmedicine,* March 1981, p. 106.

protein, red blood cells, and other substances in the urine. The condition may be caused by reduction of blood flow to the kidneys during an hour or more of jogging. The condition cures itself within 2 days, but doctors do not know whether it leads to kidney damage. If you think you are suffering from this condition, it's best to consult a physician and cut back on your running time.

"Runner's nipple" is caused when clothing rubs against the sensitive areas of the breasts. This condition can affect men and women, and although it is not a serious problem, runner's nipples can be very painful. It primarily affects long-distance runners. The remedy: applying ointment to the breasts before running or taping on gauze pads for protection. A good running bra takes care of the problem for women.

In summary, there is an ever-present risk of injury when you are exercising, but there are ways to minimize the risk. Careful, well-thought-out exercise programs can minimize most of the potential dangers, and Executive Health Examiners believes that the potential benefits of regular exercise—especially for those who live largely sedentary lives—far outweigh the risks of physical injury.

16.

Heart Disease, Diabetes, and Asthma: The Value of Exercise

Is it possible for executives with heart disease to undertake an exercise program safely? The answer is a qualified yes. It is possible for recovering heart attack patients to undertake such a program, but not without clearance from their personal physicians and cardiologists.

More and more doctors are finding that exercise can be beneficial to a recovering heart patient. A real estate executive had a massive heart attack not long after he retired 3 years ago at age 69. He came through a double-bypass operation and 3 months later was fitted with a pacemaker. Three months after that he enrolled in a cardiac rehabilitation program that emphasized daily walking and thrice-weekly workouts on a stationary bicycle.

His exercise sessions were directed by a trained nurse who monitored her exercising patients' heartbeats and other vital signs. Progress reports were sent to the patients' cardiologists. "I can't say enough about my exercise program," the executive said recently. "It makes me feel stronger and healthier. Our nurse works very closely with the doctors, and any time there is the slightest problem, my cardiologist calls me in for an examination."

After 2 months of cardiac rehabilitation, this man felt well enough to return to his normal daily activities. This case is not atypical. Younger recovering heart attack patients often return to work in a matter of weeks after beginning cardiac rehabilitation programs, and they return in good physical and mental condition. "It is my belief that, with a professionally supervised exercise program, many heart attack victims may not just return to work, but they may restore their hearts to a state far better than before the heart attack, and so prevent subsequent attacks," writes Robert C. Cantu, M.D., of the Emerson Hospital in Concord, Massachusetts. Dr. Cantu and other experts are quick to point out, however, that cardiac rehabilitation is not complete unless obvious cardiac risk factors—hypertension, obesity, cigarette smoking, including the sedentary lifestyle—are eliminated or tightly controlled.

Exercise After a Heart Attack

Terence Kavanaugh, M.D., of the Toronto Rehabilitation Center, has specialized in treating post-heart attack patients with exercise therapy. His program takes patients as early as 6 weeks after their heart attacks and concentrates on walking and running. A group of Dr. Kavanaugh's patients made history in 1973 when they entered and completed the Boston Marathon. The seven middle-aged former heart attack victims who ran in the marathon were monitored by Dr. Kavanaugh throughout the race. They reported no respiratory problems.

Jack Scaff, M.D., of Honolulu, also specializes in exercise programs for postcardiac patients. Since 1973 he has entered more than 1000 of his patients in the Honolulu Marathon. As is the case with Dr. Kavanaugh's charges, Dr. Scaff's runners are constantly monitored and train especially for the marathon for many months. None of his runners has had any serious cardiac complications.

"These feats are important as dramatic illustrations of the value of the medically supervised post-heart attack exercise program," Dr. Cantu writes. "They point out just how far one's exercise prescription can be upgraded if one desires to put in the time and effort. But it is certainly not necessary to make such a commitment. A program just three or four hours a week is sufficient to gain the physiological and psychological benefits desired."

Exercise programs for postcardiac patients should be taken under the close supervision of cardiologists. Especially important is the time to begin initial exercising. In the past, the accepted medical thinking was to give cardiac patients as much bed rest as possible. They were told to avoid straining and were cautioned to avoid such comparatively easy tasks as climbing stairs.

In the last decade medical thinking has changed on the subject of when heart attack patients should begin exercising. Many doctors now advise beginning an exercise program as soon as the patient has recovered enough strength to handle light walking. Although Dr. Kavanaugh's Toronto program takes patients as early as 6 weeks after their heart attacks, some doctors encourage patients to begin exercise programs even earlier.

A 1981 study of staff members of the University of Washington's Division of Cardiology examined the effects of early exercise programs on patients who had acute myocardial infarction. The conclusion was that while such low-intensity exercise programs do not improve the health of patients, they also do not have any demonstrable deleterious effects. The conclusion was optimistic: "If one assumes that a sedentary lifestyle is a risk factor and that exercise is a desirable preventive measure, then starting an exercise program during hospitalization when patients are highly motivated may well help to establish a habit of exercise."

Other Diseases and Exercise

Many executives are concerned about physical problems other than injuries or heart attacks when embarking on an exercise program. "Doctor, I have diabetes. Does this mean I can't exercise on a regular basis?" This is a question EHE doctors often hear. There is one rule of thumb concerning exercise and diseases such as diabetes, asthma, and arthritis: The patient must be ultraconscious of his or her particular disease while exercising. If there is the slightest sign of any abnormality, we strongly recommend that you immediately consult your physician. From our experience with setting up exercise programs for hundreds of executives with various diseases, here are some specific recommendations.

Diabetes   Executive Health Examiners has found that exercise can benefit most diabetic patients. We have treated diabetic patients who, after adopting a regular exercise program, have been able to decrease their insulin requirements. There are even cases of people with adult-onset diabetes who no longer needed insulin after adopting an exercise regimen.

"Quite clearly, the vast majority of epidemiological and clinical studies lend credence to the belief that regular physical activity promotes good health and these observations are supported by the physiologic changes which can be documented in an actively exercising individual," writes Dr. Thomas M. Flood of the Joslin Diabetes Foundation in Boston. Dr. Flood warns, however, that any diabetic about to embark on an exercise program should work closely with his or her physician to set up a regimen tailored to the patient's particular condition. "Observation of a few commonsense rules," Dr. Flood writes, "with special attention to diet and potential insulin changes during the early, evolutionary stages of an exercise program, will . . . enable diabetic patients to derive greater benefit from their exercise."

Arthritis   We do not recommend running for arthritic patients with hip or knee conditions. Swimming is ideal for those problems. The best choice for the arthritic patient is a program in which the affected joints are not exposed to potential damage. People suffering from rheumatoid arthritis should not begin an exercise program without consulting a physical rehabilitation specialist.

It now appears that contrary to popular opinion, runners, cyclists, and other regular exercisers do not have greater risk of developing osteoarthritis. However, there is some evidence that specific joint injuries can cause this form of arthritis, and so it is especially important to have severe joint injuries attended to quickly and thoroughly.

Asthma   There is no reason why a person with asthma cannot take part in a balanced exercise program. One word of warning, though. Exercising in extremely cold or polluted air can trigger an asthma attack. It is very important for those with asthma to warm up thoroughly before exercising and to begin aerobic exercises slowly and gradually.

Doctors at the University of Western Australia in Nedlands have found that exercise, when undertaken with a physician's permission and with commonsense precautions, can help most asthmatics. Research shows:

> Even persons with moderately severe asthma can often participate [in exercise] if a few simple guidelines are followed. Regular vigorous activity has been shown to bring several benefits, including increased physical fitness, enhanced tolerance of attacks and a greater social and psychological independence. Far from

being a barrier to involvement in physical pursuits, asthma should perhaps indicate an even greater need for such involvement.

Lower Back Pain   Most lower back pain is preventable, and the secret is usually exercise. For some back pain, including herniated disks, no exercise should be done without consulting a physician, but for most lower back problems stretching exercises often provide relief. "From a preventive standpoint [exercise] is one of the simplest and most important prescriptions for a healthy back," EHE director Dr. Richard E. Winter has written. "Low back pain for millions of Americans is simply another health concern for which we have responsibility and, fortunately, over which we can exercise control."

There are a number of specific exercise programs offered at places like YMCAs that are designed to focus on strengthening back muscles and alleviating back pain. Yoga exercises concentrate on the back muscles, but it is important to remember to consult your exercise instructor or yoga teacher before undertaking a program.

Hypertension   High blood pressure is one of the risk factors associated with cardiovascular disease. In cases of mild to moderate hypertension, a regular aerobic exercise program can be a valuable supplement to the treatment routine. Approval from your physician is necessary before starting such a program. Since exercise programs usually reduce weight and combat stress, they also can lead to lowered blood pressure. EHE medical records contain evidence of many patients who experienced a lowering of blood pressure after 6 to 12 months of exercising. There is no direct proof that the exercise leads directly to the lowered blood pressure, but we believe there is a correlation.

It's a Lifetime Commitment

It's customary in books of this kind to conclude with an exhortation designed to encourage the reader to begin an exercise program immediately. Before we get to that, we would like to present a few sobering thoughts.

First of all, exercise is a lifetime commitment. It's not a fad or something to dabble in when the mood strikes. In order to get the full benefits of exercise, you need to practice all three components on a regular basis. If you stop, you will lose nearly everything you have gained. This is especially true for aerobics exercises, but it also goes for the stretching and strength-building components of the exercise program.

Executive Health Examiners has found that the number one reason executives abandon exercise programs is boredom. "I just can't stand to pedal that damn stationary bike one more minute," an exasperated New Jersey insurance executive told EHE doctors recently. "I've been pedaling diligently three times a week for a year and a half, and I can't take staring at the walls any longer."

Combating Boredom

The answer for this woman and for all others who become bored with their regular exercise routines is to find ways to make exercise sessions enjoyable. If your exercise is fun, you will look forward to doing it. For bored indoor cyclists, we suggest moving the bike in front of the TV or radio or buying a portable tape recorder so that you can listen to music while pedaling.

Another way to combat boredom is to vary your routines slightly without abandoning them altogether. Runners, walkers, and outdoor cyclists can change their routes or the time of day they venture forth. You can vary your aerobic routines according to the season, switching to running in warmer weather and indoor cycling during cold weather, for example.

You can exercise with friends to alleviate boredom. Since the pace of aerobic exercises is designed so that you can hold a normal conversation, running, walking, and cycling are perfect for two people to exercise and chat at the same time. Any time you have company during your usually solitary exercise routine, a bit of adrenaline pumps into your system and you seem to glide effortlessly through the routine. This is good so long as you do not overdo it and go beyond your capacity.

We have suggested getting family members involved in exercise routines. Cajoling a lazy spouse out of bed at 6 A.M. will not only get you an exercise partner but will also give you a chance to show your partner what you are doing in the early hours of the morning.

Most exercisers find that after several months they begin changing their routines naturally. They find themselves adding twists, abandoning others, inventing new types of stretches, running in unexplored directions, and exercising at different times of the day. Some executives have switched to yoga from calisthenics after experimenting with a beginner's yoga class. You will find that the more you exercise, the better you will get to know your body, and this will help you think up more variations to alleviate boredom.

A New Type of Behavior

You are aiming for a type of behavior modification. You are trying gradually and slowly to mold yourself from a totally sedentary individual into a person who easily and readily takes part in a balanced exercise program consisting of aerobic, stretching, and strength-building routines.

This is by no means an easy task. During the first 6 to 8 weeks especially, you might hear a persistent internal voice urging you to give up. It's easy to listen to that voice. You will think of a million rationalizations for quitting. We suggest that when that voice whispers the reasons why you should quit, you should respond with the reasons to keep going and try to remember that the first 6 to 8 weeks are by far the hardest.

Things will get a lot easier as your cardiovascular system increases in capacity, your muscles get stronger, and your body becomes more flexible. You may even experience "runner's high," a feeling of euphoria that some runners claim they get after running for long periods of time. Or you may never experience any type of euphoria. But we can promise that you will feel stronger and more confident while you are exercising and between sessions. If you follow the guidelines in this book, you will feel mental and physical benefits that should give you all the incentive you need to continue your exercises.

Consider the words of David A. Field, who began exercising regularly when he was 45 years old in 1963. By 1981, after averaging about 950 miles a year, running an average of 268 days a year, Field discovered that he had made considerable improvements in his physical conditioning. Nevertheless, what mattered most to him, he wrote, was the following: "As long as the daily workout remains fun I will continue. . . . My workouts helped me to be very aware of the beauty around me: the warm weather that follows a winter that has remained too long, a crisp fall that follows a sweltering summer. All have made daily exercise well worth my time."

Perhaps the final words belong to Dr. Cooper, writing about the difficulties and rewards of getting through the first 6 to 8 weeks: "Once you're past that period, I can promise that you'll begin to enjoy your workout. After eight to ten weeks, you sense the change. You'll find yourself looking forward to your exercise, longing for it as an accustomed pleasure."

PART III

Executive Stress

Introduction

As an executive, you have to cope with stress; there is no escape. Stress is as much a part of the business world of today as the annual report. It's felt by the young man or woman driving upward, by the middle-aged executive whose career may have peaked, and by the person at the top with heavy responsibilities.

Of the thousands of businessmen and -women we see at Executive Health Examiners each year, as many as 20 to 25 percent show evidence of stress and stress effects. And the stress-related symptoms of at least 5 percent are serious enough to require professional help.

For the businessman or -woman, how can stress be anything but virtually unavoidable, considering the ever-mounting complexities, uncertainties, and pressures of business, often coupled with complex family, economic, and social factors?

When stress gets out of hand, it can create potentially serious damage. At the least, it may lead to irritability and a lowered threshold for anger or frustration. But sometimes it is incapacitating, provoking anxiety or depression. Physically, it can trigger or exacerbate a wide variety of disorders: hypertension, heart disease, ulcer, colitis, and more.

Stress, however inevitable, nevertheless is widely misunderstood. No concept dealing with human functioning and health has produced more confusion. According to conventional wisdom, stress is to be avoided if at all possible. But it cannot be. And even if it were, its avoidance would probably be calamitous to the individual and to society.

The need is not for stress evasion but for effective ways of coping with stress. To that purpose, this section is dedicated. May it help executives at all levels handle stress successfully in their business and family lives.

17.

Stress: What Is It?

Pick up almost any newspaper, magazine, or medical journal today and you are likely to read something about stress.

What, precisely, is this phenomenon which, we are often told, "has surpassed the common cold as the most prevalent health problem in America"?

In a way, we all know what it is, and yet we do not. The word *stress*, very often loosely used, seems to mean different things to different people. Many use it to connote both an external condition, loss of job, for example, and the body's internal reaction to that condition.

Among medical scientists, however, stress has to do with the bodily response. And any external conditions which arouse the response are considered to be *stressors* or stressful life events.

IT STARTS WITH PRESSURE

Stress begins with pressure.

When we speak of ordinary pressures, we mean the daily routines, responsibilities, and chores that keep us going, usually in some kind of work schedule or what might be called a "social harness." They are stable expectations guiding or harnessing both work and recreation. These activities are the normal pressures of life—far too loosely called the "normal" stresses of life.

However, there is a fundamental difference between pressure and stress. *Pressure* is a stimulus, external or internal, to which we respond. *Stress* results from our perception of a need and our gearing up for the response. It is a coupled response.

Thus, one's need to rouse from sleep (perhaps this is the end of a "need" for sleep) is the pressure. The stress, if present (we awake late and must rush), derives from the way we perceive and respond to the pressure of wakefulness.

Daniel X. Freedman, M.D.
Editor of the *Archives of Psychiatry.*

The Flow of "Juice"

Prehistoric people, we now know, survived because of the stress mechanism. That same mechanism works for us in primal fashion as it did for them.

Consider this situation:

You are relaxing after dinner, reading. Everything is quiet until, suddenly from another room, you hear a noise. Someone is moving about, and no one should be there.

You look up from your book. Without question, something strange is going on. You are about to get up when the door to the other room is flung open. In rushes someone you have never seen before.

Instantly, striking physical changes are set in motion in your body. You were relaxed before, even somewhat drowsy after your dinner as more blood went to your gut to aid digestion and less went to your brain. You breathed slowly and evenly, your heart beat was slow and regular, your skin was dry and warm.

But now, digestion stops. Blood is shunted away from the gut to your brain, which is now highly aroused, and to your muscles, which are tensed for action. Your heart pounds, your blood pressure shoots up, and your skin (as the blood moves away from it, too, to feed brain and muscles) becomes cool and somewhat clammy.

A lot more is going on within you. Blood sugar (glucose) is released from storage in the liver into your blood: This is an extra supply that can be burned fast for energy. While blood cells flow into the blood from the spleen; they too are an extra supply ready to fight off infection. Your supply of blood platelets—tiny ovoid bodies in the blood—increases, ready to produce clotting in case of injury.

You have experienced an alarm reaction, a quick readying for flight or fight.

From your nervous system, a message has gone to the adrenal glands atop the kidneys to secrete a hormone, adrenaline, the "juice" that increases heart action and relaxes and enlarges the airways so more air can reach the lungs more quickly. In addition, adrenaline reaches the pituitary gland at the base of the brain, which responds to it by secreting hormones to cause the thyroid, parathyroids, and other glands to pour out their hormones, all to complete the almost instantaneous mustering of your body and mind forces to deal with the stress situation. These responses account for some of the seemingly superhuman feats of action that are often exhibited under stress.

Homeostasis, a Nice Balance

Any organism, including the human body, tries to maintain internal balance.

For example, we need a certain amount of sugar (glucose) circulating in the blood to nourish tissues bathed by the blood. But not very much glucose—about one-sixtieth of an ounce for each pint of blood—is needed at any one time.

Normally, the body makes sure that blood sugar concentration stays relatively stable no matter how much or how little sugar you may eat in a given day or how much energy you burn up. Let blood sugar fall below its proper level and the pancreas puts out a hormone, glucagon, which tells the liver to release some of its stored sugar. Other hormones as well get into the act to reestablish proper blood sugar levels.

Conversely, if blood sugar rises above normal levels, glucagon and other hormones are turned off and the liver, rather than release stored sugar, pulls more in for storage. And the pancreas secretes more insulin, which helps push glucose from the blood into muscles and fat cells. The body thus makes constant adjustments to achieve a normal balance.

It was Dr. Walter Cannon who introduced the term *homeostasis* to indicate the maintenance of internal balance. A monumental figure credited with doing much of the groundwork which helped to stimulate intensive research on stress, Cannon published his landmark book *Bodily Changes in Pain, Hunger, Fear and Rage* in 1929.

Cannon investigated how such emotions as fear and anger contribute to animal survival. He studied the stressful effects of pain and hunger. He demonstrated how the pouring of adrenaline into the bloodstream from the adrenal glands in an "alarm" reaction readied an animal for flight or fight. And he made the observation, too, that psychological stress could produce bodily changes that in time could lead to disease.

In 1953, Dr. Harold G. Wolff, another major contributor to the growing concept of stress, wrote his important book *Stress and Disease*. He investigated how people respond to stressful stimuli and defined such stimuli as being any influences that produce responses from such tissues as muscles, nerves, or glands or that increase any body function or process.

He considered that certain stimuli are "noxious." They can have damaging effects on individual body cells or tissues or on the health of the entire person. A noxious stimulus, he observed, can be not only a physical problem, such as a broken bone, but even a change in a human relationship which may have threatening connotations.

Wolff also noted that what may be a noxious stimulus for one person does not necessarily have to be noxious for another. Is one person demoralized, for example, by a serious illness which might, on another, stimulate positive, creative action? Such an illness, in the case of Charles Darwin, led him to the idea of evolution. Severe illness, too, stimulated Florence Nightingale to push for nursing reform.

Hans Selye and Biological Stress

Unquestionably, Hans Selye, M.D., is a preeminent figure in modern stress research. He is currently president of the International Institute of Stress.

Selye is the scientist who has helped to give stress some of its modern meaning as what he calls a *nonspecific* response of the body to any demand upon it.

As Selye has pointed out, any demand made upon the body obviously is specific. If you are exposed to cold, you shiver to produce more heat. If you become hot, you sweat and the evaporation of the perspiration has a cooling effect. If you run up half a dozen flights of stairs, your muscles need more energy, so your heart beats more rapidly and strongly and your blood pressure rises to speed delivery of nourishing blood to the muscles.

Drugs and hormones also have their specific actions. A diuretic drug, a so-called water-pill, increases urine production; adrenaline augments pulse rate and blood pressure and at the same time increases blood sugar. On the other hand, insulin decreases blood sugar.

> Yet [says Selye], no matter what kind of derangement is produced, all these agents have one thing in common: They also make an increased demand on the body to readjust itself. The demand is *nonspecific*, it requires *adaptation* to a problem regardless of what the problem may be. That is to say, in addition to their specific actions, all agents to which we are exposed produce nonspecific increase in the need to perform certain adaptive functions and then to reestablish normalcy, which is independent of the specific activity that caused the rise in requirements. *This specific demand for activity as such is the essence of stress.*

It doesn't matter whether the agent or situation is pleasant or unpleasant. What counts is the intensity of the demand for readjustment or adaptation. In Selye's words:

> The mother who is suddenly told that her only son died in battle suffers a terrible mental shock; if years later it turns out that the news was false, and the son unexpectedly walks into her room alive and well, she experiences extreme joy. The specific results of the two events, sorrow and joy, are completely different, in fact, opposite to each other; yet their stressor effect—the nonspecific demand to readjust to an entirely new situation—may be the same.

Is it difficult to see how such essentially different things as sorrow and joy, heat and cold, drugs and hormones can produce the very same biochemical reaction?

But there are everyday analogies, Selye points out. One example is the home in which heaters, refrigerators, bells, and light bulbs produce heat, cold, sound, and light quite specifically, yet depend for their functioning on one common, nonspecific factor: electricity.

"The Syndrome of Just Being Sick"

Selye got a hint of what he was later to call the general adaptation syndrome when, in 1925, he was studying medicine at the University of Prague. In one of the lectures, students were shown several patients in early stages of various infectious diseases. The professor pointed out all the specific signs and symptoms characteristic of each disease. But what struck Selye was that each patient felt and looked ill, had a coated tongue, complained of diffuse joint aches and intestinal disturbances. The patients had a common syndrome, but the professor attached little significance to the signs common to all the diseases, since they were nonspecific and of "no use" to a physician in diagnosis.

More than half a dozen years later, Selye had occasion to think about that syndrome again. It was 1936 and he was working in the Biochemistry Department of McGill University in Montreal, trying to isolate a new hormone in extracts of cow ovaries. He injected the extracts into rats to see whether their organs would show changes that could not be attributed to any known hormone.

The extracts changed the rats in three ways: Their adrenal glands enlarged; their thymus, spleen, and lymph nodes shrank; and deep, bleeding ulcers appeared in their stomachs and upper guts. The changes varied from slight to pronounced, depending upon the amount of extract injected.

At first, Selye thought that the changes proved that there was a new hormone in the extract. But he soon found that he could produce the same three changes by injecting extracts of kidney or spleen or toxic drugs.

Gradually, he began to realize that the reaction he was producing with his impure extracts and toxic drugs was an experimental replica of that "syndrome of just being sick" he had noted years before. Subsequently, the reaction became known as the biological stress syndrome or general adaptation syndrome.

Selye suggested the name "alarm reaction" for the initial response, arguing that it probably represents the physical or somatic expression of a generalized call to arms of the body's defensive forces.

The Three Stages

The alarm reaction, Selye determined, is certainly not the entire response. Rather, it is the initial response and can be followed by two other response stages, those of resistance and exhaustion.

In the first reaction of alarm, the brain recognizes the attack of the stressor, which may be anything from the approach of a lion to the appearance of a threatening memorandum in the office. It signals the pituitary gland to produce a hormone, ACTH, which, moving into the blood and reaching the adrenal glands, causes the latter to discharge adrenaline and other hormones. As a result, the three changes take place, and there are also effects on heart rate, blood pressure, sugar level in the blood, and other conditions.

If the stressor is extremely drastic, death may occur within the hours or days of the alarm reaction.

If the initial stage is survived, the second stage, resistance, follows. Now the fight is on—even when the body is, in effect, acting against the mind because the stressor is a psychological one. The body combats the stressor or hastens to avoid it and begins to repair the damage. The body has adapted.

But if the same threat or stressor continues for a prolonged period, the third state, exhaustion, develops. The capacity for adaptation is exhausted.

Our supply of adaptation energy, Selye believes, is finite. Once we use it up, we face senility and finally death.

We can, of course, endure stressful work for days, even weeks, and find resistance and adaptability restored after a rest. But chronic stress, year after year, eventually can use up all our reserves.

Disease of Adaptation

Since Selye first introduced the biological stress concept, there has been considerable progress in analyzing how hormones participate in stress reactions. Moreover, he now has concluded that various derangements in the secretions of these hormones can lead to *diseases of adaptation*— so called, he explains, because they are not directly due to any particular stressor but, rather, to a faulty adaptive response to the pressures induced by some stressor. Selye observes:

In this sense, many ailments, such as various emotional disturbances, mildly annoying headaches, insomnia, upset stomachs, sinus attacks, crippling high blood pressure, gastric and duodenal ulcers, certain types of rheumatic or allergic afflictions, as well as cardiovascular and kidney disease, appear essentially to be initiated or encouraged by the body itself because of its faulty adaptive reactions to potentially injurious agents.

One question which undoubtedly occurs to you is this: Why should the same stressor—for example, a reprimand from a superior or a financial worry—cause such different lesions as ulcer in one individual, migraine in another, a heart attack in still another?

This, notes Selye, has been traced to conditioning. The conditioning can be internal, as by genetic predisposition, age, or sex, for example. It can be external, too; treatment with certain drugs or dietary factors are examples. "Under the influence of such conditioning factors," Selye writes, "a normally well-tolerated degree of stress can become pathogenic and cause diseases of adaptation which affect predisposed areas of the body selectively."

A Scale of Stress Factors In Our Lives

Early in this century, Adolph Meyer, M.D., Johns Hopkins University, kept "life charts" on his patients. From these, he repeatedly found that his patients tended to get sick when clusters of major changes occurred in their lives.

Thomas H. Holmes, M.D., professor of psychiatry at the University of Washington School of Medicine, has built on Meyer's work. He drew up a list of events that seemed to play a role in triggering various illnesses: the common cold, skin outbreaks, colon diseases, tuberculosis. Some were negative events, such as being fired from a job or serving a jail term. But many were ordinary events, like a move to a new home, a new job, a promotion, a visit from an in-law.

Diverse as they were, they did have one thing in common: a change in life pattern. Holmes concluded that a person can get sick when something happens that calls for adaptive behavior or social readjustment, when coping requires effort that may weaken resistance to disease.

Holmes and a colleague, Richard H. Rahe, M.D., then gave 394 people a list of 43 life events ranging from a change in sleeping habits or trouble with the boss to marital separation or death of a spouse. The two physicians asked their subjects to rate the events as to the relative degree of adjustment called for by each.

The highest-ranking event, the one believed to provoke the most stress, proved to be the death of a spouse with a score of 100, as compared with marriage, which carried a score of 50. Others in the top ten were divorce, marital separation, a jail term, death in the family, personal injury or illness, marriage, discharge from a job, marital reconciliation, and retirement.

In further studies, individuals were asked to list by year for a number of years any major life events they had experienced. These lists then were compared with the individuals' medical histories. In case after case, the year in which several major life events occurred was followed by a year in which serious illness developed.

The greater the life change and burden of stress, the lower the body's resistance to disease and the more serious the illness that develops.

The death of a spouse is especially likely to bring on illness. Holmes and Rahe found that death is 10 times more frequent among widows and widowers in the year following the spouse's death than it is among all others in their age group. Also, a study in Sydney, Australia, showed that in the year following bereavement, 32 percent of a sampling of widows experienced a marked deterioration in health. Their illness rate was 16 times greater than that of married women of similar age and background.

Holmes and Rahe found, too, that divorced people, in the year following the divorce, have an illness rate 12 times higher than that of married people.

They also determined that the individual who accumulates a score of 300 stress points within one year has a 90 percent chance of becoming seriously ill or of having a major accident. If fewer points are experienced within one year, the odds of a major health change may be 50/50.

What is your score?

As you see, and as Dr. Holmes emphasizes, stress is not limited to negative change but may also be associated with positive events such as marriage, promotion, and personal achievement.

Even such positive events carry strain with them, however. Marriage is regarded as a happy event, yet bride and groom are under stress. Often, prior to marriage, people may have some doubts about their future spouse, themselves, and even the whole idea of marriage.

The man or woman who has worked at a job for a number of years will experience considerable anxiety and stress when suddenly promoted to a new position, even though the new role has been eagerly sought. Both the new vice president and the new office manager are likely to have some doubts as to whether they can do the job now that they have it.

A changing situation forces us to find new ways of adapting, and there can be no certainty how well the new ways will work out. There is always a possibility that we will be worse off rather than better off following change.

With change, the status quo is threatened and, no matter how poor it may seem, it provides some degree of security. Change may mean gains, but it also means loss on the psychological level. Whatever the rewards resulting from change, there is still stress because of loss of the old and familiar.

The Holmes-Rahe scale may have several values for you. It indicates the life events that lead to extra stress as perceived by a substantial sample of people. It may help you, if you are feeling stress, to realize why.

It may suggest to you the need, more or less urgent, to develop ways to cope with the stresses in your life more effectively, with much less of the wear and tear and other consequences we will be looking at in Chapters 18 through 26.

THE HOLMES-RAHE LIFE EVENT-STRESS SCALE

Rank	Life event	Mean value
1	Death of spouse	100
2	Divorce	65
3	Marital separation	65
4	Jail term	63
5	Death of close family member	63
6	Personal injury or illness	53
7	Marriage	50
8	Fired at work	47
9	Marital reconciliation	45
10	Retirement	45
11	Change in health of family member	44

Rank	Life event	Mean value
12	Pregnancy	40
13	Sex difficulties	39
14	Gain of new family member	39
15	Business readjustment	39
16	Change in financial state	38
17	Death of close friend	37
18	Change to different line of work	36
19	Change in number of arguments with spouse	35
20	Mortgage over $10,000	31
21	Foreclosure of mortgage or loan	30
22	Change in responsibilities at work	29
23	Son or daughter leaving home	29
24	Trouble with in-laws	29
25	Outstanding personal achievement	28
26	Spouse begins or stops work	26
27	Beginning or ending school	26
28	Change in living condition	25
29	Revision of personal habits	24
30	Trouble with boss	23
31	Change in work hours or conditions	20
32	Change in residence	20
33	Change in schools	20
34	Change in recreation	19
35	Change in church activities	19
36	Change in social activities	18
37	Mortgage or loan less than $10,000	17
38	Change in sleeping habits	16
39	Change in number of family get-togethers	15
40	Change in eating habits	15
41	Vacation	13
42	Christmas	12
43	Minor violation of the law	11

18.

Are You
a Stress Victim?

Although he does not look it or even know it, R.G. is a victim. At 41, a division manager in a packaged goods company, he appears calm, assured, on top of his job. Yet he has frequent attacks of neck pain. They come as often as weekly and last usually a day or sometimes two days. They can be relieved to some extent with analgesics, especially when the drugs are coupled with heat and massage. The pain, R.G. is certain, is simply the result of awkward sleeping positions he must be getting himself into.

N.D. is a victim, too. A 37-year-old executive in a financial firm, dynamic, ambitious, dedicated to her work, she appears to be happy in it. Her only concern: Every once in a while she suffers from an eczematous rash. Starting with small patches on the backs of her thighs, it weeps, itches, and spreads. It responds to her self-treatment with salves and ointments, usually with the help of a weekend she devotes to complete relaxation. She is allergic to something, she thinks, but no allergist has been able to pin down the culprit.

At 46, L.B.R. has just become vice president in a large corporation. Married for 14 years, he has three children, the oldest just reaching adolescence. His new job requires considerable traveling and he has increased his time at work. His having less time to spend with his family has led to tensions at home.

As alienation develops, he experiences some concern over his diminishing libido. L.B.R. has an extramarital affair but it arouses feelings of guilt. More and more, his job performance suffers. A major new special project, to which he has contributed significantly in the planning stage and to which he has expected to be assigned, is given to someone else.

He suffers from insomnia. He takes sleeping pills at night, "uppers" and megavitamins in the morning. But he becomes more and more moody, irritable, depressed. Less than a year after his promotion, he experiences chest pains for the first time. By the end of the year, he is drinking excessively and his marriage is on the edge of divorce. His 13-year-old daughter is arrested for the possession of marijuana.

Fourteen months after his promotion, he has a heart attack, which he survives.

Are these three persons stress victims? Very much so. And they are only three among millions of such victims.

If stress is not the *most* significant, common, and far-reaching influence on health and well-being in the United States, it ranks high.

"A Bewildering Array"

The United States Clearing House for Mental Health Information recently reported that the nation's industry has had a $17 billion annual decrease in its productive capacity over the last few years because of stress-induced mental dysfunction. Other studies estimate even greater losses (upward of $60 billion) arising from stress-induced physical diseases.

In 1977, a study done by the National Science Foundation concluded:

> Stress is a major problem in the contemporary United States. It negatively affects the daily lives of scores of millions of Americans. It causes a bewildering array of physiological, psychological and social malfunctions. On an economic level, the effects of stress probably cost the nation over $100 billion annually. Moreover, available evidence suggests that stress-related maladies are on the rise.

In the scientific literature of just the last 5 years, the number of study reports on stress has almost doubled, now totaling more than 200,000 entries.

Stress can affect people at all levels. For executives alone, one estimate has it, American industry is losing as much as $20 billion annually in lost workdays, hospitalization, and early deaths caused by stress reactions.

Today's Problems "Squeeze and Clutch"

We have seen a drastic change in the nature of sickness in recent decades.

Throughout the eighteenth and much of the nineteenth centuries, much of illness was ascribed, even though somewhat vaguely, to the mind—largely to despair and melancholy. Then Pasteur and Koch showed that germs cause disease. One after another, they and their colleagues and successors identified and began to conquer infectious organisms. Out of these advances grew scientific medicine. It was mainly concerned, at first, with all the bacteria, viruses, fungi, and other organisms capable of producing disease. And, indeed, the once-terrible infectious scourges—diphtheria, typhus, smallpox, and the like—have largely vanished. They are no longer to be found in any modern list of leading causes of serious illness and death.

Yet doctors are busier—and hospitals are fuller—than ever. Consequently, in recent years medicine has had to take another hard look at disease causes. This look has led to a growing recognition of the role of stress.

Not New, Yet Very New

Stress itself is certainly nothing new. Primitive people had their stressors—mortal combat with foes, problems of getting enough to eat, among others.

We may not face the threat of jousting with fierce animals, but we know the threat of criminal attack on the streets. In the United States, 1.3 million cases of violent crime were reported in 1980. There were 101 major crimes per 1000 persons recorded in New York City, property crimes as well as violent offenses, and this figure is exceeded by rates of 114 per 1000 in Phoenix, 129 in Newark, 143 in St. Louis, and 157 in Miami.

Even if we do not confront them in person and on the scene, we are, with our virtually instantaneous communications, almost constantly aware of threats and actualities of wars and other catastrophes wherever they occur. They do not leave us free of anxiety or disturbing dreams.

Has the machine age been kind to us? Has the automobile, for example, given us many advantages? Is it a source of joy—or stress—when you find yourself trapped in traffic on the Long Island Expressway or any of its many equivalents?

Industrialism has brought us change—and change can be stressful. Yesterday's world was relatively stable. To be sure, change took place. There is always some change. But in yesterday's world, new things came along at a slower pace. There was opportunity to assess them and their impact. We could become accustomed to them before another change had to be faced. In recent years, changes have been coming so fast that we may have lost much of our ability, individually, to adapt.

The communications overload to which we are exposed provides so much information and so many sources of information that, as often as not, the result is confusion and, with it, sometimes also a sense of insecurity.

Today's world is one of social upheaval. Once, many social institutions, marriage among them, gave form and structure and provided some stability to our lives. Today, they may no longer do so because of changing norms and patterns.

Conflict develops between parents and children. To some extent, it always has done so. But now, teenagers, backed by peer pressure and even prodded by it, reject parental values outright. Is there an "empty nest" syndrome, which affects some families when children, having grown up, move out? At the same time, are not other families experiencing a "crowded nest period," when children are grown but not yet out of the home?

Value systems are changing. Hoodlums are on the streets in vast numbers. Vandalism is commonplace. Immorality appears to be all too usual among public officials. The quality of goods and services seems to—and often, in fact, does—deteriorate. Discourtesy appears to be almost the norm.

"The Most Ubiquitous Stressor"

Change has been called the *most ubiquitous stressor* in the work setting.

It's easier, obviously, to adjust to what we consider beneficial than to what seems threatening. But, in fact, an expectation of change, whether good or bad, can be stressful, perhaps even more so than the actual change itself.

Many executives face not only the drastic change involved in loss of a job, but also the change, perhaps somewhat less drastic, of relocation—or of merger, takeover, or divestiture. Let a new executive assume command at the top and, almost inevitably, changes occur down the line, sometimes markedly altering management style. And other kinds of changes in the workplace—new equipment, new materials, new products, new job classifications—may be disconcertingly stressful.

THE STRESS OF CHANGE

Our society is quick to recognize the positive effects of change but slow to acknowledge and deal with the stresses and instability that invariably accompany it. There is no doubt in my mind that a significant part of the vague uneasiness and apprehension that so pervade our society is the result of all the changes taking place around us that we cannot control.

It's easy to become overwhelmed so that we either throw up our hands and feel there is *nothing* that we can control, or we rigidly hang on to what we have, fearing that even that will be lost. It's no wonder that people tend to resist change, and the more unstable a person's life, the more desperately he clings to what he has even if what he has isn't very good.

John C. Connelly, M.D.,
The Menninger Foundation

Stress Effects

Stress, a normal part of life, is not all bad. It may account for a lot that gets accomplished in the world.

It's another matter, however, when stress becomes too great or continues at a high level too long—and when the individual cannot cope with it effectively. It is then that stress becomes disturbing.

It can have many effects. It can trigger a physiological arousal mechanism—a series of nervous, glandular, and other reactions that involve many body systems and that may become manifest as symptoms. They may mimic symptoms of a variety of diseases, such as chest pains, palpitations, hot and cold spells, chills, shaking, insomnia, headache, musculoskeletal pains, diarrhea, choking sensations, and others.

Stress can produce an organic or a physical reaction—exacerbating an already present disease or setting the stage for a new one. It may lower natural resistance and thus allow infection or another pathological disturbance to develop.

A BIG DIFFERENCE

Dr. Jeremiah A. Barondess, president of the American College of Physicians, has noted that:

Unfortunately, in our society "physical illness" is more respectable than "mental illness"; symptoms believed to be physical in origin are more acceptable to most people than symptoms thought to be of emotional origin. Patients therefore tend to endure the consequences of stress while they're mainly emotional or psychological—and usually they don't see the doctor until they think they're sick in the more conventional sense—that is, physically. At that point, the patient's welfare depends very heavily on the physician's understanding of stress and its consequences, of how these consequences manifest themselves, and of how to differentiate the patient's symptoms from those of true organic disease.

The Curious Phenomenon

Stress makes some people tick; it sickens others. K.W. is a woman who, in her mid-thirties, has come up the organizational ladder fast— *very* fast. Recently placed in charge of rescuing a losing operation that was seemingly headed nowhere but down, she has huge responsibility. She dotes on the pressures. She is at work by 7 A.M., rarely leaves until far into the evening, and usually works Saturday. Her phone almost never stops ringing.

"My day," she says, "is very long and pressure is very much a part of my job. The pressure of responsibility, to make the operation profitable, the pressure of being a symbol of what women can do. But I need pressure to function—the more the better. It's what I run on. It motivates me."

L.M. has a different problem. He was moving up well in the company, handling one assignment after another effectively, taking the usual pressures and some unusual ones as well. Then he landed in a position under a boss who disturbs him intensely. "He makes petty demands, changes his mind constantly, and makes his job far bigger than what it really is. He makes me smaller than what I am. He wants to make me over—in his own image."

L.M. comes home at night exhausted, frazzled. He can offer his wife and kids only irritability. He feels his guts constantly tied in knots. He gets headaches—agonizing ones. He controls his feelings on the job, but it takes tremendous effort. He sticks, sickening with the stress.

It's a curious phenomenon, stress. Serious enough for anyone, very serious for some people. It's curious, too, in what it really is (there are many misunderstandings about it), the mechanisms involved in it, the marked differences in the ways in which it can affect different people.

There is growing conviction among many investigators that how people cope with stress is far more important than the frequency and severity of stress episodes. Some people cope remarkably well—almost as if by instinct. But there are other factors involved in effective coping, and they can be understood and put to use by others.

THE PRICE OF DENYING STRESS

If you hold your breath beyond your capacity while swimming underwater, you begin to panic. Your anxiety is triggered because the brain gets a warning of serious threat to the body from the respiratory system. Immediately, the brain issues orders for escape.

Normally, for example, the brain gets messages about blood pressure from nerves sensitive to pressure changes. If the messages indicate high pressure, the brain tells the heart to slow its beat and calls on blood vessels to dilate. Both responses will help to lower pressure. Interference with this process is what Schwartz calls *disregulation*. "But why," he asks, "should the brain act in this seemingly self-destructive way? One possibility is that high blood pressure offers people a short-term advantage in stressful situations."

When, for example, Rockefeller University experimenters injected rats with a drug to elevate blood pressure, they found that the animals gradually became less sensitive to electric shock and less motivated to escape it. Humans, the experimenters speculated, may develop hypertension in a similar way, in response to persistent stress. By always denying feelings of anxiety, frustration, or anger under stress, people may gradually condition themselves to raise their blood pressure.

"Messages from the arteries calling for lowered pressure," observes Schwartz, "would then be short-circuited in the cortex and ignored, until high blood pressure becomes habitual."

Schwartz's final conclusion: While the usual approach is to use drugs to treat high blood pressure—and there is a place for such intervention—the medicines often treat effect rather than cause. More promising may be measures to make people more sensitive to their bodies and capable of controlling pressure consciously, and other measures to help them handle a threatening environment in ways that make it less stressful. "In the long run," he says, "we may be better off trying to modify the causes of stress than tuning out the body's danger signals."

19.

Stress in Executive Life

At an international symposium on the management of stress held in Monte Carlo, Dr. John H. Howard of the University of Western Ontario reported on a recently completed study in which 300 managers from 12 major companies were asked what they found to be the principal sources of stress on the job. Analyzing their responses, Dr. Howard found four general characteristics of executive jobs that seem most stress-producing:

A Feeling of Helplessness Executives often see problems, understand them, find reasonable solutions for them—yet find themselves unable to act because of organization constraints. As Howard notes, feeling unable to influence a situation can be extremely stressful; power—the ability to act—is a great antidote for stress.

Overwork The sheer quantity of work is a common problem. Executive jobs often are characterized by "much work at an unrelenting pace."

Urgency   Actually, Howard looked into this characteristic in a separate study and found that, "on average, managers do something different every 7 minutes. Their jobs are characterized by brevity and fragmentation and stress."

Ambiguity and Uncertainty   Often, problems are not clearly defined; company policies are also ambiguous. When there is considerable uncertainty, decision-making is difficult.

These characteristics—"the major underlying dimensions of stress in a manager's job," Howard calls them—originate in a number of different situations, according to the study.

The Situations

Howard categorizes the troublesome situations thus:

Poor Management or Boss   This tops the list of stress sources, in the view of the 300 executives in the study. They pointed to lack of planning and direction along with chronic indecisiveness as causing the most tensions. They also noted poor communications, often caused by a failure by top management to communicate total plans.

Lack of Authority or Blurred Organizational Structure   It is most frustrating to be given an assignment and the responsibility for implementing it—and then to have no authority to properly carry out the job. This ranked as the number two stressor. Blurred organizational structure was defined in terms of unclear job descriptions and too many bosses.

Promotion and Recognition   Uncertainty about future promotion and frustration for lack of praise and recognition from top management were considered to be significant stressors by many executives. Many complained they had no idea of the criteria by which they were currently being judged or what were supposed to be the prerequisites for the next position up the line. As some put it, they often don't know which "hoops to jump through."

Basic Work Problems   These problems, common in virtually all businesses, include constant telephone interruptions, meetings that take up too much valuable time, and the inability to find time to concentrate on a single problem long enough to solve it.

Company Politics   Always a source of stress, office politics most often plays a role in promotions, transfers, division of authority, and allocation of supplies and equipment. Among the comments was this one: "There is a type of 'buddy' system among top management as they are very protective of each other. This results in the wrong people in key jobs and the right people in a position of no authority."

Personnel Problems   These problems center not only on employees unsuited to their work but also on the difficulty of handling personal problems of employees.

Volume of Work   The need for heavy volume, combined with insufficient time and inadequate staff, can be stressful, and in more ways than one. "Most managers," notes Dr. Howard, "initially blame themselves for this lack of time. They often see their inability to adequately delegate work as the culprit. However, after considerable soul searching, managers come to realize that it is frequently an impossibility to complete all the work. It is only with this realization that the situation can be solved or coping strategies devised."

Midlife Transition

Contrary to what many people think, you do not have to be over 50 to experience a midlife crisis. For many, it comes earlier.

As young executives move along in their early thirties, they often experience some reorientation in attitudes. Some begin to question their value and to wonder whether their drive to get ahead is really worth the effort. Many grapple with the idea of a possible change of career. And, commonly, there is increasing concern with "making it," a more intense recognition that how far they can advance in their thirties may have very much to do with their ultimate success.

As they get beyond 35, many of the ambitious become impatient at not moving ahead fast enough. They may intensify their efforts to get promoted. And some become increasingly resentful, and even depressed, because they are seemingly not appreciated.

The onset of middle age, usually put at about 40, often is a stressful time.

For many, as psychiatrist Theodore Lidz, M.D., has put it, the start of middle age is ushered in by several difficult years that have been termed the midlife crisis or midlife transition.

> The crisis is not set off by any significant event but, rather, by the realization that more time stretches behind than stretches before one. The balance of life is upset by awareness of the limits of life's span. . . .
>
> Two of the world's literary masterpieces start on this note. The Divine Comedy opens with the lines, "Midway in the journey through life, I found myself lost in a dark wood, having strayed from the true path." Goethe's Faust finds that although he has studied philosophy, medicine, and law thoroughly, he is fundamentally no wiser than the poorest fool, and he makes a pact with Mephistopheles in an attempt to salvage something in life.

At the start of middle age, Dr. Lidz notes, there is still time to make changes, perhaps even to start afresh, or at least to make the best of the years remaining. But there can be no further delay.

So, commonly, middle age is a time of stocktaking, of assessing how life is going to turn out. "Will dreams be fulfilled? Must one come to terms with getting by?" Dr. Lidz asks. "Or must one accept disillusionment and failure?" Then he observes:

> However, the stocktaking concerns more than external success. It has to do with inner satisfaction and the hope of achieving a sense of completion and fulfillment. Are achievements compatible with one's ego ideal derived from early expectations? How great are the disparities between one's way of life and what provides a sense of self-esteem? For some, middle age brings angry bewilderment because neglect of meaningful relationships in the striving for success makes life seem empty.

The Three Questions Faced at Midlife

Stanley H. Cath, M.D., professor of psychiatry, has, as a primary clinical interest, emotional disorders in middle and later years of life. In his view,

It is paradoxical that at the midpoint of life when one is confronted by a very personal meaning of aging through the aging and death of one's parents, one's own decline is counterpointed by the emergence, if not exploding into life, of sexuality and creativity in one's offspring. Most families experience these developments as a critical challenge of transition, albeit in slow motion. As a common heritage, the decades after age 35 contain at least three questions.

- With whom do I live, age, and relate in this way?

- How much longer do I have to live at my best, or to correct my ways?

- How will I age, with what human supports, and how will I die— with integrity or despair?

Every reflective human being goes through a series of self-monitoring inventories and self-assessments, a life review, a reassessment of goals. . . . The task of confronting the self is enormous.

Loneliness and the Image

In a study made for the American Management Association by Ari Kiev, M.D., professor of psychiatry at Cornell University Medical College, and researcher Vera Kohn, covering 2659 executives in top and middle management one of the questions they asked was: Who is the person with whom you can talk about your personal internal problems and concerns?

Typically, 60 percent of the executive husbands answered thus: "I don't want to burden my wife. She does not understand my business problems and she wants to talk about the world when I come home. In fact, there is nobody I could really trust."

One executive even added solemnly, "And when I want to talk to my dog, he runs away!"

Yet the most common complaint of the executives' wives, that is, of 45 percent of the women questioned, proved to be: "My husband never talks. I hear about the things which happened from others weeks later at social meetings."

It's a fact that many executives, as they advance up the ladder and take on more responsibilities, become more isolated and independent at a time when they most need emotional support. Many balk at sharing their worries at home for fear of appearing weak or inadequate. The very personality traits that help to make for the successful executive — drive, combativeness, emphasis on individual strength and ability — can also make it hard to recognize when stress is getting out of hand. And they can make it still harder to seek help.

In many cases, there are symptoms that signal distress, including extreme irritability, sleeping difficulties, waning appetite for food or sex or both, frequent headaches, and periods of deep "blues." They may be so frightening that the executive feels they must be kept submerged.

And, too often, submerged they remain despite their effects on performance and productivity; sometime later, they become somatized into physical disturbances and can be treated as a "real illness."

20.

Stress and the Heart

At a recent American Heart Association meeting, Eugene Sprague, M.D., was given an arteriosclerosis research award for young investigators. The brilliant young University of Texas scientist had pointed to a mechanism by which stress is related to atherosclerosis, the artery-clogging disease that leads to heart attacks and strokes.

Sprague had been studying seventy-seven Air Force pilots, including some with atherosclerosis. He had found that those with evidence of the artery disease also showed aberrant levels of cortisol, the adrenal gland hormone whose release is known to be promoted by stress.

Usually, our cortisol level is highest at about 8 A.M. and then gradually decreases until about 3 P.M., when it begins to rise back to the 8 A.M. level.

But, in the pilots with atherosclerosis, the 8 A.M. levels, although not unusually high, did not decrease as much as did those of the pilots without significant artery disease. In the latter, cortisol declined from 19 milligrams per deciliter of blood to 8 milligrams between 8 A.M. and 10 A.M., but the levels of pilots with atherosclerosis declined in that time from 20 to 12 milligrams.

To determine whether the change in cortisol concentration could be playing a role in atherosclerosis, Sprague set about reproducing the higher cortisol levels of the atherosclerosis pilots in adult male monkeys. Some of the monkeys were placed on a high-cholesterol diet; others received both a high-cholesterol diet and cortisol.

After a year, the animals were sacrificed and their arteries were examined. Approximately twice as much area was affected by atherosclerosis in arteries from the monkeys getting the combination of high-cholesterol diet and cortisol as in the others.

"I expected to see an increase in atherosclerosis in the monkeys on the high-cholesterol, high-cortisol diet, but I was surprised it was so high," Sprague says.

The Sprague study is only one of the latest indicating stress as a significant promoter of heart disease.

THE HEAD AND THE HEART

The observation that in humans, the head can influence the heart is hardly new. Almost 2000 years ago, a first-century Roman physician, Celsus, recognized that "fear and anger and any other state of the mind may often be apt to excite the pulse."

In 1628, William Harvey, discoverer of the fact that blood circulates in the body, reaffirmed Celsus's observation by noting that "every affection of the mind that is attended with either pain or pleasure, hope or fear, is the cause of an agitation whose influence extends to the heart."

Later, the interrelationship between psyche and heart was noted by the great eighteenth-century Scottish physician and physiologist John Hunter, in a self-fulfilling prophecy: "My life is at the mercy of any scoundrel who chooses to put me in a passion."

Human Heart Attacks and What Precedes Them

Irving S. Wright, M.D., is a distinguished cardiologist who has served as national chairman of the Intersociety Commission for Heart Disease Resources. At a special symposium on stress a few years ago, he made a point of noting that while some skeptics had doubted over the years whether stress could be related to a sudden heart attack, experienced physicians have seen many examples. He reported:

> In my own experience, these have occurred many times after business failure, indictment for a crime, death of a spouse—how often a partner of many years dies shortly after the death of the first—anger at a business meeting, and so forth. . . .
>
> Sports events now are recognized as a very common precipitating cause, so much so that mobile coronary care units are increasingly used at race tracks and football stadiums. Their use has been more commonly for the spectators than the athletes. Some patients cannot even tolerate exciting sports events or other stressful shows on television without angina or serious reactions.

Recently, Canadian physicians published a study on the immediate antecedents of heart attacks in 102 active men, between 30 to 60 years of age. On the day of the attack, twenty-four of the men had experienced unusual annoyance; twenty-seven had had to face an unusual business problem; twelve had been bothered by an unusual social or domestic problem; and four had had an unusual financial problem.

More recently, Dr. James E. Skinner and colleagues reported an intriguing observation:

> Medical researchers have shown that a variety of severe life stresses, among them bereavement, marital troubles, job insecurity, even carrying a large mortgage, are often associated with heart attacks. But they have been unable to describe the exact mechanism that leads to these puzzling cases when an otherwise healthy person suddenly drops dead.
>
> My colleagues and I may now have discovered a missing piece of the puzzle. Recent studies in our laboratory show that heart rhythm and force of contraction are regulated by the frontal cortex of the brain, the same center that mobilizes the body and focuses the sensory receptors when an animal is threatened. Under extra stress, the frontal cortex may—by a process not yet fully understood—send heart muscles into fatal fibrillation [a useless quivering of the heart].

The Type A Personality

Most commonly, heart attack victims have coronary heart disease caused by atherosclerosis, or the laying down of fatty deposits that narrow the channels of the coronary arteries that feed the heart muscle. Investigators over the years have established a whole series of influences—risk factors—that are likely to bring on the disease: high levels of blood fats, high blood pressure, family history of heart disease, obesity, sedentary living, cigarette smoking.

But not all heart patients have high cholesterol levels; not all are hypertensive; not all have an impressive collection of other risk factors. And even when many such factors are present, there is no certainty that a heart attack will ensue.

Because largely physical factors alone do not provide the complete answer, many researchers have come to consider that stress can be a major influence. And, of late, more and more have been concluding that so-called Type A behavior is a prime candidate as a major psychological cause of heart attacks. In a nutshell, those who exhibit Type A behavior live under nearly constant stress, and much of that stress is self-imposed.

Although the connection between the A behavior pattern and coronary heart disease was first proposed in 1959, almost two decades passed before it received any general acceptance. In December 1978, a panel of twenty-five distinguished cardiologists, epidemiologists, and psychologists met under the auspices of the National Heart, Lung and Blood Institute of the National Institutes of Health to review the available data on Type A behavior. They concluded that it was indeed a serious risk factor for coronary heart disease.

One possible reason for the delay has been recently noted by one of the originators of the Type A concept, Meyer Friedman, M.D., who has observed:

> We were taking what is widely believed to be just the sort of behavior and personality necessary for successful living in Western society and calling it a disorder. And many of our fellow cardiologists themselves suffered quite severely from this same Type A behavior.

The Clues

More than 40 years ago, Drs. Karl and William Menninger of the Menninger Clinic were among the first psychiatrists to become interested in studying the personalities of patients suffering from coronary heart

SELF-EVALUATION: THE GLAZER-STRESSCONTROL LIFE-STYLE QUESTIONNAIRE*

As you can see, each scale below is composed of a pair of adjectives or phrases separated by a series of horizontal lines. Each pair has been chosen to represent two kinds of contrasting behavior. Each of us belongs somewhere along the line between the two extremes. Since most of us are neither the most competitive nor the least competitive person we know, put a check mark where you think you belong between the two extremes.

	1	2	3	4	5	6	7	
1. Doesn't mind leaving things temporarily unfinished	—	—	—	—	—	—	—	Must get things finished once started
2. Calm and unhurried about appointments	—	—	—	—	—	—	—	Never late for appointments
3. Not competitive	—	—	—	—	—	—	—	Highly competitive
4. Listens well, lets others finish speaking	—	—	—	—	—	—	—	Anticipates others in conversation (nods, interrupts, finishes sentences for the other)
5. Never in a hurry, even when pressured	—	—	—	—	—	—	—	Always in a hurry
6. Able to wait calmly	—	—	—	—	—	—	—	Uneasy when waiting
7. Easygoing	—	—	—	—	—	—	—	Always going full speed ahead
8. Takes one thing at a time	—	—	—	—	—	—	—	Tries to do more than one thing at a time, thinks about what to do next
9. Slow and deliberate in speech	—	—	—	—	—	—	—	Vigorous and forceful in speech (uses a lot of gestures)
10. Concerned with satisfying himself, not others	—	—	—	—	—	—	—	Wants recognition by others for a job well done
11. Slow doing things	—	—	—	—	—	—	—	Fast doing things (eating, walking, etc.)
12. Easygoing	—	—	—	—	—	—	—	Hard driving
13. Expresses feelings openly	—	—	—	—	—	—	—	Holds feelings in

14. Has a large number of interests   Few interests outside work, Ambi-
                                                                                   tious,
15. Satisfied with job   — — — — — — —   Wants quick advancement on job
16. Never sets own deadlines   — — — — — — —   Often sets own deadlines
17. Feels limited responsibility   — — — — — — —   Always feels responsible
18. Never judges things in terms of   — — — — — — —   Often judges performance in terms of
    numbers   — — — — — — —   numbers (how many, how much)
19. Casual about work   — — — — — — —   Takes work very seriously (works
                                             — — — — — — —   weekends, brings work home)
20. Not very precise   — — — — — — —   Very precise (careful about detail)

SCORING: Assign a value from 1 to 7 for each score. Total them up. The categories are as follows:

Total score = 110–140: Type A$_1$.   If you are in this category, and especially if you are over 40 and smoke, you are likely
                                         to have a high risk of developing cardiac illness.

Total score = 80–109: Type A$_2$.   You are in the direction of being cardiac prone, but your risk is not as high as the A$_1$.
                                         You should, nevertheless, pay careful attention to the advice given to all Type A's.

Total score = 60–79: Type AB.   You are an admixture of A and B patterns. This is a healthier pattern than either A$_1$ or
                                         A$_2$, but you have the potential for slipping into A behavior and you should recog-
                                         nize this.

Total score = 30–59: Type B$_2$.   Your behavior is on the less-cardiac-prone end of the spectrum. You are generally re-
                                         laxed and cope adequately with stress.

Total score = 0–29: Type B$_1$.   You tend to the extreme of non-cardiac traits. Your behavior expresses few of the re-
                                         actions associated with cardiac disease.

This test will give you some idea of where you stand in the discussion of Type A behavior that follows. The higher your score, the more
cardiac prone you tend to be. Remember, though, even B persons occasionally slip into A behavior, and any of these patterns can change
over time.

* This questionnaire was designed by Dr. Howard I. Glazer, director of behavior management systems at EHE Stresscontrol Systems, Inc.

disease. They noted that many such patients appeared to be aggressive—but under the surface.

A decade later, another psychiatrist, Flanders Dunbar, examined a large group of coronary patients and found them to be hard-driving individuals with single-direction personalities seeking refuge in work. She also concluded that they had less interest in sports, more illnesses, and less sexual tranquillity than noncoronary subjects.

Almost at the same time, another distinguished psychiatrist, J. A. Arlow, found that these coronary patients seemed to share a secret insecurity, a belief that they were shams. Because their real accomplishments failed to assuage that belief, they had an incessant need to go after new successes.

But it remained for Dr. Friedman and his colleague, Ray H. Rosenman, M.D., to establish, much later, an impressive case for the importance of personality and behavior in coronary heart disease.

The Testing

In 1955, Drs. Friedman and Rosenman became distinctly impressed by the presence of certain traits, later to be identified as indicative of Type A behavior, in almost every one of their middle-aged and younger coronary patients. They were traits not seen nearly so often in patients with noncardiac disorders.

Friedman and Rosenman proceeded to do a simple thing that brought a jolting response. They questioned some 200 business executives and about 75 physicians who were treating heart patients. What, in their opinion, caused heart attacks in friends and patients? Three-fourths of both the doctors and the executives incriminated the same things: excessive drive and deadline-meeting.

Friedman and Rosenman then asked a group of laypersons to select from among friends and associates those who seemed most obviously to have a pattern of Type A behavior. The names of eighty-three men were furnished. Union executives then were asked to choose, from among members of their organizations, eighty-three individuals who exhibited most obviously just the opposite behavior pattern, Type B. In addition, the investigators studied forty-six blind men who manifested chronic anxiety and insecurity.

The dietary intake of total calories, total fats, and animal fats was investigated and found to be essentially the same for all three groups, as was the amount of physical activity. Blood and electrocardiographic studies were made.

The findings: 23 of the 83 Type A men (28 percent) showed evidence of coronary heart disease, while only 3 of the Type B men (4 percent) and 2 of the 46 anxiety cases suffered from the disease. Thus, Type A men had 7 times as much coronary heart disease as Type B men.

Those figures do not mean that any large group of Type A people will have 7 times as much disease as a large group of Type B's. For, in this study, most of the Type A and most of the Type B persons chosen as obviously "typical" were of the fully developed or extreme type. The researchers later found a much lower proportion of the fully developed cases in large, unselected groups. But the results do suggest that subjects with Type A behavior are relatively prone, and those with Type B are relatively immune, to early occurrences of coronary heart disease.

Women were also studied: 125 with Type A and 132 with Type B behavior, all chosen by lay people. Most of the A's worked in industry or the professions; most of the B's were primarily homemakers. The A women turned out to have almost 5 times as much coronary heart disease as the B women.

Interplay: Type A, Stress, and Heart Attack

For years, working at the University of Texas, Dr. David C. Glass, a psychologist, has focused his research on the interplay between Type A personality, life stress, and heart attack.

As he has noted, stress can make a heart attack more likely by increasing levels of cholesterol in the bloodstream. Also, it can cause the same result by increasing blood pressure so that blood passing through the arteries under high pressure increases the likelihood of tears in the arterial walls, around which fatty deposits can form. Further, stress can cause release of hormones which, in the process of mobilizing the body to cope with danger, speed up blood clotting, increasing the likelihood that a vessel-blocking blood clot may form.

In his own laboratory, Glass has found high cholesterol levels in extreme Type A men as young as 19 years of age. He has also determined that in Type A men, blood pressure increases sharply when hostility is aroused. Moreover, the blood-clotting time of Type A is significantly faster than that of others and, Glass notes, some evidence indicates that they react to stress with greater hormone secretion.

Glass has also found that in Type A's, the push to achieve leads them to press their bodies to the limit. He asked subjects to walk continuously on a motorized treadmill at increasingly sharp angles of incline until they gave up. Every few minutes, as they walked on the treadmill, they rated their level of fatigue. Glass then measured the subjects' aerobic capacity individually to see how close they had pushed themselves to their lungs' capacity to absorb oxygen.

Type A subjects reached 91.5 percent of capacity; Type B's, only 82.8 percent. "Even so," says Glass, "A's admitted to less fatigue than B's did. The hard-driving A's ignore or deny their body's tiredness in their struggle to attain their goals—in this case, a superior performance on a treadmill."

As Glass sees it, Type A persons have to master challenges out of a need to control their world, and the concept of control helps explain under which circumstances such persons are more vulnerable to heart attack. Given concern about controlling the environment, a Type A person should be upset by threats to that control, and even more distressed when a threat is beyond the person's control so that, regardless of effort, he or she can do nothing to master the situation.

In one study, Glass compared a group of men aged 35 to 55 hospitalized for heart attack with a group hospitalized for other kinds of disease and with healthy, nonhospitalized men. The heart attack victims had stronger Type A patterns than either of the other two groups. But Glass comments:

> Of greater interest, though, were their scores on a Loss Index, a 10-item scale that asks a person to describe the incidence during the last year of stressful events in his life over which he had minimal control, such as a loved one's death, being fired, or a significant financial loss. Within the year preceding their illness, both hospitalized groups experienced more such losses than had the healthy group. Life events that leave a person feeling bereft and helpless can lead to disease. In the face of uncontrollable losses, a Type A person is likely to have a heart attack, while one lower in Type A traits will more often develop some other disease.

Sudden Death

That stress may produce sudden death is no new idea. Since biblical times, instances have been noted of the apparently sudden deaths of people while gripped by rage, fear, humiliation, and even joy.

Is there any scientific foundation for the idea? Many animal studies have strongly associated psychological stress with abnormal and fatal heart rhythms. Moreover, the most effective way of inducing such stress and its fatal consequences has been to subject animals to situations beyond their control.

It is difficult, of course, to conduct controlled studies with humans to establish a relationship between stress and sudden death. But there have been instances in which eletrocardiographic monitoring of the hearts of humans performing stressful tasks has shown serious, even potentially fatal, rhythm disturbances.

For example, investigators have reported the case of a 38-year-old man with conflicts about his work who was studied 6 weeks after a heart attack. During an hour-long interview, his heart rhythm was continuously monitored while his facial expressions were filmed. As judged from the filmed interview, periods of stress correlated well with the appearance and frequency of abnormal rhythms. During treadmill-exercise stress testing, however, very few such rhythms developed, suggesting that the man's heart was more sensitive to emotional than to physical stress.

There have been other significant studies as well. Some years ago, researchers investigated a then remarkable community in Pennsylvania, Roseto, where rural people of Italian descent consumed a diet very high in fats and cholesterol, yet had a very low death rate from heart attacks. The families were closely knit and stable. But more recently, with increasing urbanization, disruption of family units, and growing stress, the sudden-death rate of Roseto has risen markedly and is approaching the rates of nearby communities.

Several studies have shown the correlation between recent bereavement and sudden death, especially among men. In one study, the mortality rate for widowers in the year following bereavement was 12.2 percent, compared with 1.2 percent in a matched group of married men of similar age and background.

It has been noted, too, that among patients recovering from heart attacks, sudden deaths occur significantly more often in conjunction with rounds by the chief surgeon than at other times. These deaths, according to investigators, are provoked by the patient's excitement, anxiety, and sometimes disappointment in relation to his or her progress and prospects for quick discharge from the hospital.

Hypertension

High blood pressure, as we saw in Chapter 4 in the section on nutrition, is a serious health problem. (See pgs 50–55 for a discussion of what hypertension is, how it is measured, how it affects your body.) High blood pressure can be the result of kidney disease. Some cases stem from tumors, often benign, of the adrenal glands. But in 90 percent, or even more, of all cases of hypertension, there is no such organic cause and the hypertension is called "essential" or "primary," that is, of unknown cause.

But, even though exact causes are unknown, certain predisposing factors have been established.

Heredity is one. If, for example, one of your parents is hypertensive, chances that you will develop the disease are 2 to 3 times greater than for the general population.

Obesity is another factor. Studies have shown that among men and women over 35, the incidence of hypertension averages twice as high in the obese as in the normal population. Also, clinical studies have found that blood pressure commonly declines when excess weight is lost.

Excess salt in the diet is still another significant factor. Studies have shown that primitive tribes, for example, without salt in their diet suffer no hypertension. Even at age 60, men of one Brazilian Indian tribe have been found to have blood pressures averaging 100/60.

Stress as Culprit

Many studies have demonstrated the marked effect of stress on blood pressure.

Researchers have monitored blood pressures of several dozen men whose jobs were threatened. They checked pressures for each man while he was anticipating loss of his job, as soon as he knew he had lost it, during the time he was out of work, during trial reemployment, and finally, when he had a regular job again.

They found that pressures stayed high all through the period of stress, which lasted from the time of threatened job loss right through to the time when regular work could be resumed; only when the men felt secure once more did pressure drop.

In experiments at Michael Reese Hospital, Chicago, persons with normal blood pressure were deliberately exposed to anger-provoking situations. In those who bottled up their anger, blood pressure shot up; in those who freely vented their anger, there was less elevation.

As the American Heart Association has pointed out:

> Wrapped up somehow in the whole business of high blood pressure is the subject of emotion. When a person is angry or afraid, his blood pressure may go up. It may increase just because he knows he is going to have his blood pressure taken. Rises like these, during times of stress, are perfectly normal.
>
> But some individuals react to even mild life stresses with an excessive rise in blood pressure. (When the stress has passed, the blood pressure returns to normal.) These men and women are called hyper-reactors or pre-hypertensives. Chances are that in time many of them will develop hypertension. Their bodies simply get used to responding to daily life as if it were a series of emergencies.

The significance of stress in hypertension is highlighted by the fact, too, that while drugs are effective in lowering elevated pressure, in many cases such stress-reducing techniques as biofeedback and meditation reduce the quantity of drugs needed or even eliminate any need for them.

21.

Stress and the Gut

Tom Little first appeared at New York Hospital in Manhattan in 1941. As a child, Tom had swallowed steaming-hot clam chowder which burned and blocked his esophagus, making it useless. He required surgery to provide an artificial, external opening into his stomach. At the age of 9, he learned to chew his food, remove it from his mouth, and introduce it into a funnel attached to a rubber tube leading to his stomach. Later, he married, and only his family and close friends knew about his injury; he never ate with others.

Then one day in New York, while doing physical labor, Tom began to bleed from the stomach opening. Apparently his movements at work had irritated the area. He had to be hospitalized, and while he was recovering in the hospital, two medical researchers, Drs. Stewart Wolf and Harold Wolff, then investigating the effects of emotions on the body, persuaded him to be a subject for the study.

The two researchers noted that when Tom became resentful or angry, his stomach changed, much as if it were about to receive a meal, its pink color becoming red and its juices flowing freely. When food was introduced, it would be out of his stomach in less time than usual because of the excessive gastric juice flow.

On the other hand, when he was sad, fearful or depressed, the stomach lining became pale, secretions decreased, and, when depression was severe enough, even introduction of food made no difference. The stomach remained pale and juice flow was restricted. When food was introduced while he was depressed, it might remain in the stomach, undigested, for many hours.

Unpleasant consequences can arise from such emotionally induced effects on the stomach. For example, excessive acidity, when stimulated by anger or other emotions, may aggravate or even possibly induce a peptic ulcer. If some of the excess acid is carried with a gas bubble back from the stomach and up into the esophagus, there can be heartburn.

Nor are the consequences of emotional disturbances limited to the stomach. Anger, resentment, anxiety, humiliation, and feelings of being in overwhelming situations can increase mucus and other secretions in the intestines and increase contractions and other activities there, producing diarrhea and other discomfort. Depression, fear, dejection, feelings of futility or defeat can have the opposite effects, producing constipation and other disturbances.

Behind Indigestion

It goes by many names: dyspepsia, upset stomach, nervous indigestion, acid indigestion, acute indigestion, or just plain indigestion. Few of us escape an occasional experience.

It can sometimes produce midriff discomfort, or, sometimes, upper abdominal pain and distention, gas, belching, nausea, and heartburn singly or in combination.

Stress, of course, is not the only cause.

Possible triggers include gallbladder or liver disease, kidney stones, peptic ulcer, appendicitis, intestinal obstruction, food poisoning, or milk or other food intolerance.

For some people, eating food with high fat content, partaking liberally of such foods as cucumbers, beans, radishes, cabbage, turnips, or onions or such seasonings as garlic, chili, or pepper can produce it.

Normally, stomach mobility or food-churning and food-mixing activity is stimulated when the stomach is only moderately full. With overeating, the activity is inhibited, causing sensations of fullness and nausea. Foods high in fat or fried in fat also tend to slow stomach activity and prolong the stomach's emptying time. Thus, an excess of fatty food can have the same effect as overeating.

Stress can enter the picture in the same way, and in other ways as well. Fear, shock, depression, or other emotional upset tends to slow stomach activity. Eating during an emotional upset may involve eating too rapidly, chewing inadequately, and swallowing a lot of air.

Rapid eating and inadequate chewing of food can prod the stomach into secreting more acid to aid digestion of the food chunks. The additional acid, combined with excessive air swallowed during hurried chewing and swallowing, can irritate the stomach lining.

Mild indigestion often will disappear if you do nothing more than not eat for a few hours. Some relief, too, can be obtained by lying down on the right side, a position that puts gravity to work to help the stomach move its contents along to the small intestine. Antacids, although certainly not essential, may help to provide relief.

When indigestion is severe or occurs frequently or chronically, medical advice is needed. The possibility of organic disease has to be considered. But when such disease is exonerated, the likelihood, for a busy executive under stress, is that stress is the culprit and that the solution to the problem lies in better means of coping.

The Irritable Bowel: Common "Nervous" Gut

It *is* extremely common—so common that as many as half of all the people with abdominal complaints have it, and some estimates go as high as 60 percent.

It is *not* just a matter of abdominal pain alone or constipation alone.

Its symptoms can be highly variable. There may be abdominal distention; sharp, knifelike or deep, dull abdominal pain; cramps that may mimic those of appendicitis when they occur on the right side (but they sometimes occur on the left).

Frequently, victims suffer from constipation, sometimes alternating with diarrhea. Sometimes, stools appear pencillike. Some victims see "pus" or "worms" in the stools; they are, in fact, large amounts of mucus.

Many victims complain of lack of appetite in the morning, nausea, heartburn, or excessive belching and, not uncommonly, of weakness, palpitation, headaches, sleeping trouble, faintness, and excessive perspiration.

Life-threatening? Not at all. The condition never leads to cancer and very rarely to any serious complications. But the symptoms can be distressing.

The irritable bowel syndrome comes down to a disturbed state of intestinal mobility—with no anatomic cause.

The Disturbed Balance

An abnormality in the behavior or function of an organ or part of the body in the absence of organic disease is known as a *functional disorder*.

The colon (also called the large intestine or large bowel) consists of the last 5 feet of the digestive tract. Its main function is to conduct indigestible portions of food or waste material out of the body. Any disruption of this function can lead to symptoms. But it does not mean that the colon is damaged or diseased.

A Stress Factor

Although knowledge of why the colon malfunctions in the absence of organic disease is incomplete, certain causative factors are well established.

Biological predisposition may be a factor. In some people more than others, colonic activity may be more susceptible to disturbance. There seems to be some tendency for the irritable bowel syndrome to run in families.

In the particularly susceptible, many agents may irritate the colon and trigger symptoms. In some cases, coffee, alcohol, spices, salads, and certain other foods can provoke attacks. There are those who are allergic or highly sensitive to certain foods. Milk-sugar intolerance, for example, is a common problem, but one readily treated by avoidance of milk and milk products.

Infections, acute illness, environmental factors, or even a weather change may bring on symptoms.

There is some evidence that inadequate dietary fiber may be a factor for millions of Americans who eat highly refined, overprocessed carbohydrates. In some cases, benefits have been reported from a switch to a high-fiber diet or from the use of a high-fiber supplement such as bran.

But there is no question about the role of stress. "In most patients," reports that American Digestive Disease Society, "the symptoms stem chiefly from emotional stress."

It has been noted that stress is commonly associated with the appearance of symptoms and that still more stress exacerbates the symptoms. Some studies have even shown that symptoms sometimes correlate with a victim's particular mood; that patients experiencing pain and constipation are full of anger while, in contrast, patients with diarrhea are more anxious and feel helpless; and the very same patient may have both types of symptoms, depending upon his or her mood.

Peptic Ulcer

Is It Really the "Executive Wound Stripe"?

So it's been frequently called. But the definition is a myth.

Executives get ulcers. So do a lot of other people. Although the incidence of ulcer in this country has been declining a little, the disease still affects 10 percent of the population at some time in life. There are estimates that more than 20 million Americans now have, or have had, the problem.

But any idea that ulcer disease is limited to people in high-pressure jobs has been—or certainly should have been—outmoded years ago. One possible reason for the notion that it is the hard-driving executive who gets the ulcer may be the executive's greater likelihood to seek medical care promptly.

Blue-collar workers as well as executives get ulcers. Several investigators have found that deaths from ulcer are more common in people at the lower socioeconomic levels than in those at higher levels. Looking at occupations, one study found that streetcar conductors show the highest incidence of ulcers. Another study, in Norway, found that fishermen have the highest rate in that country.

But none of these observations means that stress plays no role in ulcer development. It can be very much in the picture along with other factors.

The Hole and the Gnawing

An ulcer is simply an open sore, a hole or erosion, that can occur anywhere in or on the body. But the most common type is the peptic ulcer. There are two types of peptic ulcer: duodenal and gastric.

Duodenal ulcers are found in the duodenum, the first part of the small intestine, lying just outside the stomach. They are about 10 times more common than gastric ulcer—ulcer of the stomach.

Pain is the most common symptom. Usually, it is not sharp but, rather, a gnawing or burning sensation somewhat like a hunger pang. The pain of a gastric ulcer will come on one-half to 2 hours after a meal; that of a duodenal ulcer, 2 to 4 hours after eating.

ULCER MYSTERIES

There are still many puzzles surrounding peptic ulcer. One is why ulcer symptoms peak in autumn and spring; another is why bleeding from an ulcer is most frequent between September and January. Another puzzle is new: why has ulcer incidence dropped over the past few decades?

Ulcers were almost unknown in Europe before 1900. In England there were only about 70 known cases during the entire nineteenth century. But they started increasing about the time of the First World War and by World War II had become an extraordinarily common disease.

Nobody knows why the incidence started to decline. Certainly stress has not decreased. In England during World War II, the number of cases of perforated ulcers, so bad that the acid had eaten completely through the lining of the stomach or duodenum, increased in the cities that the Germans were bombing. When the Nazis shifted their bombing sites, perforated ulcers increased in people who lived in the new target locations.

The cause of the pain is unclear, but it may be related to the corrosive action of acid and pepsin on the open sore in the empty stomach or duodenum. It is often relieved by eating or by an antacid that neutralizes the acid.

Although ulcers themselves are not killers, about 12,000 Americans die each year from complications. Internal bleeding can occur when an ulcer erodes an artery. Or an ulcer can perforate the stomach or duodenum, allowing contents to leak out and cause peritonitis, a serious inflammation. An ulcer can cause internal swelling, thus obstructing vital passages.

Ulcer Causes

Many details of the ulcer mechanism have yet to be worked out. But some are clear.

The stomach secretes hydrochloric acid to aid digestion. Even when the stomach is empty, there is a normal intermittent flow of the acid; after a meal, there is a much greater flow. The acid, strong enough to dissolve even iron, does not dissolve the stomach itself because of the protective effect of the mucus secreted by the mucus glands. There is also mucus protection in the duodenum.

An ulcer may develop if there is an excess secretion of acid by the stomach or an alteration of the mucus coating.

Some ulcer patients have been found to have 2 to 4 times as many acid-secreting cells as normal. One possibility is that the large number may result from hereditary influences. Another is that extra cell formation may occur because impulses through the vagus nerves are excessive, calling for increased acid secretions, which may trigger development of more cells in response to demand.

Overactivity of the vagus nerve leading to excessive acid secretion sometimes may result from disease elsewhere—diabetes or chronic lung disease, for example. Acid production may also be increased by alcohol and smoking.

And emotional stress, including aggravation, anxiety, and worry, can trigger the vagus nerve that connects the brain and stomach.

Some studies have indicated increased anxiety in ulcer patients; others have shown that acute stress preceded the onset of ulcer. But many people under even prolonged stress do not develop ulcers.

It appears that stress, or, more accurately, inadequate coping with stress, can play a significant role in ulcer formation, especially when coupled with other factors, including heredity. (Ulcers are about 3 times more common in close relatives of afflicted persons than in the general population.)

Ulcer Healing

Ulcer treatment is directed at facilitating healing.

Often, the key measure is intensive antacid therapy. Antacids, which neutralize hydrochloric acid, have been found to be most effective when taken 1 hour after meals and at bedtime.

Other medication sometimes may be prescribed if needed: anticholinergic drugs that inhibit acid secretion; antispasmodic agents that relax stomach and intestinal muscles; and sedatives. Now in common use is a fairly new drug, cimetidine, a type of antihistamine that is a powerful inhibitor of acid secretion.

The traditional diet of milk, crackers, and other soft, bland foods, long rigidly prescribed for ulcers, has largely been scrapped. Evidence has accumulated that shows such a diet does not work and that, in some patients, it may be so burdensome that it leads to production of even more acids than rich spicy food.

Many physicians now encourage ulcer patients to eat almost anything they enjoy. What possibly should be avoided, however, are alcohol, drinks containing caffeine (coffee, tea, cola) and aspirin, which stimulates acid secretion.

When medical treatment fails or when there is a threatening complication, surgery may be required.

Is Psychotherapy Necessary?

Unless there is a severe, deep-seated neurosis, psychotherapy is probably not required. But stress factors are important in determining response to the treatment of an ulcer and the likelihood of its recurrence.

The distinguished Walter C. Alvarez, M.D., of the Mayo Clinic, observed:

> Commonly the biggest factor in the production of an ulcer is a psychic one. A hundred times, after a patient has been operated on, I have seen him get a new and terrible ulcer as soon as he ran into a new emotional jam. And a hundred times, I have seen a man lose his ulcer symptoms the day he achieved mental peace.

It can be vital for an ulcer victim to understand the stressful factors involved in this condition and to adopt effective techniques of remedying or modifying them or of coping with them positively.

22.

Headaches, Backaches, Neckaches: The Stress Influence

An enterprising pharmaceutical firm, one that specializes in developing prescription drugs for headaches, recently conducted a survey to determine whether people in some jobs get headaches more often than those in others.

"One of the things we wanted to know was whether or not life in the boardroom causes headaches," remarked an executive of the drug company. "And we discovered that more often than not, it does."

The survey found that 90 percent of chief executives experience headaches regularly, while the average for the general population is 70 percent. The majority of the executives reported having two to four headaches a week, each one lasting between 1 and 2 hours. But, perhaps to the drug company's dismay, while 80 percent use nonprescription remedies, less than 20 percent use prescription painkillers.

Are the survey results valid? Are there that many headaches at the top?

Others involved in headache research agree. "If you sent questionnaires to everyone who made $200,000 and up, you'd probably find that 90 percent of them were headache sufferers," remarks Dr. Fred Sheftel, a cofounder of the New England Center for Headaches.

"The corporate world is not necessarily one that pins medals on individuals who are footloose and fancy-free," Dr. Sheftel adds. "Control of feelings is prized. Particularly anger. And anger, when suppressed, gives rise to tension headaches."

But these problems are scarcely limited just to top executives; they are frequent and sometimes chronic among executives from the lower levels up. Not just headaches, but neckaches and backaches as well, are among their most common afflictions.

The Nationwide Headache: Headaches

An estimated 45 million Americans (one-fifth of the population) suffer from severe and sometimes disabling headaches. They lose 124 million workdays a year at a cost of $6.2 billion. They spend $1.2 billion on headache remedies, most often aspirin and related compounds. Headache was the principal cause of an estimated 18,341,923 visits to physicians during 1977–1978, the latest period for which the National Center for Health Statistics has figures.

Headaches, as you might suspect, come in many varieties. Some can be indications of such potentially catastrophic illness as brain tumor, cerebral hemorrhage, or meningitis. But such headaches are relatively uncommon.

There are some queer varieties, or so they may seem. You can get headaches from excessive caffeine intake in the form of coffee, tea, or cola drinks. We have known chronic sufferers who have been amazed at their freedom from "brow-busters" once they have cut back from 6, 8, or 10 cups of coffee and several cola drinks daily.

But it is not only too *much* caffeine that can produce headaches; too *little* can sometimes be responsible. So, if you are a heavy imbiber and want to cut down, do so gradually.

For example, there is now an explanation for why some people have weekend and holiday headaches. Late sleeping leads to early morning deprivation—and headaches—in those used to large amounts of caffeine-containing beverages taken early in the morning on weekdays.

Caffeine withdrawal can also account for the headaches of many people who, for religious or other reasons, fast even for just one day. One way of getting relief is to use a suppository containing 150 milligrams of caffeine, prepared by a pharmacist on prescription, on the morning of the fast.

The explanation may seem bizarre, but sleeping with bedcovers pulled up over the head is a recently reported headache cause. Called the "turtle headache" by the physician who literally uncovered it, it produces pain all over the head, but is greatest in front. Some of the victims are awakened by it during the night; others get it on awakening. Cure for the problem, which may be the result of oxygen shortage, is to keep the covers below one's head.

There are also the headaches caused by eating cured meats. Such meats (frankfurters, bacon, salami, ham) often contain nitrites, chemical preservatives. In the nitrite-sensitive person, they can kick off trouble.

But by far the most common form of headaches are migraine (affecting some 15 million Americans) and tension headaches (affecting close to 30 million). In both these types stress is a major factor.

Tension (Muscle Contraction) Headache

It's a generalized, steady ache. The pain is dull, bandlike. Some victims describe the pain as a feeling of tightness or as a sensation that the neck and upper back are in a cast. The headache may last for several hours, occur daily, several times a week, or several times a month. Records at some headache clinics indicate that 30 percent of patients have at least one headache a day and 20 percent have constant pain.

The tension headache, the most common kind, is related to chronic contraction of muscles about the head and neck. The reason that such muscle contraction produces headache is simple to understand. If you were to clench your fist tightly and keep it clenched, you would feel an ache very soon. And with prolonged clenching, you would develop pain similar to that of headache.

When a job requires a fixed head position—for example, because of driving against bright headlights—we often set the muscles of neck, jaw, and scalp in pain-causing postures.

But we commonly do the same thing as part of a reaction to stress. One theory holds that the setting, the muscle contraction, may be a trait carried over from our early ancestors and associated with their fight-or-flight reaction. Great apes, for example, upon assuming an aggressive stance, commonly tighten muscles to pull their heads down between their shoulders.

Tension headache victims have been said to "symbolically carry a great weight on their shoulders." Upon feeling anxiety, boredom, frustration, harassment, or other reactions to stress, they may set neck, jaw, and scalp muscles and thus develop a headache.

Muscle contraction almost always accompanies migraine. One fact, often unappreciated, is that a migraine sufferer may get muscle contraction headaches as well—combined with, as well as separate from, migraine headaches.

Migraine

While tension headaches often appear late in the day as pressures mount, migraine may start on awakening in the morning.

Actually, there are two forms of migraine: classical and common.

The *classical* starts with constriction of blood vessels. At that point there is no pain. In this prodromal period, forerunner to the headache, there are sensory disturbances such as the perception of supposedly flashing lights or other visual abnormalities including blind spots. Some victims complain of frequency of urination at this point.

Then, in about half an hour, the blood vessel constriction is succeeded by blood vessel dilation. Now comes the pain. It's mostly one-sided, often toward the eye, aching or throbbing, beating with the pulse. Often it's accompanied by nausea, vomiting, and sensitivity to light, so the victim seeks a darkened room if possible.

Common migraine develops without the prodrome of visual phenomena. The pain of common migraine is as likely to be on both sides of the head as on one.

Migraine can be induced by factors other than stress. Certain foods, including chocolate, nuts, citrus juice in large quantities, and aged cheese, as well as alcoholic drinks, can trigger an attack. Rapid changes in hormone levels, as some women experience during ovulation or before menstruation, can account for migraine. So can rapid change in blood sugar level, as in people after oversleeping or fasting.

But stress is the major initiating factor in migraine, although the migraine attack often does not begin until the stress is over. And this occurrence of headache following, rather than during, stress, some authorities maintain, can be a distinguishing feature of migraine.

Combating Chronic Headaches

For a tension headache, heat, massage, a hot shower, an aspirin or another pain reliever often helps.

Once a migraine attack occurs, ergotamine tartrate may be used to cut it short. In some cases, another drug as well—aspirin or another analgesic—may be needed to affect the accompanying tension headache.

Drug therapy may be helpful in staving off future attacks of migraine. Recently, the drug propranolol (Inderal), an agent often used for high blood pressure, has come into increasing use as a preventive to migraine.

In victims of chronic tension headaches, mental depression is sometimes a factor. Treatment with an antidepressant drug may relieve both the headaches and the depression.

When at all possible, even if not easy, the victim's best means of combating stress-related headaches of either type is to determine the causative stressors and eliminate or avoid them if feasible or to learn to cope with them more effectively.

Biofeedback, as we shall see in Chapter 26, can be of great value for many chronic headache victims, providing control often without need for drugs.

The Aching Back

If the estimates are right, on any day in the United States, some 6.5 million people are victims of backache.

The bad back has even become somewhat fashionable, a kind of "in" misery. "It has emerged," observed a popular magazine article some years ago, "as such a status symbol that sufferers boldly and openly proclaim their affliction by the way they stand—with pelvis thrust forward and one hand held casually astern in the vicinity of the fifth lumbar region."

It has been said, too, that backache has become "in" almost because of a prevailing idea that once a sufferer, always a sufferer, and that, if you have to live with an affliction, you might as well be proud of it.

A cliché would have it that ever since humans stood upright on two legs instead of crawling around on all fours, they were doomed to ache behind. But, since millions maneuver through life without ever having a twinge, the inevitability thesis has to be considered with some skepticism.

There is also an idea that once a backache victim, ipso facto, always a victim. A common notion seems to be that there are no practical known ways to avoid backaches. Most stem from "slipped" or ruptured disks, which means surgery, which is hopeless.

But all these assertions are nonsense.

The 81 Percent Likelihood

To be sure, a backache can come from a herniated disk.

The spinal column, or backbone, is a column of separate bones or vertebrae—33 of them stacked upward from the sacrum to the base of the skull. Within them is the spinal cord with its nerve cables emerging from the brain. Between each vertebra and the next is a disk, a circular cushion of connective tissue and cartilage, roughly ¼- to ¾- inch thick. The disks serve to absorb the impact of body weight and movements.

In themselves, vertebrae have no stability. Ligaments, tough and fibrous, run between them and bind them together. But more than ligaments are needed to keep the spinal column upright. Muscle action is required. It is so necessary that fainting, which interrupts muscle activity, results in immediate collapse.

There are some 140 muscles attached to the spine and they perform prodigious work. Say you weigh 180 pounds and bend forward. The muscle force needed to keep you from toppling over will be 450 pounds. And if you are carrying a 50-pound weight, the force will have to be 750 pounds.

The "slipped disk" you hear so much about is really a misnomer. A disk does not slip. Actually, in the case of a so-called slip, the rim of the disk weakens and tears, and part of the soft, gelatinlike center, the nucleus pulposus, becomes extruded. The extruded (herniated) portion may press on sensitive nerve roots, producing pain.

A disk can herniate when its tough outer rim is injured severely enough—suddenly, during a bad fall or other serious accident, or gradually, through years of constant jarring activity.

Pain may originate, too, from arthritic changes in the spine. Occasionally, it may arise from conditions removed from the spine—for example, gallbladder disease, peptic ulcer, colitis, sometimes even heart disease.

But in the great majority of cases, backache has nothing to do with any of these conditions.

Some years ago, 5000 consecutive cases of back pain were studied by a combined medical group from New York and Columbia Universities. In 81 percent of the cases—somewhat more than 4000 of the 5000—the backaches were related to muscle problems.

The Clenched Muscle Factor

The most common cause of recurrent backaches is muscle tension, or spasm.

Muscle spasm means continued, involuntary contractions of muscle. If you have ever experienced an eye tic, for example, you have had one, usually minor, form of spasm.

Spasm can have useful purposes. If a joint, for example, is injured, muscles about the joint will contract and stay contracted, serving as a kind of splint to protect the joint. If a muscle is injured or under excessive strain, it may go into spasm, and so may other nearby muscles, in an effort to splint the strained muscle and thus to prevent further damage.

Spasm can be very painful. The pain results from lack of nutrition. In muscle, as in other body tissues, blood carrying oxygen and nutrients come in through arteries; after delivering its cargo, it picks up waste products from muscle cells and leaves through veins. It is through thin-walled capillaries, very tiny vessels lying between arteries and veins, that oxygen and nutrients move from blood to muscle cells and in turn move waste from cells to blood.

When muscles contract, capillaries are squeezed shut. Normally, the contraction is brief and the exchange of material goes on normally. But with spasm, the exchange process is impaired. Waste products, including lactic acid, can produce pain when they remain in a muscle. Lactic acid, especially, is an irritant to nerve endings. Moreover, a muscle in spasm is working, since it is contracting, and the lack of oxygen causes muscle tissues to cry out in pain.

Spasm and Stress

Muscle spasm can be induced by injury or excessive demand. Strain a back muscle by lifting a heavy load—or even a moderate one in the wrong fashion—and you can expect spasm.

Excessive demand on muscles is not a matter only of lifting. You have seen guy wires supporting a telephone pole. Stomach muscles act somewhat like guy wires for the spinal column. When these muscles are weak, as they commonly are because of lack of adequate exercise, we have a tendency to fall backward. But we maintain balance by shifting body weight, leaning forward slightly, and hanging our weight on muscles of the back. This solution, however, puts excessive loading or demand on these muscles. They can become fatigued, a condition that increases the likelihood of spasm.

Moreover, emotional tension can induce spasm, and it commonly does. It arouses muscle tension, which is a normal biological response to emotional tension. Muscles tense to make possible fighting or fleeing. But in many instances, however provoked we are by emotional stress, we can neither fight nor flee. Our bodies are prepared for physical action of some kind but we take none—at least, none of the fighting or fleeing kind.

Nevertheless, our muscles tense in the situation, and they may remain tense, in a state of semicontraction, even during sleep, for days, weeks, or months.

This is chronic muscle spasm. Depending upon the muscles most sensitive and most involved, it may lead to headache or neckache or backache. It is a very common factor in backache.

Stress, sometimes enough in itself to trigger spasm and pain, often is a compounding influence. Over a period of time, a chronically tensed muscle can shorten and lose its stretch; this limitation may induce painful conditions. It can also lead to awkward movements, which would make the muscles more susceptible to injury.

Combating Backache

Stress-related backache can be prevented, and it can be combated once it occurs.

The immediate cause of pain, as we have noted, is spasm. Not only does the spasm lead to pain; a vicious cycle can be set up, with the pain then leading to more spasm, which, in turn, can lead to still more pain.

For relief, both spasm and pain must be attacked.

A backache attack, even a severe one, often can be relieved with relatively simple home remedies if they are used properly. But aspirin or an equivalent pain reliever is not likely to be enough. Taking a pain reliever should be the first step, but treatment should not stop there.

- Lie down with as little delay as possible. Apply heat, using a heating pad wrapped in a Turkish towel. After 30 minutes or so, change position to avoid stiffness. (For some people, cold may provide quicker relief than heat; if you are one of these people, gently rub the painful area with ice cubes or crushed ice in a pillowcase.)

- Follow this treatment with a gentle rubdown of the painful area with any commercially available counterirritant.

- Continue taking aspirin or its equivalent, such as acetaminophen, two tablets every 3 to 4 hours as needed.

- Repeat the hot or cold applications. If heat helps and you can get into a tub, take a 30-minute hot bath and repeat several times.

- By the next day, you may find the pain beginning to ease. Continue the pain reliever and the hot or cold applications. As the pain lessens, begin gentle exercises, moving arms and legs, arching and curving the back.

It is the combination of measures, directed at the spasm as well as the pain, that often works.

Neck Pain

Another favorite target of stress-induced chronic muscle tension, as we have noted, are the muscles of the head and neck, with resultant tension headaches.

Some people develop toothaches from the tension of jaw muscles. If this tension goes on long enough, bones in the gums may be affected and premature tooth loss may result.

Neck pain, too—with or without headache—commonly involves stress-induced muscle tension. Chronic neck pain almost invariably stems directly from persistent spasm of neck muscles. This is the spasm that can develop as the result of acute muscle stretch from whiplash movement of the head in an accident. It sometimes arises from irritation of the nerve roots supplying the neck muscles, with the irritation coming from osteoarthritis of the spine in the neck region.

It may also be the result of, or may be aggravated by, stress.

Stress-induced spasm often affects the trapezius muscle, which runs from the middle of the back up the tips of the shoulders and attaches to the occipital protuberances, two projections of bone on the lower part of the back of the skull.

When the trapezius goes into spasm, it can tug strongly on the periosteal covering of the skull, a fibrous membrane, producing painful constricting headaches. When in spasm, it can also produce neck pain and, sometimes, pain in the upper back.

And there are many opportunities for the trapezius to go into spasm.

You may have noted that a cat, when alarmed or otherwise disturbed by something, usually arches its back and hunches its shoulders. In this way, it is preparing to pounce or to flee. We humans go through much the same procedure even if not so obviously. Often, we tend to elevate the shoulders just a bit when under stress. Even though not very great, the elevation can be enough to contract the trapezius muscle. And, like any other muscle, the trapezius, if contracted long enough, can go into spasm.

Combating Neck Pain

If you suffer from frequent neck pain caused by tension, you might try relatively simple measures to help reduce their frequency and severity.

- On any day, and especially on a day full of stress, take a brief time out to elevate your shoulders. Bring them up close to your ears, then shake them down. Wiggle your shoulders up and around. Roll your head around, too, in gentle circles. In carrying out these movements, you are, of course, contracting muscles. But you are also causing the muscles to relax and the relaxation helps to prevent spasm.

- If spasm-induced neck pain does appear, keep in mind that as the spasm triggers pain, the pain in turn leads to more spasm. The cycle must be interrupted as soon as possible. In addition to aspirin or another pain reliever, the technique mentioned earlier for relieving muscle spasm affecting the back often can be used effectively for relieving tension neck pain.

- Heat or cold can be applied to the trapezius muscle in the back of the neck. A counterirritant, too, may be used, often more effectively when it follows heat application.

- Massage can be useful. With your fingertips, rub the area from the back of your skull down your neck and across the top of your shoulders, repeating the procedure several times.

23.

Depression: "Dark Night of the Soul"

Abraham Lincoln went through recurring bouts of depression that began in young manhood. Nathaniel Hawthorne at one point became so overwhelmed that for 12 years he rarely left his room. "I have made a captive of myself," he wrote Longfellow, "and put me into a dungeon, and now I cannot find the key to let myself out."

Winston Churchill called his depressions "my black dog." Once, he recalled, "for two or three years, the light faded out of the picture. . . . I sat in the House of Commons but black depression settled on me."

While experiencing depression, F. Scott Fitzgerald described it by writing, "In a real dark night of the soul, it is always 3 o'clock in the morning."

Much of their suffering could have been relieved today. Of all mental illnesses, depression has come to be recognized in recent years as the most common.

Studies by the National Institute of Mental Health reveal that an estimated 8 million Americans are suffering from depression serious enough to require treatment, that 125,000 are hospitalized each year for the condition, and that probably another 200,000 should be hospitalized. These figures, however, may be conservative; some authorities have estimated that the number of depressed people is as high as 15 million.

"A lowering or decrease of functional activity. Absence of cheerfulness or hope: emotional dejection." This is one dictionary definition. But it hardly begins to picture the distressing human experience.

Who are the victims? Almost anyone can be, at any age, in any station in life, male or female.

And, because stress can foment depression, it is no stranger in the lives of many executives, although it is not always recognized early enough as depression.

The Real Thing: How Serious Can It Be?

Severe depression is something quite different from the ordinary blues. It hangs on; it can be overwhelming, making it difficult, sometimes even impossible, for its victims to function. At the very extreme, it can lead to suicide.

But, short of that, consider a case of severe depression in a 49-year-old executive vice president of a major industrial company.

It infiltrated R.D.'s life over a 3-month period. At first, he simply felt extraordinarily tired. "A terrible tiredness," he called it. He had been entirely well before, and had enjoyed his work very much. But now it became burdensome. He had to put out great effort to do his desk work. Without even fully realizing what he was doing, he found excuses for avoiding his usual business trips.

In another few weeks, he was experiencing generalized aches and pains. He was an excellent squash player but now he stopped playing: He was too tired, too achy, and he felt a mounting fear that he might suffer a heart attack. Day by day, he felt worse and worse. Living through the day became an effort. He found himself not wanting to wake up in the morning. At that time, he felt worst of all.

He had begun to worry about a possible heart attack when he had experienced some shortness of breath. Now lack of breath intensified. So did sleeping difficulty. He could fall asleep all right. But he was up, unable to get back to sleep again, hours before it was time to get up for the day. He was experiencing headaches, very severe. And he felt tight pains in the back of his neck all the time, sometimes spreading behind his eyes.

There was a hospital workup. Many tests were taken. All were negative.

Diagnosis: Depression.

The Continuing Cloud: Symptoms and Disguises

Significant depression can produce a wide range of physical, emotional, and mental symptoms.

Depression has been called the *great masquerader* because often, despite mood and behavioral changes, physical symptoms seem overriding. Fatigue and slowing of physical and mental energy are prominent. There may also be appetite loss and digestive difficulties, heart palpitation, insomnia, headache, reduction or loss of sexual drive, dizziness, and visual disturbances.

Frequently, a victim's concern with physical discomforts may be so great that little attention is paid to the other indications of depression or they may be thought to be the results of the physical symptoms. And, commonly, when medical help is sought, the patient may detail the physical complaints and fail to mention others.

Unless the victim is aware of the importance of the mood and behavioral disturbances, or unless the physician is alert to the possibilities and makes an effort to ferret them out, treatment may be focused— uselessly—on the symptoms instead of—beneficially—on the causes.

Some studies have indicated that the elapsed time from onset of depression to its recognition can range up to 36 months, during which time patients, if they receive any treatment, often may be treated for other illnesses.

One recent study involved 100 consecutive patients seen at the University of Mississippi Medical Center and Jackson Veterans Administration Hospital, who were referred by physicians and found to be depressed. Many had seen physicians on several occasions because of sleep disturbances, had asked for sleeping pills, and, in almost 100 percent of the cases, had received them, though the depression was overlooked.

Many others had been treated with analgesics for aches and pains; some had received antacids; still others had been given antinausea drugs. When carefully interviewed at the Center and the Hospital, they admitted to many other symptoms suggesting depression.

Causes

What actually brings on depression?

Many investigators believe that some underlying genetic or biological vulnerability is involved, but having this predisposing factor does not mean that the illness is inevitable.

"The situation is somewhat analogous to diabetes," says Frederick K. Goodwin, M.D., distinguished researcher at the National Institute of Mental Health. "Someone who has an inherited vulnerability to diabetes may not get it if that person keeps his or her weight under control. The same is true of depression except that here we're talking about the interaction of psychological and biological factors."

Stress is the major psychological factor in depression.

"Most depressions are brought on by stress events—principally stress due to a loss," says Richard C. Proctor, M.D., professor in the Bowman Gray School of Medicine of Wake Forest University.

Triggering loss can be of many kinds. "You may lose someone you care about very much through death, divorce, or just because that someone has moved to another part of the country," observes Dr. Proctor. "The loss could be more personal. What is more personal than losing your hair, putting on too much weight, or realizing one morning when you look in the mirror that you are not 18 years old or even 38 years old anymore?"

Dr. Proctor continues:

> Here are other examples: The esteem in which you may have been held by others might be shattered. This can cause stress, just as can loss of self-esteem or self-confidence. What of loss of your security, or your cherished dream or a symbolic loss, you might ask? Often, it is not so much who is lost, but what is lost and the "what" will vary from one person to another. What is important to one individual may be not as important to another.
>
> Whether you are part of the management structure of a large corporation or running your own business, there can be an unending list of stresses coming from your work. You may feel lonely or develop feelings of inadequacy. Adapting to an unaccustomed social position or a new culture and environment can bring on stress.
>
> If personal values run counter to values in your business, that

can precipitate guilt, which in turn is followed by depression and anxiety.

Treating Depression

It may be hard to believe that only 300 years ago in Europe and Great Britain, depression victims were likely to be chained in rat-infested prisons. And in the early days of the United States and for decades thereafter, the depressed and other mentally ill persons were stored in infamous "snake pits" that passed as mental hospitals. Even early in the nineteenth century, some American physicians were using such treatments as purgatives and a "tranquilizing" chair that restrained the patient with leather straps and wooden helmet and looked somewhat like the modern electric chair.

With the development of modern psychiatry, we now have a therapeutic, rather than a punitive, approach to emotional and behavioral disorders, and treatment for depression has become increasingly effective. For the depressions that primarily involve a psychological state with sadness, loss of interest, hopeless feelings, and inability to enjoy, some form of psychotherapy is often helpful. When a depression is severe enough to disturb sleep, inhibit appetite and energy, and interfere with normal functioning, antidepressant medication may be needed. In many cases, a combination of drugs and psychotherapy is successful.

In one study of patients with moderately severe depression, drugs and psychotherapy as treatment were compared. The investigators determined that:

Patients who got drugs alone had marked improvement in the physiological symptoms of depression. Sleep, appetite, energy level, and ability to function all returned essentially to normal. But low self-esteem and interpersonal difficulties remained.

With psychotherapy alone, self-esteem and interpersonal relations improved but the physiological symptoms did not.

Patients who received both drugs and psychotherapy improved in both areas.

No matter which treatment or combination of treatments is used, it is even more important than many realize that treatment continue past the point of feeling a little better to the point of assurance that recovery is well on the way. Meanwhile, medications can be lessened in strength and other types of treatment decreased in frequency, until full recovery occurs.

Drugs for Depression

Many antidepressant agents are available and new ones keep coming. Some examples of those in common use are Tofranil, Elavil, Aventyl, Pertofrane, Norpramin, and Sinequan.

Commonly, antidepressants take about 3 weeks to begin to work and another few weeks to exert their full effects. The drugs are not identical chemically, and a person who does not respond to one may respond to another. All told, about 80 percent of people with major depressions will have a virtually complete remission with one or another of the drugs, according to reports.

Side reactions, when they occur, are usually more annoying than serious. The most common are dryness of the mouth and some constipation. For the first few days of treatment, there may be some sleepiness, and occasionally a patient may feel a bit unusual or peculiar for a brief period. When side reactions are troublesome, a switch may be made to another antidepressant which, in the individual case, may combat the depression with fewer, less bothersome, or no undesirable effects.

Psychotherapy

Psychotherapy is often a valuable aid to the depressed patient. It may be used to uncover the emotional background of distress and to help change personality and living patterns so that recurrence of depression is less likely.

Although a number of techniques are used in psychotherapy, there are basically two approaches: insight-oriented treatment and behavior-centered treatment.

With insight-oriented therapy, an effort is made to uncover the roots of the patient's emotional problems, to find the emotional factors involved in the depression. The objective is to increase the patient's understanding of his or her own behavior and not solely to attack the symptoms. This therapy suggests that earlier events, even those occurring in childhood, may exert a powerful influence on later behavior.

Behavior-centered psychotherapy, in contrast, is aimed at modifying behavior directly rather than by probing into underlying causes. The goal is to help the depressed person to get rid of old, bad habits and to acquire new responses to stress.

In recent years, group psychotherapy has become common. It is based on recognition that psychological disturbances are often a product of relationships with other persons—and that learning new ways of interacting with others is often best achieved in a group that offers opportunities for such interaction.

24.

Stress and the Woman Executive

Women executives, of course, encounter many of the same stressful problems that men do. They may experience quite a few others as well.

As women have begun to take their place in increasing numbers in American offices, no longer only as clerical helpers but also as professional colleagues and executives, it has seemed to many men that the office is no longer what it once was, a kind of male club.

Men have had to make adjustments. No longer appropriate are some of the old, easy ways of relating among men—the jokes and bantering. To some men, having a woman boss has loomed as awkward, even to some extent threatening.

On the other hand, for women, the office may still seem to be a male club, strange and hostile.

In a recent report dealing with occupational stress, Dr. Tobias Brocher of the Menninger Center for Applied Behavioral Sciences talked of "the growing number of female executives in an all-male world who are in isolated positions, surrounded by men who are either courteous in a stereotyped but phony way, or openly hostile and derogative in their competition."

"Ulcers, gastrointestinal disorders, and emotional distress prevail in these women as a result of common male prejudice," Dr. Brocher remarked.

Recently, too, Dr. Leon J. Warshaw, also a specialist in occupational health, observed:

> In part, the woman worker's problems reflect the fact that she is a newcomer. . . . As a colleague put it, "She doesn't know how to behave in that male locker room and the men don't quite know how to react to her presence."
>
> The aggressiveness that the woman has to muster to enter this domain and her justified resentment in instances when she had to be better qualified and accept lower pay to win the job are sometimes translated into an abrasiveness that makes her hard to take.

Some studies have suggested that a woman who gains a leadership position can expect, almost as a matter of course, to meet resistance from the staff—and the resistance may not be confined to men only. Accustomed to having a male leader, both male and female workers may feel that they cannot be properly represented by a woman. They may assume that the man to whom she reports may be the real authority, threatening the integrity of the group.

Some men in the group may also make some effort to undermine a woman executive's authority by covertly performing functions that should be hers and by treating her not as a superior but as an equal.

Stereotypical attitudes

Despite the gains of women in recent years, there still remain, even if a little less widespread, some stereotypical attitudes which hamper the full utilization of women in management.

Some employers hold the view that it does not pay to train or promote women, especially in professional or managerial positions, because they will marry and leave the company, thus causing an investment loss to the employer.

Yet, this allegation was refuted in a study by the Aetna Life Insurance Company as far back as 1973. It showed that women in technical, supervisory, and managerial positions turned over at the rate of 8.5 percent a year, while men in comparable jobs turned over at a 9.0

percent rate. Absence rates were found to be identical for men and women, which, the U.S. Department of Labor points out, is also consistent with the national data.

Still, it is often argued that if women in management fail to move ahead as far and as fast as men even when both have equal credentials, such as an M.B.A. degree, slower advancement is to be expected, for women bear the brunt of family duties. They are more likely to work only part-time for some period in their careers and to turn down assignments requiring travel and long hours because of child-rearing responsibilities.

A study shedding light on these questions was conducted by Columbia University's Center for Research in Career Development. It considered forty men and forty women graduates of the 1969 through 1972 classes at Columbia's Graduate School of Business, all carefully selected so they had comparable social, economic, and academic backgrounds.

The study found that among the women earning over $50,000, some 65 percent were married, as compared with about 60 percent of those earning less than $50,000 (and about 75 percent of the men in the group). Moreover, two-thirds of the married women earning over $50,000 had children.

Mary Anne Devanna, research coordinator at the Columbia center and the author of the study, says: "There isn't any overwhelming indication that women have to give up human roles to succeed." Family concerns, she adds, "aren't what is keeping women from getting ahead."

Conflicts

The difficulties encountered when juggling a busy career with a demanding home life can take a heavy toll, however.

M.T., a 28-year-old account executive for a large Wall Street brokerage firm, is married to a busy lawyer. They both have full days professionally that leave them tired at the end of the day. They also have a 3-year-old child who requires attention from both of them evenings and weekends.

For the past year, there has been increasing friction concerning M.T.'s domestic role. Although they employed a daytime baby-sitter, the responsibility of preparing dinner and keeping the apartment clean had routinely been accepted by M.T., while her husband spent time with

STEREOTYPES OF THE WOMAN EXECUTIVE

Unlike men, women who strive do not automatically get community approval, spouse appreciation, and peer-group support. They are accorded just the opposite, suggests S. P. Hersh, M.D., in his book *The Executive Parent*. He writes:

"When executive women are overtly aggressive in their pursuit of excellence and/or success, they quickly become aware of uneasiness, guardedness, and disapproval in others. Women executives are clearly more hard put to find the sources of emotional sustenance that assist *everyone* in life, whether the stresses they deal with are ordinary or great.

"They are constantly drained of energy by conflicting demands, double messages, and opposing expectations. To cope, they mobilize styles of behavior, "marks," and other defenses. The struggles to mobilize these defenses can produce subclinical depressions that evolve into chronic mood states of dissatisfaction and feelings of isolation.

"In their attempts to cover these states, women executives not infrequently resort to increased activity or the actual assumption of one of the expected caricature roles, such as the 'aggressive, castrating bitch,' the 'deceptively helpless, manipulative maneuverer,' or the 'seductive, moody, loyalty-changing climber.'"

Yet, Hersh points out, women who cope successfully with "these incredibly challenging stresses" do exist. They are able to remain in touch with themselves; they deal with the system without letting it distort their basic values and without making the kinds of accommodations that lead to chronic repressed anger.

There are other sources of stress on women executives, including what Hersh terms "the reality that if they choose to be executives *and* have husbands and children, they take up a struggle which puts them in the category of 'superfemale,' 'supermomma,' and 'superwoman.'"

The energy required of such women is extraordinary, says Hersh:

"They have little time for insight and introspection as they superhumanly switch roles from executive to homemaker (another form of executive), to wife, mother, and lover. Usually, a woman handles this struggle by creating stages in her life (mother stage, work stage, and many other variations on this theme) or by compartmentalizing her activities while relying heavily on housekeepers and relatives to fill in for her at home."

their son. They rarely had an evening out, since they felt the obligation to stay home at night. M.T. increasingly resented this aspect of her domestic role, and her feelings led to frequent disagreements that resulted in marital discord and the onset of frequent tension headaches.

During her company-sponsored physical examination, the physician noted that M.T. complained of fatigue, yet had trouble sleeping at night. The EHE doctor asked M.T. to return with her husband for an appointment with the staff psychologist. Subsequently, they were advised about the importance of sharing at home; taking turns with meal preparation and playing with their child; getting a baby-sitter two nights a week to allow an evening out with each other and/or friends; and getting away with the entire family on weekends to avoid the necessity of domestic preparations. They were also convinced by the psychologist that their combined professional income was substantial enough to hire a regular housekeeper to handle the routine cleaning and upkeep of the apartment. In addition, with the help of a learned relaxation response, M.T. is sleeping better and has far fewer headaches.

If both spouses are busy executives, they must work together in a spirit of sharing and mutual cooperation and remember not to be pennywise and pound-foolish. Investing wisely in domestic help provides vital time for important family relationships to develop.

Working Women and Heart Disease

By entering the 9-to-5 rat race, have women increased their risk of developing coronary heart disease (CHD) over what it would have been had they remained housewives?

Generally no, according to a study by Drs. Suzanne Haynes and Manning Feinleib of the National Institutes of Health's Heart, Lung and Blood Institute Epidemiology Branch. The 8-year study, using data from the Framingham Heart Study (which began in 1948), concluded that working women did not have significantly higher incidence rates of CHD than housewives. However, some exceptions were found when women were placed in specific occupational and marital categories.

Beginning in 1965, a 300-item psychosocial questionnaire was given to 1319 participants (352 housewives, 387 working women, and 580 men). The questionnaire assessed employment and occupational status, personality types, situational stress, reactions to anger, sociocultural mobility, and family responsibilities. The participants were aged 45 to 64 and were free from coronary heart disease at the start of the study. Occupations were classified in three categories: white-collar, clerical, and blue-collar.

A working woman was defined as one who had worked outside the home for more than half her adult life. Regardless of employment status (currently employed, unemployed, retired), women reported more symptoms of emotional stress than men. In addition, working women experienced more job mobility than men, more daily stress, and more marital dissatisfaction than housewives or men. All these differences were statistically significant.

Although the overall data indicates that working women did not experience statistically different incidence rates of CHD than housewives (7.8 versus 5.4 percent), women in clerical occupations had nearly double the incidence of CHD (10.6 percent) than housewives had. CHD rates were also higher among working women who were, or had been, married, especially for those who had raised three or more children.

The study results indicate that women in clerical positions (secretaries, stenographers, bank clerks, bookkeepers, and sales personnel) are at a higher risk of developing coronary heart disease than other women. The risk increases with family responsibilities (that is, having children), and is greater (21.3 percent) if a woman in a clerical occupation has children and is married to a man doing blue-collar work. The most significant predictors of CHD among women in clerical occupations were suppressed hostility, having a nonsupportive boss, and lack of job mobility (staying in the same job for a long time).

Previously, it was thought that a man's lifespan was shorter than a woman's because of the man's occupation. Researchers were fearful that with more and more women entering the work force, the incidence of chronic disease such as CHD in these women would begin to show the same mortality statistics as for men.

Dr. Haynes noted that "the Framingham data show that employment of women, in itself, is not related to an increased risk of coronary heart disease. In fact, the women who were employed the longest period of time—the single working women—had the lowest rate of CHD."

25.

Coping Effectively

A poem called "The Shoelace," written by Charles Bukowski, contains these lines:

> It's not the large things that
> send a man to the
> madhouse...
> not the death of his love
> but a shoelace that snaps
> with no time left....

But why? How come so much impact, conceivably, from a minor nuisance?

Dr. Richard S. Lazarus, a distinguished University of California stress researcher, likes to refer to those lines from "The Shoelace" to make a point: When people get upset over what appear to be trivialities, it's because, for them, the trivial symbolizes something of great import.

When the shoelace breaks, the psychological stress, Lazarus points out, can stem from the implication that you are unable to control your own life, that you are helpless in the face of stupid trivialities, "or,

284

even worse, that such things happen because of your own inadequacies in the first place."

But there is another, more broadly significant, point to be made: Stress is neither good nor bad in itself. The effects of stress are not determined by stress itself, but by how we view and handle the stress, by how we appraise and adapt to an event.

We either handle it properly or let its negative effects get the better of us and we suffer distress.

Tuning In

To make stress work for you instead of against you, a first vital step may be to recognize that you are overly stressed, possibly distressed, in one way or another. The recognition process may seem, at first glance, to be unnecessary. Yet our experience at Executive Health Examiners is that executives, like a lot of other people, often tune their bodies to tune out the fact that they are miserable. They keep going on automatic pilot.

Our experience, too, is that while there are a substantial number of valuable techniques for combating stress, the starting point for effective use of one or more of them almost has to be your own recognition that stress is getting to you.

If these are your particular responses to stress, you should be aware of them.

Ten Stress Signals You Should Heed

- Are you finding yourself restless and seemingly unable to relax?

- Are you irritable and given to anger if things don't go your way?

- Do you have periods of prolonged or excessive fatigue?

- Do you have concentration difficulty?

- Have you lost interest in your usual recreational activities?

- Are you worried about things that worry can't help?

- Are you working excessively even if not entirely effectively?

- Are you taking more and more work home?

- Are you smoking more? Drinking more?

- Do you suspect now and again that you are losing, or have lost, perspective on what's really important in job and family areas, and maybe in life?

The Competent Copers

People differ in their ability to cope with stress-producing situations. What distinguishes the more successful copers from the less successful ones?

In trying to find out, John M. Rhoads, professor of psychiatry at Duke University School of Medicine, carried out an interesting study with fifteen men he knew personally to be "effective, successful, and physically and mentally healthy." The group included corporate vice presidents and several physicians, lawyers, and academics. All had a work week of at least 60 hours.

The subjects completed a questionnaire on lifestyle, attitude toward work, and personality. Results were compared with an earlier study of fifteen professionals who worked equally long hours but who had developed a syndrome of "overwork" characterized by exhaustion states mimicking serious physical illness.

"Long hours of work," Dr. Rhoads determined, "are not what makes one ill. If the work is enjoyed and provides a reasonable amount of freedom of time and judgment away from immediate supervision, there is no good reason for an individual to become ill. Linked to the work situation are personality factors that enable the individual to cope.

"Perhaps the most striking" of these personality features, Rhoads reports, "is the ability to postpone thinking about problems until it is appropriate to deal with them."

All the healthy, successful subjects had this ability. In contrast, the overworked men "were never free of ruminating or of being obsessed about work problems, often to the point that it interfered with the ability to do anything else," Rhoads found.

Although the overworked were in jobs giving them some freedom and independence, they could not tell when they were working so hard that they had gone beyond their endurance. As their productivity diminished through exhaustion, they lengthened their already-long work-day to try to compensate.

In contrast, the healthy men were able to spot fatigue. Most responded by quitting work early or taking time off within a week. They differed from the overworked in other important ways: They avoided stimulants, tranquilizers, alcohol, and tobacco abuse; they scheduled and enjoyed vacations; they had stable family situations; they had the ability to form and maintain friendships.

Almost to a man—fourteen of the fifteen—the healthy subjects engaged in regular physical exercise; the overworked men were, almost to a man, sedentary.

The healthy subjects, Rhoads found, also were more likely to have interests outside their work and had a high degree of altruism as reflected by their charitable contributions. They also had what Dr. Rhoads called a "crucial" attribute: a sense of humor and ability to laugh at themselves, while the overworked subjects were notable for their lack of humor.

Although many people utilize the variety of relaxation techniques described in Chapter 26, there are other, less structured pastimes that may be equally effective in helping you slow down and relax. Some of the more common diversions noted by the clients of Executive Health Examiners are reading, listening to music, gardening, painting, sculpturing. There is something for everyone. For example, one of our patients, R.P., is the very successful president of an international conglomerate. As you can imagine, the stress and tension of supervising profit centers worldwide are imposing. However, this individual copes very effectively with his demanding schedule. As well as exercising moderately, he raises exotic orchids, and each evening after returning home, he retreats to his greenhouse for 30 to 45 minutes to care for and enjoy his flowers, a pastime that he finds relaxing and which totally removes him from the stress of his professional life.

In addition to specific relaxation aids, however, do not lose sight of the essential need for *regular vacations* and a sufficient amount of *sleep*. Six hours is a minimum, and you probably need more.

Other Attributes of Competent Copers

Out of other studies of executives successful in coping with stress has come a conviction among some experts that many such executives have in common an awareness of the stress potential in a situation, sensitivity to their own reactions, capacity to find appropriate responses.

Commonly, the studies suggest, the competent copers analyze stress-producing situations and decide on what is worth worrying about and what is not.

Rather than carry the entire load, they make a point of delegating responsibility, and they may delegate more and more tasks when tension starts to build.

They set priorities and establish goals to achieve the most important objectives.

They are realistic about perfection—when it is achievable and when not.

When tension begins to build, they talk. They talk with others on the job; they may even have "bitching" sessions with peers; and they commonly talk things through with their spouses. They blow off steam.

Sensitive to their own responses to stress and aware that excessive responses can land them on a frustrating and less-than-full-productive merry-go-round, they are given to taking a break—withdrawing physically from the situation for a while—when that makes sense.

As much as possible, they try to foresee upcoming stress-producing job situations and events and, if possible, try to schedule them so they all do not occur at the same time.

They realistically expect that there will inevitably be some unanticipated stress situations and try to leave some coping time and capacity open for them.

Many of the competent copers compartmentalize work life and home life. They work hard on the job but, once home, they take their attention away from any job pressures and problems by becoming involved at home, for example, with reading, gardening, photography, embroidery, or other hobbies.

And most engage in physical exercise as an aid in releasing tension and building health. The building of health also means building coping energy.

Changing the Language and Thinking of Stress

Competent copers have their attributes.

Those who do not cope well, who suffer from stress, also have theirs. Among these, certain patterns of thinking and perceiving, which need not be immutable, are emphasized by Dr. Frank Gardner, a Hofstra University Health Center psychologist specializing in stress.

Emotional stress immediately follows, not a situation, but rather, what an individual tells him- or herself about that situation. Gardner notes, "I've never seen anyone in a coma feel tense. We have to think to feel."

And, because it is a medium of thought, language is important in stress reactions. "There is a great deal of evidence that the words we use to describe things affect our emotional responses," Gardner explains. "We respond to the messages we tell ourselves. We appraise things via language."

Often, stressed people repeat to themselves such messages as "This is terrible (or dreadful, or unbearable). Life shouldn't put things in my way which are terrible to me. Why do 'they' keep messing up my life!" These are stress-producing and stress-accentuating messages.

To cope with such thoughts, it is essential to be aware of them. "You have to separate the situation and your reaction to the situation," says Gardner. "We make a lot of assumptions—and a lot of illogical inferences from those assumptions."

Typically, Gardner finds, either one of two treacherous thinking and perceiving patterns, black-and-white thinking and catastrophizing, can contribute significantly to stress.

People who see the world in black-and-white absolutes, of good and bad, of should's and shouldn'ts, pave their way to angry feelings. "On an intellectual level we all know that the world can't always be the way we want, but in a situation we don't always act that way," Gardner says. "The world is *supposed* to be 'screwed up'! Take this sentence with you; it will make you much happier."

Black-and-white thinking sometimes turns back on the self in frustrated perfectionism. But it's important to accept human fallibility. "The best accountant is going to add wrong sometimes; the best therapist is going to misdiagnose sometimes. There's nothing wrong is desiring, only in *demanding*, to be the best."

Catastrophizing blows up things out of proportion and leads to anxiety, or, as Gardner puts it, "expectations of horror." People with such tendencies see a scratch on their car and fear that the entire chassis is about to fall apart.

"You have a right to be tense and angry. Sometimes you may want to go with the feelings. I am not saying things don't matter," Gardner points out, "but that there's a more appropriate 'in-between' reaction.

Instead of being highly anxious, be somewhat aroused; instead of being furious, be somewhat annoyed."

Try new ways, he urges, and expect you may have to argue with yourself as you try. "At first when you say to yourself, 'It isn't that bad,' there may be a little voice telling you, 'It really *is* terrible!'"

Try new ways first on the little things. "The little things are really what takes the toll, the nudgy little things that happen all the time," says Gardner.

Have a go at annoyances first for a reason even more significant than their abundance. "People get into a rut. They don't believe they can do something." Early successes with a little annoyance can demonstrate that doing something isn't impossible and can encourage continued change.

26.

Coping Aids

As we saw in Part II, exercise is an excellent help for the often desk-bound "sedentary" executive lifestyle, as well as an adjunct to a good dietary program. It is even more than that: Many studies have established that physical activity is one of the best antidotes for mental and emotional tension; that it is difficult, if not impossible, to remain tense during vigorous activity.

At the University of Southern California some years ago, Dr. Herbert de Vries set about comparing the effects of exercise with those of tranquilizers. In a tense, emotionally upset person, almost invariably muscles become tense. Measuring muscle tension offers an effective, objective method of determining emotional state and any changes in it. De Vries found that even as little exercise as a 15-minute walk is more relaxing than a tranquilizer.

That was no unexpected discovery. Many years ago, the distinguished heart specialist and physician to presidents, Paul Dudley White, observed:

> It has been said that a 5-mile walk will do more good to an unhappy
> but otherwise healthy man than all the medicine and psychology

291

in the world. Certainly it is true that, in my own case, nervous stress and strain can be counteracted and even prevented by regular vigorous exercise. It is my strong belief that all healthy persons, male and female, should exercise regularly no matter what their ages.

When, a few years ago, Thaddeus Kostrubala, a psychiatrist at Mercy Medical Center, San Diego, decided that he needed regular exercise, he took up running. Before long, some of his psychiatric patients were running along with him three times a week, an hour at a time. Changes in the patients, he has reported, were striking. Those with depression had fewer symptoms; even a schizophrenic patient could be taken off medication.

In studies at the University of Wisconsin Medical School, investigators reported finding that thirty to forty-five minutes of jogging three times a week is at least as effective as talk therapy for the moderately depressed.

At the University of Arizona Medical School, Dr. William P. Morgan has found exercise effective in decreasing anxiety.

One of the stressors many of us suffer from is that of our pent-up aggressive drives. When those drives are expressed in physical action, we're likely to be better off.

One EHE client, the chief executive officer of a major New York City advertising agency, now in his early fifties, keeps very fit by skipping rope during the week and chopping wood every weekend. He is especially fond of the chopping, which he says is a great tension-breaker because of the impact, the striking of the logs.

In fact, some physicians at Executive Health Examiners, noting a marked increase in the popularity of indoor racket sports, such as racquetball, among executives, consider that it may be due not only to the vigorous play but also to the great release of tension one gets from striking something.

Other Values

Regular exercise can help overcome excessive fatigue.

Physically, it helps by enhancing muscular strength and endurance, of course, and additionally by increasing coordination and efficiency of body movement.

Fatigue, moreover, often has psychological aspects. The human body has the capacity to generate as much as 14 horsepower with maximum effort but generates only 1/10 horsepower at rest, according to studies by Dr. Peter Karpovich, professor of physiology at Springfield College. In many sedentary people, unused horsepower builds into tension, which then becomes a factor in fatigue as well as other complaints. By counteracting tension, exercise may reduce undue fatigue.

The American Heart Association's Committee on Exercise reports that regular, vigorous activity enhances the quality of life by increasing the capacity for both work and play.

There is evidence, too, that physical activity may improve the quality of sleep.

Working with a group of people accustomed to regular exercise, Dr. Frederick Baekeland of the State University of New York Downstate Medical Center, Brooklyn, monitored their sleep in a sleep laboratory during a period when they were engaging in their customary exercise and again during the month-long period when all exercise was banned.

During that month without exercise, the subjects complained that they did not sleep as well. Monitoring instruments also revealed a basic change in sleep patterns: less deep sleep, indicating anxiety, during the no-exercise period.

Evidence that the more a person exercises, the deeper the sleep has also been shown in studies by Dr. R. B. Zloty of the University of Manitoba, Canada, and Dr. Colin Shapiro of Johannesburg, South Africa.

Which Activities?

Almost any form of exercise, if practiced regularly, can serve as an antidote to stress.

Possible exceptions may be competitive sports for those who tend to be compulsive about achieving a standard of performance or about winning. For them, it's possible for recreational athletic activities to become as stressful as work pressures.

Aerobic exercise, including running, jogging, brisk walking, swimming, cycling, or any activity that is rhythmic and leads to a sustained increase in breathing and heart rate, is valuable for relieving stress and at the same time may be helpful for the heart.

Mild exercise, too, such as calisthenics performed during exercise breaks a few times a day, can be useful in relieving stress-produced tension.

One important precaution: For anyone over 35 who has long been sedentary, there should be no sudden leap into full-fledged, vigorous activity. Instead, proceed slowly, gradually increasing the intensity—preferably after clearance following a medical checkup.

Relaxation Therapy

Breathing, a Simple Aid

Breathing techniques are part of many effective forms of relaxation therapy. They may also be of value in themselves.

A regular, relaxed, slow pattern of breathing—moving the diaphragm rather than the upper chest—helps to lower the arousal level. It can almost immediately change many of the physical indicators of a stress response. For example, skin response to an electric stimulus diminishes while skin temperature rises.

Dr. Leon J. Warshaw, an occupational health physician, recalls that early in his career he encountered people who were building up tension and anxiety to the point of interfering with their performance and producing discomfort. It was, he knew, futile to tell them to "just relax." They had heard that many times. So he devised what he calls "a little ritual."

Asking his patients to close their eyes and to stand if they did most of their work sitting or to sit if they usually stood or walked about while working, he had them breathe in and out slowly and rhythmically, counting silently or aloud as they preferred, until they reached some number, such as 100. In tough cases, he had them start with a higher number and count back to zero. Often, while they breathed in such a pattern, he had them bend and extend their arms, shoulders, and neck slowly and gently.

The breathing exercise, which took only a few minutes, was repeated several times a day. Furthermore, there were strict instructions that during the exercise period, no calls were to be taken or interruptions allowed.

A Simple Technique: Relaxing with a Memory

At the University of California at Davis, Drs. Alfred P. French and J. P. Tupin have developed a simple, meditationlike relaxation method that may be learned in a few minutes and that often is helpful in relieving moderate anxiety. Often, report French and Tupin, the technique is also effective in relieving insomnia, moderate pain, and emotional responses to illness.

They suggest this three-step method:

- First, sit comfortably with feet on the floor and eyes closed, and relax your breathing—really letting your breathing become relaxed so that air flows gently into and out of your lungs, after which you can allow your muscles to relax.

- Next, simply allow your mind to be as relaxed as your muscles are, and let your mind drift, very naturally and very gently, in the direction of a memory which is very pleasant, relaxing, restful, and reassuring. In most cases, this becomes possible within a minute.

- Finally, simply present that memory very gently to your mind. Allow yourself to be there and experience that memory. Don't concentrate or think about it in the usual sense, and if your mind wanders off simply bring yourself back, very gently and naturally, by presenting the memory to your mind again.

The method usually is learned in 3 or 4 minutes and, French and Tupin find, in many cases it produces an immediate sense of both relaxation and well-being.

Meditation: Using It to Unwind

Several years ago, in its business pages, the *New York Times* ran a story headed "Management: Using Meditation to Unwind." The article noted that at 6 o'clock every morning, the board chairman of a major midwestern brewery settles himself into an easy chair, closes his eyes and, for 20 minutes, meditates, silently repeating his mantra (a phrase chanted repeatedly) and keeping his mind free of all but the most fleeting thoughts. Before dinner that evening, he repeats the procedure.

Meditation, he says, tunes up his mind, prevents him from getting "worn out," and helps him keep cool under stress, according to the *Times* report.

Meanwhile, in his Manhattan apartment, a partner in a large accounting firm wakes at 6:30 A.M., moves to a chair near his bed, and meditates for 20 minutes. Later, he spends another 20 minutes meditating in his office.

Although he calls himself a "devout skeptic" by nature, he reported to the *Times*: "Now I react very differently to a stressful situation. Occasionally in my work, there'll be somebody yelling at the other end of a phone, or something will come up that is really high pressure. I have no anxiety in the pit of my stomach. I can handle it more efficiently and more easily."

Also reporting to the *Times*, the manager of branch operations for one of America's largest corporations, says that he meditates at 5:45 A.M. at home, and again at 2:30 in the afternoon, sitting on a couch in his office.

"I don't understand all the physiological things that occur," he says, "but I know I'm a lot sharper and more acute. My retention level is higher. I'm not a faddist, and I didn't go into this for a couple of years after hearing about it, but it's done wonders for me."

The three businessmen are graduates of a formal transcendental meditation class. Clearly, TM is not for everyone. For example, fully half of one group of insurance company executives who began the practice were dropouts within a few months.

But enthusiasts can be passionate about the benefits not only of TM but of other forms of meditation, notably the relaxation response and a technique called CSM (clinically standardized meditation).

Transcendental Meditation

In 1959, Maharishi Mahesh Yogi, a guru who early in his life had studied physics, left India, bringing with him a revised form of yoga. He set up an organization to train instructors who in turn could teach his technique. By the early 1970s, an estimated 10,000 Americans a month were getting training in transcendental meditation (TM).

TM requires no intense concentration, no rigorous mental or physical control, and the relatively simple technique is easily learned.

It has four essential elements: quiet surroundings, a passive attitude, a comfortable sitting position, and a mental device. The device is a secret word, the mantra—a sound or phrase which is given to you by an instructor and which you promise not to divulge. It is often derived from Hindu scripture and allegedly is chosen to suit the individual.

In two 20-minute periods a day, one in the morning, usually before breakfast, and one in the evening, usually before dinner, the meditator, sitting comfortably, repeats the mantra over and over silently as an aid in preventing distracting thoughts. If such thoughts come into mind, the meditator disregards them, going back to the mantra.

Feelings produced by TM can vary considerably. Some people experience feelings of restfulness and quiet, others a sense of pleasure and well-being, and still others report a feeling of nearly ecstatic deep relaxation.

Various physiological effects may occur. Often, oxygen consumption falls off by 10 to 20 percent as much as during sleep, reflecting a drop in body metabolism. Heartbeat slows and breathing rate and depth decline. Blood pressure drops, especially when it is high to begin with.

One of the major benefits claimed for TM is that it eases stress. There have been reports, too, of improvement in job performance, significant reduction in high blood pressure, peptic ulcer healing, curing of insomnia, and relief of many stress-related disorders.

The Relaxation Response

Herbert Benson, M.D., director of the Hypertension and Behavioral Medicine Sections of Boston's Beth Israel Hospital, studied TM and confirmed its value in reducing tension and high blood pressure. But he became convinced that meditation could be as useful as TM when stripped of the latter's mysticism. It could be used, quite simply, in noncultic fashion, to elicit what he calls an innate *relaxation response*.

The Benson procedure shares with TM the four essential elements of quiet surroundings, passive attitude, comfortable sitting position, and mental device, which in this case is just the word "one."

Benson teaches patients to sit quietly in a comfortable position with eyes closed, to deeply relax all muscles, beginning at the feet and progressing up to the face, and to keep them relaxed.

The patients are then instructed to breathe through the nose, to become aware of the breathing, and, as they breathe out, to say the word, "one" silently to themselves. They are to continue doing this for 10 to 20 minutes.

Benson further instructs:

- You may open your eyes to check the time, but do not use an alarm. When you finish, sit quietly for several minutes, at first with your eyes closed and later with your eyes opened. Do not stand up for a few minutes.

- Do not worry about whether you are successful in achieving a deep level of relaxation. Maintain a passive attitude and permit relaxation to occur at its own pace. When distracting thoughts occur, try to ignore them by not dwelling upon them and return to repeating "one." With practice, the response should come with little effort. Practice the technique once or twice daily, but not within 2 hours after any meal, since the digestive processes seem to interfere with the elicitation of the relaxation response.

What feelings accompany the relaxation response? They vary, Benson reports. Most people feel a sense of calm and great relaxation. A small percentage experience ecstatic feelings. Various individuals have told of feelings of pleasure, refreshment, and well-being. Still others have noted relatively little change in feelings. But, regardless of reported feelings, Benson notes, the physiological changes, such as decreased oxygen consumption, take place. He maintains:

> The case for the use of relaxation response by healthy but harassed individuals is straightforward. It can act as a built-in method of counteracting the stresses of everyday living which bring forth the fight-or-flight response. We have also shown how the relaxation response may be used as a new approach to aid in the treatment and perhaps prevention of diseases such as hypertension.

Clinically Standardized Meditation

Clinically standardized meditation (CSM) is a variation of transcendental meditation developed by Dr. Patricia Carrington, Princeton University lecturer in psychology. It falls somewhere between TM and the Benson relaxation response.

Like Benson, Dr. Carrington brushes aside TM's mysticism and secretiveness. But, she believes that meditation, like TM, can be learned more effectively and quickly when taught by a qualified, experienced "supervisor." She encourages patients to use the self-instructional audiocassettes that she has developed for home reinforcement of the CSM technique.

With CSM, a subject may choose a mantra from a list or devise one. Dr. Carrington's nonsecret mantras are usually melodic words or nonsense syllables (such as "vis-ta," "shan-ti," "shi-rim") rated by volunteers as pleasant and soothing.

CSM is permissive. No effort need be made to concentrate on the mantra or coordinate its use with breathing. And distracting thoughts are allowed to drift in and out of consciousness while the subject attends passively to the sound of the mantra. This permissiveness, Dr. Carrington believes, allows subjects to desensitize themselves to disturbing thoughts.

One indication of the efficacy of CSM is a program to treat a group of New York Telephone company employees who reported very high levels of on-the-job stress. With CSM training, they experienced a marked decrease in anxiety, in hostility and depression, and in physical symptoms associated with stress. The firm has adopted CSM training in a companywide stress-reduction program.

Biofeedback

Biofeedback is, in effect, an extension of the normal way in which we learn.

In learning, we receive "feedback" cues from such sources as our eyes, ears, hands, and feet. Swing a golf club, for example, and you feel your arms move, see how the club connects with the ball, and watch where the ball goes—all cues to guide you so you can try to correct your swing for possibly better ball placement next time.

In most people, the face tends to be extraordinarily expressive of mood and emotion. Some people have argued quite seriously that the body feels what the face feels; that the face may be the key cue to the rest of the body.

Usually, however, we get few feedback cues to what goes on within the body. But sensitive electronic equipment can provide such awareness. With electrodes attached at various points of the body, the equipment can detect, amplify, and display small internal fluctuations in the form of sound beeps or light flashes, for example.

The potential of biofeedback is very closely tied to what has amounted to a virtual revolution in an old medical theory. That theory held that the human being is unable consciously to exert control over the automatic nervous system. Ordinarily, without our awareness, this system regulates such processes as pulse rate, the secretions of glands, oxygen consumption, and other complex mechanisms which, upon being disturbed, often trigger stress disorders.

This theory was challenged, however, by Dr. Neal E. Miller of Rockefeller University. By drugging rats with curare to inactivate their skeletal muscles, then using electric shock as a teaching aid, Miller and his coworkers established that the rats could be taught to control interior processes.

Rats, it turned out, can learn to control blood pressure levels to obtain suitable awards. Miller even had one rat which could be regularly brought to send enough blood to one ear to produce a blush there, while the other ear blanched.

At the Menninger Foundation in Topeka, Kansas, one of the first institutions to study the use of biofeedback for migraine headaches, notable successes have been achieved by taping temperature sensors to a patient's finger and forehead. A meter shows the difference between head and hand temperature.

While watching the meter the patient is asked to do such things as relax while repeating a calming phrase (such as "I feel quiet") in order to relax blood vessels in the hands and thus increase hand temperature. When he or she succeeds, the meter needle moves. With the relaxation and warming of the hands comes a redistribution of blood that reduces pressure in blood vessels in the head, ending the migraine headache.

Once a patient develops the ability to move the needle, the same technique can be used, without the biofeedback equipment, to cut short a migraine episode.

Investigators at Menninger have reported that 74 percent of migraine sufferers have improved and have gained the ability to increase blood in the hands in almost 100 percent of situations in which they detect the onset of a headache.

Biofeedback has also been found to work well for tension headaches, which are the most common kind, involving contraction of forehead, scalp, and neck muscles. Improvement rates of up to 80 percent have been reported.

Patients with tension headaches may have sensor electrodes applied to the forehead to record muscle tension. If the level is high, the biofeedback equipment emits a series of rapid beeps that the patients hear through earphones. As tension is reduced, the beeps slow.

Biofeedback gives a patient a precise measurement of his or her physical state as it pertains to headaches. It also offers the gratification of knowing that the sufferer can alter that state. In effect, the signal beeping at the desired pace tells a patient, "You're in charge of yourself."

Among the disorders other than tension headaches for which EMG biofeedback shows promise, according to reports from various investigators, are anxiety, phobias, insomnia, alcoholism, drug abuse, asthma, high blood pressure, menstrual distress, and some intestinal disorders such as ulcer or colitis.

Modifying Type A Behavior

Type A behavior, as we have seen earlier, is now recognized as a major risk factor for coronary heart disease and heart attack. Additionally, it can be an internal source of pressure and stress. It is a behavior common to many executives.

Can it be modified?

Research is now under way on a substantial scale to evaluate methods for modification and the benefits of modification as well. At Colorado State University and the University of Montreal, studies with coronary heart disease patients have shown significant reductions in blood pressure and blood cholesterol levels following Type A modification. In a study at the U.S. Naval Hospital in San Diego, a modification program was set up as part of post–heart attack rehabilitation. Participants showed significantly less heart morbidity and mortality than post–heart attack patients who received only standard rehabilitation measures.

In what is believed to be the first mass attempt to alter the A behavior pattern, Dr. Meyer Friedman, one of the pioneers in the study of Type A behavior, is working with 900 post–heart attack patients. Both Friedman and Ray H. Rosenman, M.D., another pioneer investigator of Type A, believe modification is possible but not easy.

One difficulty is that the Type A person tends to have what Friedman calls "some vague sort of Horatio Alger complex." Such a person believes that the complex—the competitive drive, time urgency, speed, and hyperarousal—has been primarily responsible for his or her major accomplishments and that any change will lead to diminished income, power, and prestige.

When Type A people finally recognize the true nature of their behavior, they try to modify it. "They begin to realize that Type A behavior has actually impeded their socioeconomic progress rather than enhanced it," Dr. Friedman observes. "They become aware that this behavior may be a failure-inducing, not a success-producing, pattern."

It is also helpful when the patient realizes that Type A behavior over many years may have impoverished various aspects of personality. Friedman points to Charles Darwin who, when he discovered that sad fact about himself, wrote:

> My mind seems to have become a machine for grinding out large collections of facts, but why this should have caused the atrophy of that part of the brain alone on which higher tastes depend, I cannot conceive. . . . The loss of these tastes (the enjoyment of poetry, music, painting, reading of general literature, etc.) is a loss of happiness and may be enfeebling the emotional part of my nature.

Two other realizations can be critical. One is that modification does not mean changing a Type A person into a Type B but, rather, tempering the A behavior. The second is that, with modification, there can be not only a reduction in coronary heart disease risk and self-induced stress but also gains in efficiency and productivity, along with gains in general health, sense of well-being, and life satisfactions.

Evidence that this is so comes from the Montreal study, mentioned earlier, in which participants went on working the same number of hours and carrying the same responsibilities as before behavior modification but reported enjoying life more now.

Modification Strategies

Changing Type A behavior may best be done with the aid of a trained counselor. But, short of that, executives who already recognize themselves as Type A or who wish to reevaluate themselves and make valuable changes may find the following guidelines useful. They are based upon methods used by Drs. Friedman, Rosenman, and others in a growing number of programs.

Observing yourself   Often, Type A people are unaware of their actual behavior. Self-observation can be a vital first step.

It can teach you, as Dr. Rosenman puts it, "to witness such daily experiences as the struggle in commuting to work, the schedule bulging with activities without adequate breaks, the battle with the clock, and the impatience and irritation with others that too often are manifested in facial tension and vocal outbursts."

Log yourself. Keep a record, for a week or two, of the situations that make you angry, anxious, or frustrated, or that make you very much aware of the clock and give you a dominating sense of time urgency.

That record can serve several purposes, beginning with helping to motivate you to make changes. It can also pinpoint particular behaviors that most need change and then serve as a kind of benchmark against which you can measure progress.

Contracting One at a time, make a series of small contracts with yourself, written commitments to changing particularly undesirable daily patterns of behavior. There should be no effort to change yourself completely overnight. That is almost certainly doomed to failure.

Instead, take one specific thing at a time. For example: Rather than say in general terms that you are going to slow down at work, determine instead to walk, instead of rush, to work and to walk in a relaxed fashion.

Contract to slow down in other ways—one at a time. Slow your speech when you talk. Drive more slowly.

Contract to listen to music as an aid in relaxing when you drive rather than to dictate or become frustrated by other drivers.

For at least one coffee break a day, contract to replace the coffee with a brisk walk.

Contract, in due course, to get 20 to 30 minutes of exercise a week.

Evaluating Yourself Consider your life's goals. Perhaps determine what they were when you started out and what they really are or might be today if you attend to them seriously now. "Concentrate on what is worth *being* rather than what is worth *having*," somebody has remarked. It might be that you would really like to follow this suggestion.

Managing your environment Type A people often fail to manage their environment effectively in terms not only of getting work done properly but of doing so without causing themselves distress.

Delegate whenever possible. If that's difficult for you, if you feel too often that only you can do the task, give delegation a trial anyhow. You may be surprised, and all the more so if, in delegating, you explain with patience exactly what must be done.

Eliminate needlessly excessive obligations. Must you take on so many extra duties, get involved in so many committees at and away from work? Get rid of the trivial.

Try setting priorities the first thing you do each day. Then stay with them, going from one thing to another in due course, taking up a new task only when you finish with one that has higher priority.

Learn how to schedule your appointments realistically, so you are not always rushing from one to another.

Learn, too, how to manage requests, and even demands, from others. Let them know how much time and effort you can give, and when you cannot oblige. One expert in stress management suggests: "Get the person who wants you to take on another task to help you evaluate the urgency of the request and determine where it fits among your priority items."

Try getting up 15 minutes earlier in the morning so you can begin the day in less rushed, more relaxed fashion.

When you are up against a deadline, concentrate on the job. But try taking an occasional break: Walk about, chat with someone, stare quietly out the window for a minute or so—anything to cut down on the tension. You may well find this no loss of time at all but an actual time-saver and aid to effective concentration.

Working at the hostility problem "A critical and difficult problem," Dr. Rosenman calls it, "the hostility that often grows out of excessive impatience and competitiveness. In the course of development of the Type A behavior pattern, hostile aggressiveness is fostered." He continues:

"Perhaps, because Type A individuals place winning and achievements as the ultimate goals, they perceive most other individuals as competitors and threats. The Type A person's band of hostility may be described as 'free floating,' reflecting its capacity to be touched off by even the slightest provocation."

Rosenman urges Type A people to observe and monitor their frustration, anger, and hostility, noting the situations that provoke them and recording them so they become clear. After doing so, efforts can be made to deal with them.

Are there particular people who especially annoy you? Perhaps, at least some of these people can be avoided. Are you wasting hostility and anger on trivial matters, even those about which you can do little or nothing, such as a delayed plane, a discourteous salesperson, or an inept waiter?

Stop demanding, if only in your mind, that others act as you do, talk as you do, move as you do. Don't interrupt them almost invariably, or finish their sentences for them, again almost invariably.

Modeling   An effective way to develop new behavior is to observe a model, to see how some other successful person carries out the behavior, how he or she gets things done in relaxed fashion, exhibiting humor rather than anger, using relaxed rather than frenetic movements.

Perhaps you can select such a model from among your acquaintances. He or she need not be aware of the selection. You can study your model's reactions to daily stressors and his or her handling of them. Imitation can be helpful.

Drug Treatment

Do drugs have any role in our dealings with our anxiety and feelings of stress?

Anti-anxiety drugs—tranquilizers—sometimes have a place, but they are not, as so many people seem to think, inevitably the answer.

Each year, American pharmacists fill over 150 million prescriptions for mood-affecting drugs. Are they justified?

Perhaps one concerned medical authority is right. He asks these questions:

> How do physicians acquire such unquestioning faith in drugs? Are they stampeded by their patients? Because they serve a public that has been brainwashed to think that there is a "pill for every ill," do they believe the patient will be disappointed if he doesn't receive something tangible in return for sharing his problems?

But he answers these questions thus:

> Many physicians feel ill-equipped to deal with the emotional aspects of a patient's illness and are unwilling to embroil themselves

in a lengthy and financially unrewarding discussion with him. No doubt a pill is the easy way out.

But it is *not* the effective way out.

Tranquilizers, of course, do not cure anxiety. They do not get at the bases for stress disorders. They can relieve symptoms and they may be valuable for that purpose when stress reactions and anxiety become so intense as to interfere with job and other aspects of living.

In some cases, physicians have found tranquilizers valuable when the patient's symptoms, emotional and physical, are so disabling that coherent communication and counseling are virtually impossible.

In other cases, the drugs may be valuable when physical symptoms are so debilitating that a patient is unable to accept the possibility that the manifestations, so suggestive of actual organic disease, may be caused only by the stresses of his or her life. Then, a suitable tranquilizer in appropriate dosage may help, through its relief of the symptoms, to convince the patient of the stress origin and lower the anxiety level enough to facilitate other therapeutic steps.

Psychotherapy

Psychotherapy certainly is not always needed to combat stress. But it often can be a valuable aid, as noted earlier, for the executive with stress-induced depression. It can be useful, similarly, for stress-provoked anxiety. It need not take the form of extended classic Freudian psychoanalysis, with years spent on the couch. The range of professional help for emotional problems is much broader now.

In actual fact, short-term psychotherapy, consisting of 10 to 15 counseling sessions and sometimes even fewer, often helps during a particularly difficult stress or an emotional situation. It is not uncommon for psychotherapy to bring some, almost immediate, reduction of discomfort. Expressing painful thoughts and feelings to a qualified counselor helps to relieve distress through sharing.

If you should need professional help, your personal physician may be in a position to suggest a suitable therapist.

How do you know if there is such a need?

As a distinguished psychiatrist has put it, summing up well the view of many specialists:

The key element of when to look for help is to listen to your own inner stirrings. When the intensity of the problem becomes too great to handle yourself or by talking with spouse or trusted friend, then look for professional help.